THE WHITE WINES
— OF —
FRANCE

Robert Joseph

Consultant Editor
Joanna Simon

641 Joseph, Robert.
.22 The white wines of France / Robert Joseph ;
23 consultant editor, Joanna Simon. -- Los Angeles :
09 HPBooks, [1990], c1987.
44 161 p. : ill., maps.
Jos

Includes index.
Bibliography: p. 161.
04166663 LC:89019949 ISBN:0895868636 (pbk.)

1. Wine and wine making - France. I. Simon, Joanna. II.
Title

2199 90MAY30

THE WHITE WINES
— OF —
FRANCE

Robert Joseph

Consultant Editor
Joanna Simon

HPBooks
a division of
PRICE STERN SLOAN
Los Angeles

Published by HP Books,
a division of Price Stern Sloan, Inc.,
360 North La Cienaga Boulevard,
Los Angeles, California 90048
Printed in Belgium
9 8 7 6 5 4 3 2 1

Library of Congress Cataloging-in-Publication Data
Joseph, Robert.
  The white wines of France.

  "A Salamander book."
  1. Wine and wine making—France. I. Simon, Joanna.
II. Title.
TP553.J67 1990   641.2'223'0944   89-19949
ISBN 0-89586-863-6

Credits

Editor:
Philip de Ste. Croix

Designers:
Roger Hyde
Carol Warren

Colour artwork:
Ann Winterbotham and Stephen Seymour
© Salamander Books Ltd

Maps:
Sebastian Quigley
© Salamander Books Ltd

Index:
Jill Ford

Filmset:
SX Composing Ltd, England

Colour reproduction:
Melbourne Graphics Ltd, England

Printed in Belgium by Proost
International Book Production, Turnhout

CONTENTS

*A*UTHOR: Robert Joseph is publishing editor of WINE magazine, which he launched for Haymarket Publishing in 1983. Having lived for several years in Burgundy, he has travelled extensively throughout France and has written on French wines for publications in Britain, Switzerland, the USA and Japan. As a taster he has been a member of the panels of the prestigious annual Clos de Vougeot Tastevinage and the Mâcon Wine Fair. He has also tasted for the *Which? Wine Guide* and *The Sunday Express,* and is a regular member of the highly-respected tasting panels of WINE magazine. He is also editor of *The Wine Lists* (Guinness, 1985).

*C*ONSULTANT EDITOR: Joanna Simon has edited two of the foremost wine journals in the English language: *Wine & Spirit* magazine, which she joined as assistant editor in 1981, becoming editor in 1984, and WINE, which she edited between October 1986 and December 1987. She has travelled extensively in Europe and Australia, has tasted for a number of wine magazines, as well as *The Financial Times,* and has written for a wide range of trade and consumer publications on wine-related subjects. She is currently wine correspondent for *The Sunday Times*, and Contributing Editor of WINE and *Wine & Spirit.*

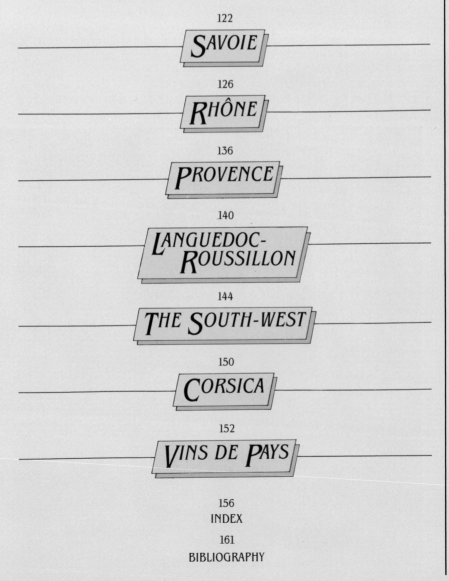

*F*OREWORD

*W*hen General de Gaulle made his now infamous remark about the impossibility of governing a country with 365 different cheeses, he might just as easily have been talking of France's wines. There is scarcely a corner of what the French themselves call ``*l'hexagone*'' in which someone has not, at some time tried to plant vines and to ferment their fruit into wine.

In some regions, those early experiments were so successful that the names of the wines – or rather the communes where they were produced – and the grape varieties from which they were made, have become familiar terms to wine drinkers throughout the world.

Others have attracted less fame and fortune; grapes like the Gros Manseng and the Ondenc have yet to climb the vinous hit parade in California, and wines such as Pacherenc de Vic-Bilh are still as hard to find outside the tiny region in which they are made, as their names are to pronounce.

This book is about all of France's white, pink and sparkling wines; the very famous and the extremely obscure. Some of the wines described feature on almost every wine list in the world; others can only be found by the most persistent search or, far more likely, quite by accident by visitors to the regions in which they are made.

The wines themselves and the way in which they are produced vary so greatly that it would be quite impossible to describe them all in detail within the covers of a single book. Entire volumes have been devoted to familiar regions such as Bordeaux, Burgundy and Champagne; other, equally long-established areas such as the Jura and the South-West of France have been far less generously served. In writing this book, I have attempted to take as even handed an approach as possible to the most familiar and the least well-known wines, in the hope that, by doing so, some at least of the latter may be rescued from their undeserved current state of obscurity.

This book has been written following years spent visiting the wine regions of France and – in the case of Burgundy – of living among the men and women

who, almost every day of their lives, have to tend their vines, top up their barrels, stick labels on their bottles and perform the seemingly endless list of chores which make winemaking such a varyingly demanding form of agriculture.

It is to these people that this book must be dedicated, for their hospitality to visitors such as myself, and for the care which the best of them at least devote to one of the most difficult crafts in the world.

Many people have helped me enormously, both with information and advice while writing this book. I should above all like to thank Sarah McWatters whose painstaking research uncovered a wealth of facts I had not previously imagined, Sally Robinson for her help in collating parts of that research, Joanna Simon for her encouragement and forbearance as commissioning editor, Jane Hunt MW for agreeing to proof read the book, Charles Metcalfe and Oz Clarke, as ever, for general advice and support, and Christina Ker Gibson for her own brand of patient tolerance.

Metric/Imperial Equivalents

The French wine industry uses metric measurements to express volumes, weights, dimensions, etc. This book, therefore, also uses metric units for such measurements. For those readers unfamiliar with the metric system, or who are more comfortable thinking in Imperial units, listed below are the necessary conversion factors.

1 metre (m) = 3.281 ft
1 kilometre (km) = 0.6214 miles
1 hectolitre (hl) = 100 litres = 22 UK gallons or 26.4 US gallons
1 hectare (ha) = 10,000m^2 = 2.471 acres
1 kilogram (kg) = 2.205lb
1 tonne = 1,000kg = 2,205lb

*T*here is no denying it – the French are spoilt. Not only do they have one of the most beautifully varied countries in the world, but they also have a long tradition of growing almost all the world's best grape varieties. The Italians, Spaniards and Portuguese all have interesting indigenous vines from whose grapes they make good pink and white wines, but few of them have sufficiently excited the interest of growers in other countries to encourage planting of these varieties elsewhere. Even Germany, home of some of the finest white wines, can boast no fine grape variety which is not also successfully grown on the other side of the Rhine.

Above: *Harvest time in Bordeaux. Although machines are beginning to take over the task, in thousands of vineyards throughout France families still work together to bring in the crop.*

France's list is like a vinous Hall of Fame: Chardonnay, Riesling, Muscat, Sauvignon Blanc, Sémillon, Chenin Blanc, Pinot Noir. As a result France can probably offer a wider variety of pink and white wines than any other country, ranging from the grapily aromatic, to the grassily refreshing, and the buttery and mouthfilling.

While winemakers in the "New World" have tried to plant all of these varieties almost side-by-side in neighbouring vineyards, the French have discovered over the centuries that some grape types make better wine when planted in particular kinds of soil and climate. So the Riesling and the Gewürztraminer are only grown in Alsace in eastern France, the Sémillon is restricted to Bordeaux and the South West, and the curious Viognier is only to be found in two small communes on the banks of the Rhône. These restrictions, dictated historically by the conditions of the vineyards, are now laid down for most of the country by *Appellation Contrôlée* law. At times they may seem overly limiting, but they certainly help to ensure that France avoids the trap which threatens those countries which seem determined to restrict the range of wines they make to ones which just happen to suit one current generation of wine drinkers.

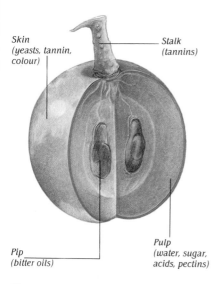

Skin
(yeasts, tannin, colour)

Stalk
(tannins)

Pip
(bitter oils)

Pulp
(water, sugar, acids, pectins)

Above: *The grape, source – the only source – of all wine. White grapes and black ones are almost identical, only their skin colour differentiating between them. The bloom on the skin harbours the natural wine yeasts.*

The accompanying table lists grape varieties and relates them to the region in which they are grown to make white and rosé wine. Any varieties grown in Bordeaux are usually also used in other regions of south-west France, such as Bergerac, Monbazillac etc.

Grape Varieties for White and Rosé Wines

Name of grape	Description	Region of cultivation
Aligoté	White – an acidic grape of humble birth and usually humble wines	Burgundy; Savoie; Alsace
Altesse (or Roussette – but not the same as the Rhône Roussette)	White – very floral	Savoie
Bourboulenc	White – making wines of usually little interest and short life expectancy	Rhône; Provence
Cabernet Franc	Black – blackcurranty-grassy	Loire; Bordeaux
Carignan	Black – flavourless to toffee'd. Used for rosé	Provence
Chardonnay	White – fresh and light to rich and buttery. Good for sparkling wine	Burgundy; Champagne; Alsace
Chasselas	White – usually dull	Savoie; Alsace
Chenin Blanc	White – honeyed and appley. Dry and sweet still wines and fair quality sparklers	Loire
Cinsault	Red – spicy, used for rosé	Rhône; Provence
Clairette	White – can be full flavoured, though often dull. Used for good sparkling wine	Rhône; Provence
Colombard	White – sometimes fruity	South-West
Folle Blanche (or Picpoul)	White – often dull	Rhône; Provence; South-West
Gewürztraminer	White – aromatic, dry or sweet	Alsace
Grenache	Red – peppery	Rhône; Provence
Grolleau (or Gros Lot)	Red – used for rosé	Loire
Gros Plant	White – acidic, basic	Loire
Jacquère	White – floral	Savoie
Maccabeu (or Maccabéo)	White – characterfully fruity	Provence; Rhône
Malbec (or Cot)	Red – used for Cahors, and for rosé in the Loire	Loire; South-West
Marsanne	White – late ripening	Rhône
Melon de Bourgogne (or Muscadet)	White – used for Muscadet	Loire
Merlot Blanc	White – not used in high quality wine	South-West
Molette	White – high yielding and dull	Savoie
Mondeuse	Black – used for rosé	Savoie
Mondeuse Blanche	White – rather dull	Savoie
Mourvèdre	Black – spicy, used in rosé	Rhône; Provence
Muscadelle	White – dry or sweet, used in blends	Bordeaux
Muscat Ottonel	White – grapey, dry or sweet	Alsace
Muscat Blanc à Petits Grains (or Muscat d'Alsace)	White – grapey, dry or sweet	Alsace; Rhône; Provence
Pineau d'Aunis (Chenin Noir)	Black – pale, used for rosé	Loire
Pinot Blanc	White – light, fruity and good for making sparkling wine	Alsace; Burgundy; Savoie
Pinot Gris (or Tokay)	White – aromatic, dry or sweet	Alsace
Pinot Meunier	Black – used for sparkling wine	Champagne
Pinot Noir	Black – used for rosé and sparkling wine	Burgundy; Champagne; Jura
Poulsard	Black – used for rosé	Savoie
Riesling	White – aromatic, sweet or dry	Alsace
Roussanne (or Roussette)	White – spicy	Rhône
Sauvignon	White – aromatic and used to make dry white and, blended	Loire; Bordeaux
Savagnin	White – nutty, grapey, and probably a cousin of the Gewürztraminer – the essential component of Vin Jaune	Jura
Sémillon	White – honeyed quality when well handled. Dry or nobly rotten and sweet	Bordeaux
Syrah	Black – spicy for rosé	Rhône; Provence
Trousseau	Black, used for rosé	Savoie; Jura
Ugni Blanc	White – dull; for blending or inexpensive dry whites	Rhône; Bordeaux; Provence
Viognier	White – characterfully floral, only used at Condrieu and at Château Grillet	Rhône

*I*t is perhaps easiest to consider the wine-grower's year by taking as a starting point the winter months following the autumn harvest. During this cold season it is necessary to tidy the vineyards, lopping off the dead wood left over from the previous year's growth. These branches are usually burned, and one of the most evocative sights at this time of the year are the thin strings of white smoke which rise against the background of the darkening grey sky.

Next comes the pruning of the vines which takes place in February and March. This is a highly skilled operation, each separate vine calling for individual attention. Different regions have their own styles of pruning, depending on the grape variety, the soil and climate, and the type of wine they produce, but whichever pruning style is used, the final size of the crop, and thus its quality, will be dictated by the number of new buds which are left on the plant. The more foliage you leave, the larger the harvest and the thinner-bodied the final wine. For this reason, French law lays down maximum yields per hectare for all quality wines. Unfortunately, even when these limits are not exceeded, they are often so over-generous that good producers choose instead to exercise more rigorous self-restraint to ensure a higher quality yield.

Planting takes place in April. Since the devastating attack by the phylloxera beetle at the end of the last century, almost all of the vines in France have had to be grafted on to American rootstock which is resistant to the pest. Winegrowers can choose from a selec-

Above: *Frost on the vines in Champagne. This can be one of the worst hazards facing winemakers in northern France.*

tion of different kinds of rootstock, depending on the soil of their vineyard, just as they can now pick one of a variety of clones of the grape variety they have to plant. Some of these clones, bred from selected parent vines which they will resemble perfectly, will produce higher yields; others may result in better quality. All should be less prone to disease than the unselected vines which were available before the development of clones. A vineyard planted with high quality clones should produce better wine than one with mixed pre-clonal vines. On the other hand, older vines (at least 30 years old) always produce more intensely flavoured wine than younger ones, as is proved by such estates as the Château de Fuissé in Burgundy which makes a "Vieilles Vignes" (literally, "old

Guyot simple

Guyot double

Above and above right: *Guyot simple and Guyot double are variations on the same classic theme. Both involve training the vines along two (or more) wires, the top to support the foliage, the bottom to bear the weight of the grapes.*

Gobelet   *Bush*

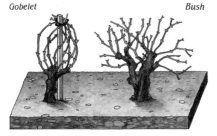

Above: *In the Gobelet and bush training methods, the vine is cut back to a few spurs which produce fruit-bearing canes.*

Alsace

Above: *The Alsace method of high training, though mainly used for white grapes, may also be used for Pinot Noir.*

Vine Cultivation: The Annual Cycle

La Taille	Pruning; undertaken in February and March, this is the essential vineyard maintenance which will determine the quantity of grapes that each vine produces and the concentration, or lack of it, of the wine it makes
Le Débourrement	The budding – usually in April or May. The weather at this time can influence the subsequent evolution of the vine.
La Floraison	The flowering of the vine – this can be as early as the beginning of June, or as late as mid-July. Here too, the weather can play a vital role in the later growth of the vine; the later the flowering, the later the harvest (there always being 100 days separating the two events) and, possibly, the lower the quality of the harvest.
La Veraison	The ripening of the grapes.
Le Traitement	Treatment – various fungicides and insecticides are used against vineyard pests.
La Récolte	The crop
Le Rendement	The yield – this may vary from less than 15 or 20 hectolitres (2,000-2,600 bottles) per hectare in Sauternes to over 100hl (13,000 bottles) in Alsace. Limits are established by law for every quality wine producing region in France and for every year. Wine produced in excess of these figures has to be sent to be distilled, but some areas permit a supplementary allowance of 20 per cent for growers who have requested it before the harvest.
Le Tri	The sorting of healthy from rotten, or unripe, grapes.
Le Ban de Vendanges	The officially established date on which the harvest may start. Some growers wait until their grapes are a little riper, risking the dangers of the poor weather of late autumn.
Les Vendanges	The harvest – more and more frequently accomplished by mechanical "*machines à vendanger*" which shake the grapes from the vines. Although such machines are undoubtedly quicker and less troublesome than teams of human pickers, the quality of their harvest and the possible long-term effect on the vines themselves, are questioned in several regions. In Champagne, mechanical harvesters are illegal.

Graft slip

Graft support

Before assembly   After assembly

Above: *This diagram shows the English type graft which is widely used in France. Grafting French slips on to American rootstock was introduced as a remedy to the phylloxera crisis.*

vines") as well as the far from ordinary Pouilly Fuissé from less venerable plants.

During the summer months, the vines need regular attention and treatment to ensure that they neither fall victim to rot nor to one of the numerous diseases which regularly lay siege to vineyards.

The harvest, whose opening date is fixed region by region by the *Appellation Contrôlée* authorities, can start as early as mid-September or – in the case of sweet wines made from individually picked grapes which have been subject to noble rot – as late as the end of December or the beginning of the January following the harvest. By tradition, the harvest takes place 100 days after the flowering of the vine. As a rule, earlier flowering, and thus earlier harvests, make for better vintages, but the climate of the year as a whole, both in terms of temperature and humidity, can save a year which started badly, or spoil one which promised well.

White wine is remarkably simple to make. Unlike red winemakers who have to concern themselves with overheating tanks and deficiencies of colour, the men and women who produce white wine can, in theory at least, leave their grape juice to ferment into wine at its own pace; fermentation is slower, cooler and less dramatic than it is for red wine. The basic process of making white wine, from delivery of the newly-picked grapes to bottling, is shown in the diagram below.

If white wine is far easier to make than red, it is, unfortunately, also far easier to make it *badly* – as anyone who has tasted a range of some of the world's cheaper red and white wines will appreciate. The two essential enemies which have to be confronted when trying to produce white wine are bacteria and dullness. The former problem, a greater hazard for whites than reds, can be dealt with simply by ensuring that the winery and everything in it is kept clean. As for the latter, this can be trickier. A white wine can be dull because it is made from dull, flavourless grapes, or because insufficient care and skill were used in the way in which the flavoursome grapes were fermented and matured.

Everything depends on the style of wine you intend to produce. If it is to be rich, full-bodied and long-lived, then you can afford to let the fermentation last for several months, possibly in the oak barrels in which the wine will continue to mature. This style suits some grape varieties better than others. The Char-donnay, for example, can benefit from being fermented and matured in *new* oak while more aromatic varieties, such as the Gewürz-traminer, would gain nothing.

If a less characterful grape variety, such as the Ugni Blanc is being used to produce a light, fruity style for drinking young, the wine can be allowed to ferment in large tanks at a cool temperature of 8-10°C, which helps to bring out the freshness of flavour such wines need. As a general rule, cool temperature fermentation tends to produce fruitier, short-lived wines, while slightly warmer temperatures can provide both greater longevity and complexity. Even so, few people nowadays like to ferment their wine at much over 20°, as this can lead to flat, tired wines.

To make sweet wines, you naturally need to use grapes with a high natural degree of sugar, enough to create a finished wine with between 11-13 per cent alcohol, but which still has a decent residual level of sweetness left over. In some cases, such as Sauternes, the sugar content of the grape should be quite sufficient; in others, such as Muscat de Beaumes de Venise, a dose of brandy is required to stop the fermentation once a desired alcoholic strength has been achieved. Such wines do not benefit from new oak maturation.

Right: *Grapes which are about to be pressed in a horizontal press similar to those in use throughout France.*

How White and Rosé Wine Is Made

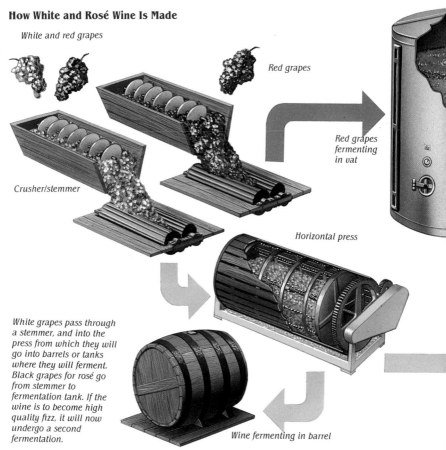

White and red grapes

Red grapes

Red grapes fermenting in vat

Crusher/stemmer

Horizontal press

White grapes pass through a stemmer, and into the press from which they will go into barrels or tanks where they will ferment. Black grapes for rosé go from stemmer to fermentation tank. If the wine is to become high quality fizz, it will now undergo a second fermentation.

Wine fermenting in barrel

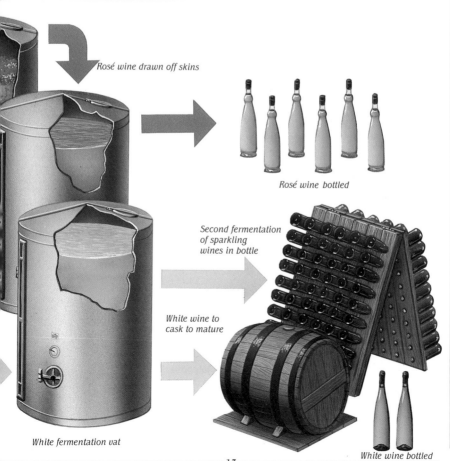

Rosé wine drawn off skins

Rosé wine bottled

Second fermentation
of sparkling
wines in bottle

White wine to
cask to mature

White fermentation vat

White wine bottled

*W*hen a passenger travelling to the USA recently asked the stewardess for a glass of rosé, she was apologetically given a quarter bottle each of red and white and asked to mix her own. History does not relate how the wine she made tasted, but one thing is certain, had a French winemaker tried to make *his* rosé that way, he would have been breaking French wine law. The only exception to this ban on the blending of red and white is Champagne rosé, and even in that region, there are those who say that this is not really the "proper" way to do things.

There are two basic legal methods to make pink wine. The first simply requires the producer to treat black grapes as if they were white, following precisely the same steps as have already been described, allowing the pigment in the skin to dye the white juice on its way through the crusher and press. The second method by contrast, is essentially red winemaking *interruptus*: black grapes are crushed and passed into the tank, just as if they were to be fermented into fully coloured red wine, but before the juice has become too deep a red, after 12 or 24 hours, the juice is drawn off. This 'bleeding' of the vat is known as a 'saignée' and it is increasingly popular in red wine regions where producers are pleased to be able to combine a means of concentrating the colour of their reds with the production of saleable rosé.

Whichever method is used – and both have their advocates, depending on regions and grape varieties – rosé-making is a trickier job than is often thought. As with white wine, it is remarkably simple to make dull rosé and, in the case of Anjou and the other sweeter styles, far too easy to overdo the sulphur. It is only when you have the chance to taste a really good, peppery, curranty rosé from Pro-

Winemaking: What the Technical Terms Mean

Le Fouloir	The stemmer-crusher through which the grapes pass on their way to the press. In some cases, the fruit may be put directly into the press.
SO₂	When the grapes are first picked, and at various other stages of the winemaking process, sulphur dioxide is used as a natural agent to kill the bacteria which so easily convert wine to vinegar. Use of sulphur is even more essential in the case of sweet wines whose sugar content confers an added risk of re-fermentation, and it is often in these wines that the unpleasant throat-tickling presence of too high a dose of sulphur can be detected.
Le Pressoir	The press. These are generally horizontal machines which work either by squeezing the fruit between round plates drawn together from opposite ends of a slotted cylinder or, in the case of some of the newest presses, by blowing up a rubber bag within the cylinder. This last method has the dual advantage of not squeezing the pips which can otherwise give the wine a bitter flavour, and of being able to handle very small amounts of grapes.
Débourbage	Following pressing, the juice is left in a tank so that any solid matter can settle before the liquid is fermented.
Le Moût	The must: grape juice which has not yet fermented into wine. The *moût d'égoutage* is the juice which is drawn from the grapes after they have simply been crushed to remove the stalks, skins and pips. The *moût de presse* is the juice drawn from the press.
Cuve de Fermentation	The fermentation tank, now often made of stainless steel with built-in cooling equipment. Wine may subsequently spend time in other tanks which are also known as *cuves*.
Liqueur	If a sweet *vin doux naturel* is to be made, such as Muscat de Beaumes de Venise, alcohol will be added to the vat to halt fermentation, maintaining the natural sweetness of the wine.
Le Fût (or Tonneau, Barrique, or Pièce)	The barrel. In some regions, most notably Burgundy, producers ferment their wine in the same new oak barrels in which it is to mature. They believe that this helps to give their wine a richer, oakier, flavour.
Chaptalisation	The generally legal (though not in all regions) addition of cane sugar to fermenting must in order to raise the alcohol level of the finished wine.

vence or a blackcurrant version made from the Cabernet grapes in the Loire, that you realise that a well made rosé is the equal of all but the very finest whites.

Above: *The bottling line at the firm of Hugel in Alsace. Here, as increasingly elsewhere, modern equipment and spotless hygiene are considered essential.*

Winemaking: What the Technical Terms Mean

La Fermentation Malolactique (Le "Malo")	The natural second fermentation which transforms the appley *malic* acid present in any young wine into creamier *lactic* acid. In some regions, such as Burgundy, all wines do their ''*malo*''; in others, such as Alsace, where producers want to maximise freshness, the process is prevented by means of a small dose of sulphur dioxide.
La Cuvée	A specific vat, possibly denoting a particular style or a higher quality – e.g. *Cuvée Personelle.*
Lie	The lees, or solid yeast particles held in suspension in all recently-made wine. Most producers aim to separate the wine from these lees by *soutirage* and *collage*, but in Muscadet there is a tradition of bottling the wine "*sur lie*", or "on its lees" in order to give it a characteristically yeasty flavour.
Soutirage	Racking – the passing of wine from one tank or barrel to another. This needs to be done to prevent the fine solids (mostly yeast) from giving the wine undesirable flavours.
Collage	Fining – usually using egg white, caseine (milk protein) or bentonite (an earth compound), all of which, when added to the wine shortly before bottling, fall to the bottom of the barrel or vat, dragging down with them any fine solids which may be suspended in the liquid.
Filtrage	Filtering – not absolutely necessary, particularly when the wine has been carefully fined, but usually practised nontheless.
Traitement à Froid	Like filtering, this pre-bottling chilling process is not really necessary, but it does serve to precipitate any tartaric acid crystals which might otherwise form like tiny diamonds in the bottom of the bottle following a spell in a cool cellar. These crystals are both harmless and flavourless, and as natural a feature of a white wine as the sediment in a red.
La Mise en Bouteilles	Bottling – normally a mechanical process, this can nevertheless still take place as it has done for centuries, simply by drilling a tap into the side of the barrel and emptying the contents bottle by bottle. This is, however rare and only makes sense where producers want their wine to remain for as long as possible in contact with its yeast.

*T*here is one very simple way to turn a still wine into a fizzy one; all you have to do is to put the wine into a sealed tank, pump in sufficient carbon dioxide for the gas to dissolve in the liquid, and bottle the result under pressure. The process works well for fizzy drinks and most gassy mineral water, and it is used throughout the world for the kind of wine you buy cheaply in supermarkets. However, this winemaking process, known as "carbonation", cannot be used to make any quality wine in France.

Every other method of making sparkling wine involves a process of fermentation in which the activity of yeast and sugar create carbon dioxide naturally. The classic way of doing this is simply to bottle the wine before it has quite finished fermenting. This is not easily achieved, and involves filtering and racking – passing the wine from one tank to another – in order to slow the fermentation down, and requires careful judgment of the amount of sugar to leave unfermented. Known as the *Méthode Rurale*, this is the most old-fashioned sparkling wine process in France; it is now only used in Gaillac, at Die and in Limoux. Wines made in this way can vary widely in their fizziness and will tend to contain a deposit of yeast.

No such deposit will, however, be found in wines made by the *Méthode Champenoise*, fuller details of which appear in the section devoted to Champagne. In basic terms, this process involves the addition of a yeast and sugar solution known as *liqueur de tirage* to fully fermented dry wine, and the refermentation of that wine in bottle over a period which can vary between nine months and several years. The longer the wine remains in contact with the yeast, the more "biscuity" the result. To remove the yeast from the wine, the bottles are stored neck-down, at an increasingly steep angle, and shaken and turned (a process known as *remuage*) either by hand or, more frequently nowadays, by mechanical *giropalettes* until all of the solid matter has settled in the neck of the now upside-down bottle. The bottles are then passed through a special cool brine or liquid gas bath which freezes the contents of the bottle neck. The beer-caps with which the bottles are sealed are then removed and the frozen, yeasty grit expelled (*dégorgement*). The space left is replenished either with more of the same wine as is already in the bottle or, generally a sweetened blend of wine, sugar and occasionally brandy, known as the *dosage*.

This method is the only one used for Champagne and the majority of other *Appellation Contrôlée* sparkling wines produced in France; the only exceptions are those made by the *Méthode Rurale*. Wine made in this way should be the best fizz you could find; unfortunately, however, putting the bubbles into the wine in the best possible way is only half the story. Everything depends on the

Below: Remuage – *the process of shaking and turning bottles daily so as to shift the sediment down on to the bottle cork whence it is expelled by* dégorgement.

Left: *A rare view of the* Méthode Champenoise *in action. The sediment in this pink Champagne has been moved down to the neck of the bottle by* remuage *and will soon be ready for* dégorgement.

filtered under pressure so as to avoid losing any of those precious bubbles, and rebottled. Proponents of this method, which is widely used in the USA and Australia, claim that it makes wine which is almost as good as *Méthode Champenoise*. This is very rarely the case and, under French law no *Appellation Contrôlée* wine can be made in this way.

Equally excluded from AOC status are wines made by the *Charmat* or *Cuve Close* method which mimics the *Méthode Champenoise* but allows the refermentation to take place in large (up to 120,000 litre) sealed tanks. Filtering and bottling take place under pressure. Wine produced by *Cuve Close* (generally inexpensive sparkling wine which has no appellation and which does not carry the words *Méthode Champenoise* or *Crémant* on its label) will tend to have larger bubbles than *Méthode Champenoise* wine, and it will almost certainly not have the delicate threads of tiny bubbles found in the best bottle fermented products.

quality of the original base wine; good and bad Champagne are made by precisely the same method.

A simpler, though rarely used, alternative process, known as the transfer method, also allows the wine to referment in bottle, but skips the labour-intensive *remuage/dégorgement* stage. Instead, the sparkling wine is passed from bottle into a tank, whence it is

---

Sparkling Wines: Explaining the Terms

There are a great many technical terms associated with the making of sparkling wine. The following are the most important:

Assemblage — The essential blending of base wines for Champagne and any other sparkling wine which uses more than one grape variety and/or wine of more than one vintage.

Crémant — Confusingly, in Champagne this means that a wine is less fizzy; elsewhere, however, as in Crémant de Bourgogne, de la Loire and d'Alsace, it simply means sparkling wine.

Cuve Close — Tank-fermented sparkling wine – also called "Charmat" after the inventor.

Dégorgement — The removal of the yeast from the wine following the second fermentation. Bollinger's R.D. (recently disgorged) Champagne is a rare example of a wine which has been left for a far longer than customary (ten rather than three years) before disgorgement.

Dosage — The process of adding sweet *liqueur d'expédition* to sparkling wine following *dégorgement*.

Giropalettes — The mechanical racks which perform *remuage*.

Méthode Champenoise — The process of fermenting wine in the bottle in which it is finally sold.

Mousse — Literally, the fizz.

Remuage — The process of shifting the yeast, by manipulation and gradual inversion of the bottle, down to its neck when making *Méthode Champenoise* wines.

To the winemakers of California and Australia, France's wine industry seems bound up in miles of red tape. Growers cannot plant the grapes they want where they want; in the best regions they are stopped from irrigating their vines, even in a drought, and, in short, the whole business seems hogtied by bureaucracy.

What that American might not realise is that the French have had stringent wine laws since long before Columbus' parents were born. Grapes have been grown in most of the areas of present day viticulture since the Roman occupation, so it is hardly surprising that, after a few centuries, farmers discovered that certain types of vine make better wine when planted in certain types of soil and in regions which enjoy a particular type of climate.

By the same token, many of the French vineyards which we take for granted as being amongst the best in the world gained their reputation over a thousand years ago. Corton-Charlemagne, for instance, one of the finest white burgundies, comes from a small vineyard which belonged to the emperor Charlemagne who lived between 742-814AD. It would have been surprising had the emperor of Europe, as he then was, not taken the best piece of land available in that area for himself, and none finer has since been discovered. As for the way in which the wine was made, Charlemagne himself laid down a strict set of rules which applied to the whole of Burgundy.

It is the basic validity of such long-established reputations, and the damage done to them by greedy producers ready to take short cuts, which in the mid 1930's led a group of Frenchmen to establish a set of wine laws which, when properly applied, are still acknowledged to be the most sensible of any wine-producing country.

In essence, France's laws acknowledge the intrinsic quality of the land and climate – or micro-climate – in which each wine's grapes have been grown; the specific nature of those grapes, the age of the vines (newly planted vines do not make good wine, so cannot produce wine of designated quality until their fifth harvest); the tonnage harvested per acre (the higher the yield, the thinner the wine); and the way in which the wine is made.

Under the aegis of the *Institut National des Appellations d'Origine* (INAO), winemaking France is divided into areas which make *Vin de Table*, the most basic level of all; *Vin de Pays*, country wines; *Vin Délimité de Qualité Supérieure* (VDQS), country wines of a higher quality and with more identifiable regional characteristics; and *Appellation d'Origine Contrôlée* (AOC), from regions and villages whose vineyards have the soil, climate and tradition required to make France's best wines. Beyond the AOC, and varying from region to region, there are further levels of individual quality which apply to specific vineyards, with *Grands Crus* at the peak of the pyramid, just above *Premiers Crus*. The higher the quality designa-

Above: Grands Crus *such as* Le Montrachet *do not have to mention the village they come from. Morgeot is a Premier Cru vineyard in Chassagne Montrachet; its wine should be better than the non-Premier Cru from the same commune. The Bourgogne is straight white burgundy, probably from a variety of places.*

tion, the stricter the edicts on yields, specified grape varieties and so on.

The rules are not cast in concrete: regions and vineyards are not often demoted, but promotion to VDQS from *Vin de pays*, and to *Appellation Contrôlée* from VDQS has been allowed in a large number of regions, while Alsace has recently created a wholly new set of *Grand Cru* vineyards.

The quality ladder is easily understood, once you have accepted the concept of some specific vineyards and regions producing better wine than others. A wine produced in the *Grand Cru* Burgundy vineyard of Le Montrachet should be better than one from the

The Quality Ladder

AOC	*Appellation Contrôlée* wine produced in France's best winemaking regions. An entire region, such as Bordeaux, may have its own appellation; so may a village, such as Sauternes, a vineyard, such as Le Montrachet, and even a style, such as the sparkling Crémant de Bourgogne. Local quality designations, usually of the *Premier* or *Grand Cru* style, may form part of the appellation.
VDQS	*Vin Délimité de Qualité Supérieure*. Regions of almost, but not quite, *Appellation Contrôlée* standard or jumped-up *Vin de Pays*, depending on your view. The INAO unofficially admits that this compromise designation is not a success and may be abolished one day. In the meantime, new ones are still being created. Fairly strict controls on yields, grape varieties etc. are applied.
Vin de Pays	Less strictly controlled, but still restricted regions which produce honest country wines, but sometimes aspire to greater recognition.
Vin de Table	Could be anything – from wine made in a designated region which falls outside the rules (through being made from non-permitted grape varieties, too-young vines, too high a yield etc) to blends from the entire country.

Examples

Specific (AOC + Quality designation	Grand Cru (Burgundy); Grand Cru Classé (Bordeaux); Grand Cru (Alsace); Premier Cru
Local (AOC Village or commune)	Meursault; Hermitage; Sancerre; Sauternes; Muscadet
Regional (AOC Region)	Burgundy; Bordeaux; Alsace
VDQS	Sauvignon de St-Bris; Vins de Bugey
Vin de Pays	Vin de Pays du Jardin de la France; Vin de Pays des Coteaux de l'Ardèche
National	Vin de Table

Above: *A typical Alsacien village seen from the vines which overlook it. Other than* Grand Crus, *all wines from Alsace are identified by grape variety, rather than locality.*

nearby *Premier Cru* vineyard of Morgeot in the commune of Chassagne Montrachet. A wine made in a non-*Premier Cru* vineyard in that same commune – in other words a Chassagne Montrachet – should, however, still be a cut above a straight white burgundy which could come from anywhere within the much larger region of Burgundy.

Unfortunately, however, life is not always quite so simple. Two villages within the same region and technically of the same quality level may differ enormously: Meursault and Mâcon Blanc are both communal appellations within Burgundy, but one bottle of the former is worth at least two of the latter. And both would probably outclass most Muscadet, a wine which enjoys its own communal appellation in the Loire.

Elsewhere, there are regions which step outside the system. In Alsace for example, although there are now *Grands Crus*, the other wines are all known by their grape varieties rather than the villages in which they are made and can thus come from anywhere within the region.

Until the middle of this century the vast majority of French winegrowers farmed grapes only as part of their agricultural endeavours. Even in regions such as Chablis, the little money they earned from their wine was rarely sufficient to feed their families and, besides, there were years when poor weather prevented the growers from making any saleable wine at all. It is against that historical background that France's wine industry evolved into its present-day form.

In French, revealingly, winemakers generally refer to themselves as *"vignerons"* or *"viticulteurs"*, both of which terms relate to the work of growing vines rather than of making wine. Even when the grower does transform his grapes into wine, he may not be very skilled at maturing that wine, putting it into bottle, and selling it.

To take on the job of turning the fruit of your own vineyard into a marketable bottle of wine calls for at least three separate skills. So it is hardly surprising that most of France's growers have traditionally been happy to leave at least some of the headaches to merchants, or *négociants*, who buy the wine in barrel or tank which it is still young, possibly blending it with other growers' wines from the same region or *appellation* and often creating in the process a mixture which is better than any of its components. Most important of all, these merchants all have, or should have, the ability to market the wine they have made. Many of the villages whose wines are now known internationally were put on the vinous map by one or two keen local *négociants*.

Other growers, however, particularly in regions such as the south, where there were traditionally few merchants, and wines are difficult to sell, embraced the concept of the co-operative. This simplifies their lives still further: they do not have to make their wine at all, but simply deliver the grapes to the local co-op which pays for them by the kilo. Co-operatives now play a major role in France, particularly in the south, in Alsace, Champagne and southern Burgundy. Part of their success has been due to the growth of supermarket, liquor store, and wine merchant chains which require the large quantities of consistent, low-price wine that the co-operatives are perfectly placed to supply.

Somewhere, sandwiched profitably in various layers between growers, co-operatives, *négociants* and commercial wine buyers, there is also the shadowy but seem-

Right: *Michel and Henri Laroche, father and son, are both merchants – négociants – and growers – vignerons – in Chablis. Most good négociants also own vineyards, indeed in Burgundy the amount of land they own has grown in recent years, since this enables a merchant to ensure that he will be able to maintain supplies of the quality he needs. The merchants' domaine wines are often sold separately.*

ingly essential profession of the *courtier*. These brokers save *négociants* the chore of choosing from too wide a range of growers' wines by seeking out samples which they know are likely to suit a specific company's needs. They are the cogs which turn the complicated wheels of the Bordeaux trade, standing between *château* and merchant, and they can save foreign buyers' valuable time by pointing them towards sources of the kind of wine they want to buy.

In recent years a battle has also developed between the different segments of the market, with growers who have discovered – sometimes thanks to the brokers – that they can sell their own wine in bottles, flying a "Small is Beautiful" flag, and implying that no wine from a *négociant* can ever be quite as fine as a wine produced by an individual estate. The merchants, for their part, argue that they are uniquely placed to provide continuity of quality and style, and both groups are united in suggesting that the co-operatives' obligation to accept their members' grapes prevents them from making anything first class. In reality, no group holds a monopoly of quality.

Left: *Throughout France – in this instance, Roussillon – small family domaines are still the most essential part of wine production. Monsieur Pujol and his son bottle and sell their own wine (which is called Domaine de la Rourède) but many of their neighbours deliver their grapes to the nearby co-operative.*

Who's Who in the Wine Industry

The Grower

Le Vigneron; Le Viticulteur; Le Propriétaire; Le Récoltant.
All synonyms for individual producers who grow their own grapes and make their own wine.

GAEC, GFA

Initials indicating domaines which are run as family businesses of one kind or another.

The Broker

Le Courtier
The (arguably) essential, but, as far as most consumers are concerned, invisible go-between who finds growers' wine for French merchants, or growers' and/or merchants' wine for other customers in France or elsewhere.

The Merchant

Le Négociant
A merchant who may buy and sell wine which is already in bottle.
Le Négociant-Éleveur
The *élevage* of a wine involves the possible blending of several *cuvées* and the use (or not) of new oak barrels, as well as decisions as to whether it will, or will not, be filtered, and the choice of when it should be bottled.

The Co-operative

La Cave Coopérative; La Cave des Vignerons; Les Vignerons Réunis.
Any of these names may appear on bottles produced by co-operatives from wine vinified from their members' grapes. Some co-operatives have the reprehensible habit of labelling their wine as if it were made and bottled by one of the members in particular.

French wine label should tell you a great deal about the stuff in the bottle. Beyond the useful details of bottle contents (70 or 75cl for example) and alcoholic strength there are six pieces of information, all or most of which may appear on any label: the name of the wine, its quality level, the region in which is was made, the wine's style, its vintage, the person or company who made it, and if and where they bottled it.

The name: this could be a brand such as Piat d'Or or Mouton Cadet; the name of the estate at which the wine was made, such as Château Carbonnieux or, as in the case of Moët & Chandon, its producer; a regional description such as Bourgogne Blanc or, particularly as in Alsace, the name of a grape variety, such as Riesling or Gewürztraminer.

The quality level: is the wine a basic *Vin de*

Table which could be a blend of wines from anywhere in France, a *Vin de Pays* or *Vin Délimité de Qualité Supérieure*, (often abbreviated to VDQS) which would be a wine from a specified region, produced from specifically permitted grape varieties and within legally established yields per hectare? Or is it an *Appellation Contrôlée* (abbreviated to AOC), in which case its production will have been subject to an even stricter set of regulations? As an *Appellation Contrôlée* wine, its label may reveal an even higher quality designation, such as *Premier Cru*, *Grand Cru*, or *Grand Cru Classé* indicating that it comes from a superb vineyard.

The region: this may have appeared as the wine's name – e.g. Puligny Montrachet, or as part of its quality designation – e.g. Vin de Pays de l'Aude or Appellation Bordeaux Con-

GRAND CRU CLASSÉ —— Classified growth (according to the Graves classification of 1959)

NB Vintage is on the neck label. Note also that there is no indication of whether this wine is dry or sweet; nor indeed of whether this is the estate's red or white wine, but as it is in a clear glass bottle there can be no doubt.

CHÂTEAU CARBONNIEUX —— Name of wine ie name of estate

APPELLATION GRAVES CONTROLÉE —— Appellation (quality category); in this case AOC

GRAVES —— Zone

MIS EN BOUTEILLES 〜〜〜 AU CHATEAU —— Bottled at the château (estate)

PRODUCE OF FRANCE

Société des Grandes Graves —— Name and address of proprietor
PROPRIÉTAIRE A LÉOGNAN (GIRONDE)

G. MOOLENAAR · BORDEAUX

Vintage

Name of négociant —— F.CHAUVENET 1984 F.CHAUVENET

Neck label

Company logo —— 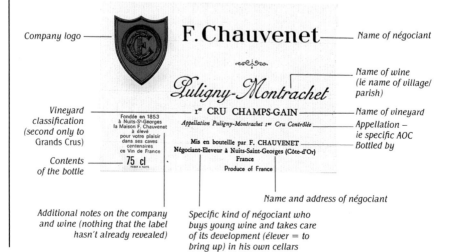 **F. Chauvenet** —— Name of négociant

Name of wine
(ie name of village/
parish)

Vineyard classification (second only to Grands Crus) — Fondée en 1853 à Nuits-S¹-Georges la Maison F. Chauvenet à élevé pour votre plaisir dans ses caves centenaires ce Vin de France

Puligny-Montrachet

1ᵉʳ CRU CHAMPS-GAIN —— Name of vineyard

Appellation Puligny-Montrachet 1ᵉʳ Cru Contrôlée —— Appellation – ie specific AOC

Mis en bouteille par F. CHAUVENET —— Bottled by
Négociant-Eleveur à Nuits-Saint-Georges (Côte-d'Or)

Contents of the bottle —— **75 cl**

France
Produce of France

Name and address of négociant

Additional notes on the company and wine (nothing that the label hasn't already revealed)

Specific kind of négociant who buys young wine and takes care of its development (elever = to bring up) in his own cellars

trôlée. Otherwise, the producer's address should reveal all – Jean Dupont, Propriétaire à Chablis.

The style: most indications of style refer to sweetness. Sparkling wines can be very dry, Brut Zéro, very sweet, Doux, or, more usually, somewhere between the two. They may be made from 100% white grapes, Blanc de Blancs, or from 100% black ones, Blanc de Noirs, and less bubbly, Crémant. Still wines can reveal their sweetness too: Sec, Moelleux etc.

The vintage: usually featured on the neck label; this can also appear on the main label itself. The expression VSR is used in Burgundy to describe a non-vintage wine. Elsewhere, the letters NV may appear.

The producer: by law no wine can hide the name of its maker. In simple terms, it may have been made by an individual grower: *Vigneron*, *Propriétaire*, or *Viticulteur*; a merchant: *Négociant*; or a co-operative: *Cave Coopérative*, though other descriptions can be used. Note, however, that pseudonyms and codes are sometimes adopted: "CCVG" could be a co-operative; the unfamiliar "Pierre Dupont, Négociant a Beaune" could be one of a number of brand names belonging to a merchant whose own name you might recognise immediately.

Where the wine was bottled: *Mis en Bouteilles au Domaine* or *au Château* does not necessarily indicate a better wine – some châteaux are not very good at bottling – but it will suggest that the producer is at least taking responsibility for his handiwork. Beware though wines made by co-operatives which claim to be "domaine-bottled".

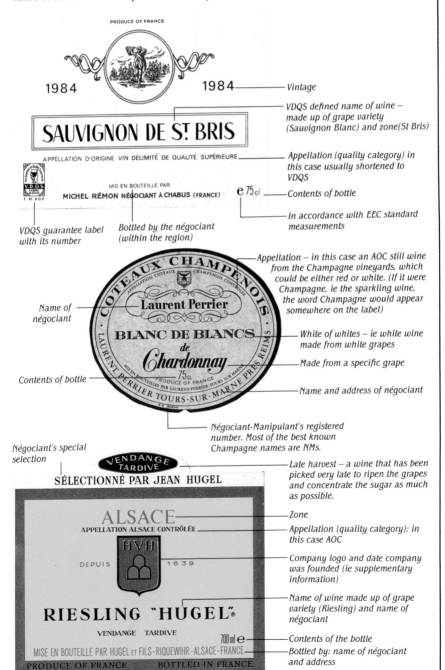

PRODUCE OF FRANCE

1984   1984 —— Vintage

—— VDQS defined name of wine –
made up of grape variety
(Sauvignon Blanc) and zone(St Bris)

SAUVIGNON DE St BRIS

APPELLATION D'ORIGINE VIN DÉLIMITÉ DE QUALITÉ SUPÉRIEURE —— Appellation (quality category) in this case usually shortened to VDQS

MIS EN BOUTEILLE PAR
MICHEL RÉMON NÉGOCIANT À CHABLIS (FRANCE)   e 75cl —— Contents of bottle

—— In accordance with EEC standard measurements

VDQS guarantee label   Bottled by the négociant
with its number   (within the region)

Appellation – in this case an AOC still wine from the Champagne vineyards, which could be either red or white. (If it were Champagne, ie the sparkling wine, the word Champagne would appear somewhere on the label)

Name of
négociant

Laurent Perrier

BLANC DE BLANCS —— White of whites – ie white wine made from white grapes

de
Chardonnay —— Made from a specific grape

Contents of bottle ——

Name and address of négociant

Négociant-Manipulant's registered number. Most of the best known Champagne names are NMs.

Négociant's special
selection

VENDANGE TARDIVE

Late harvest – a wine that has been picked very late to ripen the grapes and concentrate the sugar as much as possible.

SÉLECTIONNÉ PAR JEAN HUGEL

ALSACE —— Zone

APPELLATION ALSACE CONTRÔLÉE —— Appellation (quality category); in this case AOC

DEPUIS   HVH   1639 —— Company logo and date company was founded (ie supplementary information)

Name of wine made up of grape variety (Riesling) and name of négociant

RIESLING "HUGEL"®

VENDANGE TARDIVE   700 ml e —— Contents of the bottle

MISE EN BOUTEILLE PAR HUGEL ET FILS-RIQUEWIHR-ALSACE-FRANCE —— Bottled by: name of négociant and address

PRODUCE OF FRANCE   **BOTTLED IN FRANCE**

Once you have mastered the many intricacies and the confusion of French wine labels, there remains the question of what to buy, and how and where to buy it. Buying Champagne is arguably easier than any other kind of wine. After all, the big Champagne houses make much of the fact that they do not release any of their wine until it is ready to be drunk and enjoyed. Non-vintage Champagne is, by definition, a blend of several years' wines, married together to produce a fizz which can be uncorked the day it is bought. But the success of the world's most famous sparkling wine in recent years has changed all that. Nowadays, anyone who has tasted a wide range of non-vintage Champagne during the mid 1980's will almost certainly have encountered some extremely "green" tasting wine. By the same token, even the very best houses have felt obliged to satisfy the demand of their customers in shipping very good wine which, if asked, they would admit ought to be kept for at least six months before being uncorked.

Vintage Champagne has, however, the advantage over non-vintage in proclaiming its age on its label. Bottles of 'N. V.' can vary in age by five years or so, depending on where they are bought, with a high turnover merchant or supermarket clearing his shelves in weeks, while the corner shop allows its wine to gather dust somewhere at the back of the cellar. If you like the biscuity, nutty flavour of old Champagne, some of these forgotten bottles are worth buying. If you prefer your Champagne to taste fresh, buy from a merchant with a rapid turnover.

France's other sparkling wines should, like rosé, almost without exception be bought as young as possible, and from a supplier who

Below: *A wine shop in Sancerre inviting passers-by to taste and buy. Buying wine directly from growers, or from shops or co-operatives in the region of production is one of the pleasures of travelling in France. Excellent value for money can often be found.*

Buying Wine: A Selection

Inexpensive/Daily Drinking
Vin de Pays du Jardin de la France
Gros Plant
Bergerac
Bordeaux Blanc
Rosé de Provence
Côtes du Rhône Rosé

Mid-Price
Muscadet
Bourgogne Blanc
Bourgogne Aligoté
Mâcon Blanc / Villages
Graves
Côtes du Rhône
Gewürztraminer
Riesling

Slightly More Extravagant
Chablis
St-Véran
Pouilly-Vinzelles
Sancerre
Pouilly-Fumé
Châteauneuf-du-Pape
Tokay ''Réserve Personelle'' (or a
   similar quality Alsace)
Muscat de Rivesaltes
Muscat de Beaumes de Venise
Ste-Croix-du-Mont
Old Monbazillac

Lashing Out
Pouilly-Fuissé (but only from Château
   de Fuissé and Dom. Ferret – others
   not worth it)
Pernand Vergelesses
St-Aubin
St-Romain
Auxey-Duresses
Meursault
Alsace Vendange Tardive

For The Experience
Top Class Graves: Domaine de
   Chevalier
Meursault Premier Cru
Chassagne-Montrachet Premier Cru
Corton-Charlemagne
Le Montrachet; Bâtard-Montrachet etc
Fine Sauternes and Barsac
Alsace Sélection de Grains Nobles
Château Grillet
Château-Chalon

can be expected to shift his wine very rapidly. There are of course exceptions; Vintage Crémant de Bourgogne can sometimes be kept, and Arbois, for example, makes a slightly longer-lasting rosé. There are those who claim that Tavel and Lirac, the Rhône's two top rosés, improve with age, but I have certainly never been convinced by older bottles of these last two wines.

Inexpensive white wine, by which I mean almost all Vin de Pays and VDQS, as well as Muscadet and most other simple, dry French wines, should be drunk just as young as those rosés. These wines are not intended to improve with age – very few of the world's white wines are – and they tend to lose their freshness quickly, gaining no extra richness in the process. As for older white wines, the most likely source for these are auctions which regularly include lots sold by merchants, individuals and, on occasion, bankrupt or financially troubled restaurants. Bargains can be found in this way as can wines which are available nowhere else, but caution is advisable; dry white wines can suffer from being kept badly or for too long and a case of 1971 white burgundy which has passed through the hands of several owners might prove on opening, to be less of a snip than it did in the excitement of the auction room. Old sweet wines can be a safer bet as their sugar content helps to protect them from the perils of oxidation.

Buying young wine directly from the producer is a particular delight in France; merchants and growers have increasingly discovered that merely placing a sign outside their cellars can bring in a steady flow of passers-by, many of whom can be persuaded to leave with at least a few bottles under their arms. Many large merchants and individual estates are now geared up to receive visitors and boast English-speaking guides, audio-

Below: *Crémant de Bourgogne sparkling wine is a good inexpensive alternative to Champagne. These bottles are stored in the Caves de Bailly.*

visual displays and organised tastings galore. Such tours can prove rewarding, but if you want to meet the men and women who actually make France's wines, the smaller cellars of the growers themselves are often a better bet. If you have the courtesy to avoid visiting during the hectic bustle of the harvest, telephone to make an appointment beforehand, and do not call during the two mid-day hours when producers are having lunch, you will almost certainly be well received, and offered tasting samples of several wines. Most likely these will be drawn directly from tanks or barrels and will be of the most recent harvests. If you show an intelligent interest and genuinely appear to be a potential purchaser, the grower may then uncork a bottle or two of his older wine.

Even assuming that you feel reasonably confident in being able to spot and reject a wine which smells or tastes dirty, oxidised or faulty in some other way, if you have never tasted new and very young white wine before, you may at first find it difficult to know the qualities you should be looking for, the characteristics which will make for a bottle worth keeping as opposed to the ones which mark a wine that will never be enjoyable to drink. In fact, it takes very little practice to pick up the knack. The criteria for judging the potential of young wine are precisely the same as those for assessing older bottles; whatever its age, a wine should, above all, have *balance*. Its alcohol should never outweigh the flavour of its fruit; there should be enough acidity to keep the wine fresh-tasting and – in the case of sweet wines – to prevent them from cloying, but not enough to obscure the other flavours. A wine which seems unbalanced – overly alcoholic, too sweet or acidic – when it is first made will almost never gain balance as it ages; if there is too much acid for the fruit today, by the time that acid softens, there is a high chance that the fruit will have disappeared too.

Above: *A selection of local wines on offer in the shop window of the Fruitière Vinicole d'Arbois, a Jura co-operative. Prominent in the display is a Vin Jaune in the traditional 62cl clavelin bottle. Vin Jaune, particularly Château-Chalon, is a wine to lay down; it is expensive but lasts for many years.*

Cellars to Visit

Vouvray
  Prince Poniatowski, Clos Baudoin (47) 52 71 02
  Ch. St-Georges, Rochecorbon (47) 52 50 72
  Manoir du Haut-Lieu (47) 52 78 87
Saumur
  Bouvet Ladubay, St-Hilaire-St-Florent (41) 50 11 12
  Ackerman-Laurance, St-Hilaire-St-Florent (41) 50 25 33
Sancerre
  Dom Vacheron, Sancerre
Anjou
  Château des Fesles, Thouarcé (41) 91 40 40
Bordeaux
  Château de Malle, Preignac (56) 63 28 67
  Château Piada, Barsac (56) 27 16 13

Provence
  Château Val-Joanis, Pertuis (90) 79 20 77
  Château de Selle, Taradeau (94) 68 86 86
  Les Maitres Vignerons de St-Tropez (94) 56 32 04
Rhône
  Les Vignerons de Tavel (66) 50 03 57
Southern Burgundy
  Château de Fuissé, Fuissé (85) 37 61 44
Côte Chalonnaise
  Michel Juillot, Mercurey (80) 45 27 27
Côte d'Or
  Château de Meursault, Meursault (80) 21 22 98
  Dom des Comtes Lafon, Meursault
Champagne
  Moët & Chandon, Epernay (26) 51 71 11
  Perrier-Jouët, Epernay (26) 51 20 53
  Pol Roger, Epernay (26) 51 41 95
  Laurent-Perrier, Tours-sur-Marne (26) 51 23 89

White Wines: How Long Do They Keep?

Wine to Drink Very Young
(Within two years of the harvest)

Alsace
Edelzwicker
Other inexpensive Alsace
Burgundy
Aligoté
Country wines
Vins de Pays, VDQS
Loire
Muscadet, Gros Plant
Rhône
Côtes du Rhône
Rosé
All rosé
Savoie
Vins de Savoie

Wine to Drink Young
(Within five years)

Alsace
Gewürztraminer, Pinot Blanc
Burgundy
Mâcon Villages, Petit Chablis, most basic
Chablis, Bourgogne Blanc

Loire
Pouilly Fumé, Sancerre, dry and medium
Vouvray
Rhône
Crozes Hermitage Blanc

Wine for Keeping
(Over five years)

Alsace
Well made wines from good vintages
Vendange Tardive
Bordeaux
Sauternes and Barsac
Top class white Burgundy
Meursault, Puligny-Montrachet,
Chassagne- Montrachet, Corton-
Charlemagne, Le Montrachet (Bâtard-
Montrachet etc)
Grand Cru Chablis and
Premier Cru from good producers and
good vintages
Jura
Château-Chalon
Loire
Vouvray Moelleux, Quarts de Chaume
Coulée-de-Serrant
Rhône
Château Grillet

*T*here is possibly more nonsense talked about how wine should be served than any other aspect of the subject. Wine is to be enjoyed after all; turning the removal of a cork from a bottle into a quasi-religious ceremony removes wine entirely from the origins it shares with beer, cider and every other beverage drunk by man. As a general rule, use generously proportioned glasses with bowls which come in at the rim, capturing rather than expelling the fine aromas of the wine. Do not fill them too generously. This is a useful command with any wine – the fuller the glass, the more difficult it is to swirl the wine around to release those aromas – but it is particularly valid in the case of the wines covered in this book, all of which should be served cool. Wine will warm up more quickly in the glass than in the bottle, especially when people rest the bowl in their hand, allowing their body heat to cook the wine gently.

To cool wine, try to avoid putting it into the freezer. Far better is a spell in the refrigerator (45 minutes will usually suffice) or even more effectively, 15 minutes in a bucket full of cold water and ice. Virtual immersion of the bottle of wine in the water is far more efficient than merely surrounding the bottle with ice cubes.

Opening Champagne and sparkling wine bottles can be an extraordinarily dangerous practice. In the USA, locally produced "champagne" has to be packaged with a protective plastic capsule, complete with warning; in Britain, Champagne corks are responsible for more eye injuries than any other single item. So, rule one is: don't point the bottle at anybody or at anything which might be injured or damaged by the impact of a rapidly moving projectile.

Still white wine and rosé rarely gain much from being allowed to "breathe" before a meal, and neither is usually decanted. After all, the principal reason for decanting is to remove the sediment which is created as red wines and port age, but which is entirely absent in white and pink wines. On the other hand, do not chill all your whites and rosés to the same temperature, and certainly avoid the widely practised crime of overchilling a wine to the point at which its flavour is indistinguishable from iced water. Very nasty wines should, for this very reason, be served as near freezing point as possible, but, as a general rule, the better, richer and older a dry wine, the less cold it needs to be. The one exception to this rule are sweeter wines, which can be served far cooler; indeed at lower temperatures they will seem less sweet.

Lastly, there is the question of the natural order of things: what goes first? What comes last? There are three rules to remember: the better the wine, the later it is served; youth precedes age; and, above all, dry comes before sweet. Sometimes, inevitably, these rules may conflict, but do not worry too much about getting it wrong. Wine drinking should be a pleasure not some complicated form of social ordeal.

Above: *The best way to cool wine is to stand the bottle in an ice bucket; avoid using the freezer.*

Below: *Fish dishes such as this are ideally accompanied by a dry white wine served at a temperature of 8-9°C.*

Wine Temperatures

The following suggested temperatures (in ° Centigrade) should allow each of the listed wines to taste at their best.

5° represents about a day in the refrigerator
6° takes about three to four hours
7° takes about two to two and a half hours
8° takes about an hour and a half

9° takes about an hour
10° takes between half an hour and an hour
11° takes about half an hour
12-14° would be the temperature of your cellar

Cheap white or rosé ..4°	Bordeaux Blanc ....8°	Savoie ....10°
Sauternes ....5°	Saumur Mousseux ....8°	Côtes de Provence ....10°
Doux Champagne .....5°	Alsace ....8°	Mâcon Blanc ....10°
Alsace Sélection de	Muscadet ....8°	Condrieu ....11°
Grains Nobles ....5°	St-Péray ....9°	Bourgogne Blanc ....11°
Muscat de Beaumes de	Graves ....9°	Arbois Rosé ....12°
Venise ....5°	Pouilly-Fumé ....9°	Château Grillet ....12°
Vouvray Moelleux ......5°	Sancerre ....9°	Chablis ....12°
Quarts de Chaume ....6°	Vouvray Sec ....9°	Pouilly-Fuissé ....12°
Alsace Vendange	Châteauneuf-du-Pape .....9°	Chablis Premier Cru ......12°
Tardive ....6°	Crozes-Hermitage ....9°	Meursault ....12°
Blanquette de	Non-vintage	Top class Graves ....12°
Limoux ....6°	Champagne ....9°	Meursault Premier
St-Péray Mousseux ....6°	Anjou Rosé ....9°	Cru ....13°
Demi-Sec	Vintage Champagne ......10°	Corton-Charlemagne .....13°
Champagne ....6°	Graves Supérieur ....10°	Le Montrachet ....14°
Bonnezeaux ....7°	Tavel Rosé ....10°	Vin Jaune ....14°
Coteaux du Layon .....7°	Arbois ....10°	

*I*f you follow the dictates of the traditionalists, you will neither drink white wine with red meat, nor rosé with fish. And it is a fair bet that, by limiting your wine drinking in this way, you will also miss out on a lot of fun. Thankfully, and despite the rearguard action of a number of Californian winemakers who seem eager to handcuff specific foods to particular wines, nowadays practically anything goes.

However, it should be recognised that some things do go together more successfully than others and the art of finding complementary wines and food involves not trying to bring together partners which are either too similar or too far removed from one another in character and style. A delicately flavoured dish of chicken or fish will be completely overpowered by a blockbuster of a wine, but a carefully chosen bottle can bring out the subtle flavours of a sauce. Where possible, therefore, look for associations of flavour; for example, try serving the same wine as was used for the sauce. The keyword when trying to find perfect matches of food and wine, as when trying to make the dish or the wine in the first place, is balance. A creamy sauce will, for instance, need a wine with enough acidity to combat the richness of the sauce itself.

The following recommended combinations include ones which have been found to work well over the centuries in the regions in which the wines are made – and a few which have been discovered more recently by adventurous gourmets. Just one word of caution: do not use these as absolute rules, they are intended to help you try out further experiments on your own, and are not to be viewed as utterly inflexible.

Below: *A freshly baked veal pie, perfectly matched by a cool bottle of Sancerre. The crisp gooseberry tang of wines, like Sancerre, made from the Sauvignon grape are well suited to any dish which has a reasonably full flavour and a creamy sauce or buttery pastry.*

Right: *Puddings are always more difficult to match to wine. Either the food or the drink can be too sweet, the one overpowering the other. Wines like a late harvest Gewürztraminer can be perfect partners to fruit mousses, thanks to their own inherent fruitiness.*

White and Rosé Wine and Food

Aligoté
Trout; écrevisses.

Alsace (Sélection de Grains Nobles)
Pâté de foie gras; puddings; blue cheese; smoked cheese

Bordeaux Blanc Sec (Graves)
Smoked salmon; veal; oysters; seafood.

Bourgogne Blanc
Rabbit; poulet au vin blanc; escargots; fish in light sauce.

Chablis
Oysters; trout; escargots; fish in cream sauce; fried fish

Chablis Grand Cru
Oysters; smoked salmon; trout; escargots; poulet au vin blanc

Champagne (Dry)
Everything

Champagne (Sweet)
Puddings

Chassagne-Montrachet
Poulet au vin blanc; pâté de foie gras; goat cheese; jambon persillé

Condrieu
Grilled seawater fish

Corton-Charlemagne
Smoked salmon; rich poultry; fish.

Crémant de Bourgogne
Everything

Gewürztraminer
Charcuterie; Munster cheese; choucroute; smoked fish or meat; chinese dishes; tarte à l'oignon

Gros Plant
Oysters; mussels; light fish

Hermitage
Smoked salmon; shellfish

Jura (Vin Jaune)
Coq au vin jaune; goat cheese

Jura (Vin de Paille)
Pâté de foie gras

Mâcon Blanc
Fried fish; escargots; cheese tart

Meursault
Grilled seawater fish; sweetbreads; écrevisses

Muscadet
Oysters; shellfish

Muscat de Beaumes de Venise
Pâte de foie gras; puddings

Pinot Blanc
Quiche; freshwater fish; smoked dishes

Pinot Gris (Tokay)
Pâté de foie gras; smoked dishes, venison

Pouilly Fuissé
Rabbit; goat cheese; veal; fried fish

Pouilly Fumé
Goat cheese; Andouillette (tripe sausage) de Pouilly; chicken or fish in cream sauce

Riesling
Choucroute; coq au Riesling; smoked ham and other charcuterie; smoked cheese; quiche

Rosé d'Anjou
Cold meat

Rosé de Provence
Charcuterie; salade niçoise

Sancerre
Goat cheese; trout meunière; chicken or fish in cream sauce

Sauternes
Pâté de foie gras; roquefort cheese

Vouvray (Demi Sec)
Chinese dishes; fish in cream sauce

Vouvray (Moelleux)
Pâté de foie gras; puddings

*V*intage charts are notoriously controversial pieces of work. Wine enthusiasts who try to use them as foolproof guides forget that even the most comprehensive chart – which could fill an entire book – is essentially a generalisation. If 1978 Chablis receives a higher mark than, for instance, 1976 Chablis, there is nothing to say that there are not several producers who made better wine in the supposedly "lesser" of the two vintages. By the same token, unless you take as careful a note of the name of the producer as you have of the wine name and its vintage, you may very well find some very disappointing wines from an acknowledged "great" year. Even so, some vintages do undoubtedly produce wines which are generally better than those made in other

Right: *The Ste Cathérine cask in the cellars of Hugel in Alsace dates from 1715 and is the world's oldest which is still in regular use for winemaking.*

Vintage Chart

Burgundy Chablis	61	62	63	64	65	66	67	68	69	70	71	72	73
	4	3	1	4	1	3	3	1	2	3	(5)	2	3
	74	75	76	77	78	79	80	81	82	83	84	85	86
	2	(4)	(4)	2	(5)	3	(4)	(4)	2	(4)	(4)	(4)	(4)

Burgundy Cote d'Or	61	62	63	64	65	66	67	68	69	70	71	72	73
	4	4	1	4	1	5	4	1	(5)	4	(5)	2	3
	74	75	76	77	78	79	80	81	82	83	84	85	86
	3	3	3	3	(5)	3	2	(4)	(3)	(4)	(4)	(4)	(4)

Great white burgundies such as Corton-Charlemagne and Le Montrachet from earlier vintages than those circled may still be drinking well.

Bordeaux Graves	61	62	63	64	65	66	67	68	69	70	71	72	73
	4	3	1	4	1	1	5	1	5	(5)	3	1	3
	74	75	76	77	78	79	80	81	82	83	84	85	86
	4	(5)	(4)	2	(5)	(4)	(4)	(5)	(5)	(4)	(4)	(5)	(3)

The figures only apply to truly high quality Graves such as Domaine de Chevalier; others need drinking young.

Bordeaux Sauternes	61	62	63	64	65	66	67	68	69	70	71	72	73
	3	3	2	2	0	3	(5)	2	2	(5)	(3)	2	2
	74	75	76	77	78	79	80	81	82	83	84	85	86
	2	(5)	(5)	2	(4)	(3)	(3)	(5)	(2)	(4)	(2)	(4)	(0)

Loire Sancerre	61	62	63	64	65	66	67	68	69	70	71	72	73
	4	4	1	5	1	2	2	1	5	5	5	1	3
	74	75	76	77	78	79	80	81	82	83	84	85	86
	1	5	5	2	(5)	3	3	3	3	(4)	(3)	(5)	(4)

years when the climate has been kinder. The following chart takes those climatic conditions into consideration and grades the wines with marks out of a possible five. Only white wines which are worth keeping have been listed, and for the same reason I have not included rosés, none of which really improve with time – whatever the winemakers of Tavel may say. Circled vintages should still be drinkable in 1988, whereas the uncircled vintages would almost certainly be past their best.

Vintage Chart

Loire Quarts de Chaume

61	62	63	64	65	66	67	68	69	70	71	72	73
④	3	2	③	2	2	④	2	④	③	④	2	③
74	**75**	**76**	**77**	**78**	**79**	**80**	**81**	**82**	**83**	**84**	**85**	**86**
2	③	⑤	2	④	③	②	③	②	④	②	⑤	④

Alsace

61	62	63	64	65	66	67	68	69	70	71	72	73
3	1	5	1	4	3	1	0	5	3	⑤	2	2
74	**75**	**76**	**77**	**78**	**79**	**80**	**81**	**82**	**83**	**84**	**85**	**86**
1	4	⑤	2	5	4	2	③	②	⑤	②	⑤	④

Vendange Tardive and Sélection de Grains Nobles Alsace wines last longer than dry ones.

Rhône Hermitage

59	60	61	62	63	64	65	66	67	68	69	70	71
5	2	3	2	2	4	2	5	4	2	4	⑤	⑤
72	**73**	**74**	**75**	**76**	**77**	**78**	**79**	**80**	**81**	**82**	**83**	**84**
3	4	2	④	④	3	⑤	4	2	3	2	⑤	③
85	**86**											
⑤	④											

Jura Vin Jaune

61	62	63	64	65	66	67	68	69	70	71	72	73
④	④	1	3	1	④	3	1	③	③	④	1	2
74	**75**	**76**	**77**	**78**	**79**	**80**	**81**	**82**	**83**	**84**	**85**	**86**
1	2	⑤	2	⑤	③	②	③	②	⑤	②	⑤	④

Champagne

Since each Champagne house decides for itself whether or not to declare a vintage, and some houses can be more successful in some years than others, gradings for Champagne are even more generalised than elsewhere. In 1977 for example, supposedly a very poor vintage indeed, Roederer made a great "Cristal".

61	62	63	64	65	66	67	68	69	70	71	72	73
5	2	1	⑤	1	④	3	1	3	④	④	3	④
74	**75**	**76**	**77**	**78**	**79**	**80**	**81**	**82**	**83**	**84**	**85**	**86**
2	⑤	④	2	④	③	③	④	③	③	1	⑤	④

The range of wines available to today's wine drinker – particularly if he or she lives in Britain or the United States – has never been greater. Literally thousands of new wines appear on the market each year, some wholly different from anything anyone has ever tasted before, others only slightly dissimilar from a host of styles which have been known for generations. In this changing world, only the dullest of souls would stick to one or even to a few wines.

The following list consists of a personal selection of alternatives, French and non-French, to some of the most familiar styles produced in France.

Right: *Chardonnay grapes, unarguably the world's most popular variety at the moment from New York to New Zealand.*

2   3   4   5   6   7   8   9   10

1   **11**

Above: *Typical regional bottle shapes: Burgundy (1), Loire (2), Bordeaux (3), vin ordinaire (4), Champagne (5), Côtes du* Rhône (6), Alsace (7), Provence (8 and 9), Languedoc-Roussillon (10), the Jura clavelin (11).

Famous Wines and Some Recommended Alternatives

French Wine	French Alternative	Non-French Alternative
Champagne	Saumur Mousseux Vouvray Crémant de Bourgogne Crémant d'Alsace Blanquette de Limoux St-Péray Vin de Savoie Jura Mousseux Clairette de Die Vin du Bugey	Cava (Spain) Californian Méthode Champenoise (but beware cheap, tank- fermented U.S. "Champagne") Australian Méthode Champenoise New Zealand Méthode Champenoise
Sancerre	Pouilly Blanc Fumé Sauvignon de St-Bris Vin de Pays du Jardin de la France Quincy Sauvignon de Bordeaux Touraine Sauvignon	Californian Sauvignon or "Fumé" New Zealand Sauvignon Australian Sauvignon or Fumé Austrian Sauvignon N.E. Italian Sauvignon Chilean Sauvignon
Un-oaked white burgundy (e.g. basic Chablis)	Chardonnay from l'Ardèche Chardonnay from the Loire	N.E. Italian Chardonnay Bulgarian Chardonnay New Zealand Chardonnay Chilean Chardonnay
Oaked white burgundy (e.g. Meursault)	Top quality Graves Côte du Jura Coteaux Champenois	Californian Chardonnay Australian Chardonnay Better New Zealand Chardonnay Australian (especially Hunter Valley) Sémillon Traditional Rioja (e.g. Marquès de Murrieta)
Pinot Blanc (Alsace)	—	Italian Pinot Bianco
Gewürztraminer (Alsace)	—	New Zealand Gewürztraminer, usually sold as "Traminer" Australian Gewürztraminer Austrian Gewürztraminer Californian Gewürztraminer N.E. Italian Gewürztraminer "Viña Esmeralda" (from Penedés, Spain) German Gewürztraminer
Riesling (Alsace)	—	German "Trocken" and "Halbtrocken" Riesling Chilean Riesling N.E. Italian Riesling Californian Riesling Australian Riesling (particularly from the Barossa and Hunter Valleys) Carr Taylor Reichensteiner (from England)
Vouvray	Montlouis Jasnières Anjou Coteaux du Layon	Californian Chenin Blanc New Zealand Chenin Blanc
Vin Jaune	—	Fino Sherry
Rosé d'Anjou	—	Portuguese Rosé Californian Rosé (sweet)
Rosé de Provence	Rosé de Bourgogne Côtes du Rhône Rosé Arbois Rosé Rosé des Riceys	Chiaretto di Bardolino Rioja Rosado Chilean Rosé Californian Rosé (dry)
Sauternes	Monbazillac Ste-Croix-du-Mont Quarts de Chaume	Australian Late Picked Sémillon Californian Late Picked Muscat
Muscat de Beaumes de Venise	Muscat de Rivesaltes Muscat de Frontignan	Australian Late Picked Muscat Greek Muscat Italian Malvasia and Moscato Moscatel de Setubal (Portugal)

Left: *A wine shop in Sancerre. Such shops are rarer in France than one might expect, many Frenchmen (and women) now buy* *their wine in supermarkets, or directly from the producer, but they are always found in regions where wine is made.*

Above: *Traditional Burgundian harvesting baskets, filled with Aligoté grapes. Much of the wine they produce will end up mixed with Cassis as kir.*

*W*ine buffs can, and almost certainly will, argue for ever about which of the world's wine regions produces the best red. When, however, the discussion turns to dry white wine, there can be little dispute: no matter how great the recent success of the Chardonnay growers of California, Chile and Australia, nowhere outside Burgundy has yet managed to produce a range of wines which can be as immediately appealing when young, and potentially as richly complex when twenty or more years old.

Everything seems fine until one comes to try to buy a bottle of this nectar. Suddenly, confusion is heaped upon confusion; there seem to be more names to remember than in a telephone directory; quality and styles vary alarmingly; and the only certainty one can confidently predict is that the chances of finding a Burgundian bargain are very small indeed.

To understand Burgundy one has to understand both the wine and the place: *le* and *la* Bourgogne. Settled by the Scandinavian Burgundi barbarians in the 5th century, the region enjoyed a brief period of glory in the 14th century when, for around 100 years, under a succession of dukes, the Duchy of Burgundy seemed to be the heart of medieval Europe controlling lands which extended as far as Flanders. Dijon became a capital and

the strip of land to the south of that town was allowed to develop. In a spirit of rare enlightenment, Philip the Bold, Duke of Burgundy, allowed his tax collector, Nicolas Rolin, to found a charity hospital in 1443 whose income would come from the sale of wine from its vineyards. This was the Hospices de Beaune, whose celebrated auction of wine occurs to this day on the third Sunday in November following each harvest.

As winegrowing in Burgundy developed, under the tutelage of the church, and as it became clearer that the choice of grape varieties which could produce fine wine in these soils was limited, it was also realised that this, more than any other wine region in France, is the land of the "*gout de terroir*", the specific flavour given to a wine by the specific plot of land from which it comes. Weather conditions can vary here so dramatically from hillside to hillside that the local term for a parcel of land is a "*climat*"; soils can be totally different from one side of a track to the other. And, perhaps most importantly of all, the Chardonnay, like its neigh-

Villy • Maligny
Lignorelles •
La Chapelle • 2
-Vaupelteigne 1
Milly • CHABLIS • Fleys
3 • Chichée
4
St-Bris-le-Vineux •

Key to map
1 Chablis Grands Crus.
2 Chablis Premiers Crus.
3 Chablis.
4 Petit Chablis.
5 Hautes Côtes de Nuits.
6 Côte de Nuits.
7 Hautes Côtes de Beaune.
8 Côte de Beaune.
9 Côte Chalonnaise.
10 Mâconnais.
11 Mâcon Villages.
12 Pouilly-Fuissé.
13 Pouilly-Loché and Pouilly-
   Vinzelles.

Grape Varieties

White Chardonnay, Aligoté, Pinot Blanc,
Sauvignon (both in very small
quantities), Pinot Beurot.
Red Gamay, Pinot Noir, César (small
quantities only)

Below: *Chardonnay grapes growing on
vines planted in typically chalky soil in
Chablis. The Chardonnay is an early
budding variety which makes protection
against frost essential in this area.*

• DIJON

5

• Fixin

6
• Morey St-Denis
Chambolle-Musigny •
• Vougeot
Vosne-Romanée •
• Nuits St-Georges

• Pernand-Vergelesses
Aloxe-Corton • • Ladoix
Chorey-lès-Beaune •
7 8 • BEAUNE
St-Romain • • Monthélie
Auxey-Duresses • • Meursault
Blagny •
7 • Puligny-Montrachet
Chassagne-Montrachet • CHAGNY
• Bouzeron
• Rully
9
• Mercurey

• Givry
• CHALON-SUR-SAÔNE

Saône

10 TOURNUS •

Chardonnay •

Lugny •
11 • Viré
Clessé •

La Roche-Vineuse

• Prissé • MÂCON
Pouilly-Fuissé • Pouilly-Loché
12 13
• Pouilly-Vinzelles
St-Verand •

bour the Pinot Noir, but unlike the Cabernet Sauvignon, Merlot and Sauvignon Blanc, seems to be a remarkably influenceable variety. In no other region of France is the selection of the right clone for the right plot of land more carefully considered.

This understanding of the crucial individuality of Burgundian villages and vineyards was apparent centuries before Bordeaux created its classification tables, but it inevitably led to a splitting of the region into small units of villages and vineyards. Each vineyard had its own name and each village lucky enough to possess a really great vineyard tacked that name on to that of the commune itself. Thus Auxey became Auxey-Duresses, Puligny, Puligny-Montrachet and so on. Matters were complicated still further by the revolution in 1789. Not only were the large wine estates broken up and sold; changes in French inheritance law ensured that the parcels of land thus created would grow ever smaller. Suddenly, on the death of his or her father, every child, male or female, was entitled to receive equal shares; in other words, a vineyard owner who left five hectares of vines and five heirs could, by dying, lead to the creation of five separate domaines. Obviously the same laws applied elsewhere, but, unlike Bordeaux where, over the years, families had every reason to try to maintain the integral nature of their estates, in Burgundy there was little reluctance to split up estates which were already so fragmented. Only marriage between growers' children, and sensible arrangements between heirs prevented the division of the land continuing in this fashion *ad infinitum*.

Even so, in Burgundy today, 10,000 growers share 40,000ha of vines, farming an uneconomical average of 4ha each. But in the most prestigious villages of the Côte d'Or, the figure is even smaller. Life would be easier if these two, three or four hectare estates were coherent units, but they are not. In almost every case, they are geographically divided between several different communes and appellations. So, a winegrower in Meursault would probably own vines in Puligny-Montrachet, Chassagne-Montrachet and Volnay. Worse still, his vines in each of those communes might well be split between different named vineyards; he might, in Meursault for example, own half a hectare of *Premier Cru* Perrières, a quarter of a hectare of *Premier Cru* Genevrières and three quarters of a hectare of straight Meursault. Each of these wines, however limited its production, has to be made and, more importantly, marketed, separately.

Below: *A rare view of the multi-coloured Hospices de Beaune rooftops, covered with snow. Visitors rarely imagine how cold autumn and winter can be here.*

Above: *Harvest time in the Côte Chalonnaise, close to Montagny. These well-tended vineyards make some of the best basic red and white burgundy.*

Given that background, it is hardly surprising that *négociants* moved in to instill some order into the economic chaos. Three barrels of Meursault from Monsieur Dupont could be blended with two from Monsieur Duval, and one from Monsieur Durand and, hey presto, the merchant had a large enough "*cuvée*" of Meursault to market to the public under his own name.

Some merchants are inevitably better – more skilled, more scrupulous and more honest – than others, just as the growers from whom they buy will vary in quality, but until recently, the system worked quite well. The problem came following the hard financial times of the early 1970s, when the merchants were unable to sell the wine they had bought, so had to stop buying any more. At first, the growers, 90 per cent of whose wine had been bought by the *négociants*, had no idea what to do. Given no choice, many of them embarked on the apparently risky course of bottling and selling their wine themselves.

Despite their early fears, however, and thanks to a growing international taste for dry white wine and a "small-is-beautiful" sympathy for the individual as opposed to the large company, most of these growers had little difficulty finding purchasers for their wine. As sales became easier, for many growers it became harder to resist the temptation to increase production per acre and prices per bottle. The merchants who had previously controlled the market had seen their share fall, in the case of the most prestigious wines, from 90 per cent of the harvest to 60 per cent. Rather than control prices and quality they could, in many cases, do little else but buy any wine they were offered.

It is a simplified picture, but it should serve to explain just how such a variation in quality can occur. After all, if 300 individuals all make Meursault, some of them selling some or all of their wine to 50 or so merchants, it is hardly surprising that two bottles of apparently similar Meursault can be so different. And, with a greater number of people bottling their wine than ever before, the diversity of winemaking styles becomes more apparent. Most experts acknowledge that fine white burgundy benefits from spending time in new oak barrels. But what percentage of the barrels should be new (too much new oak can give too strong a vanilla flavour) and for how long? And what about more basic white burgundy? Should ordinary Chablis, or Pouilly-Fuissé be matured in barrel or in stainless steel tank? Answers to these questions differ from cellar to cellar, in much the same way as the wines themselves do.

If the winegrowers of Chablis were really sharp, they would give up making wine and simply find a way to claim royalties on all the millions of bottles of characterless wine which American and Australian producers so shamelessly label as "Chablis". One thing is certain; if you want a vinous equivalent of chalk and cheese, there could be few better than a comparison between a glass of "chablee" and one of the real stuff.

But if it is easy to recognize, the unique character of good, typical Chablis is hard to describe precisely. It is, or should be, absolutely bone dry, but with a buttery suppleness and a fullness entirely foreign to the dry wines of Sancerre, just a short drive to the

Above: *When seen from the* Grand Cru *vineyard of Les Clos, Chablis seems exactly what it is: a small provincial town, surrounded by vines on all sides.*

west. On the other hand, the chalky soil and the cool climate of these vineyards does produce a flinty edge which is reminiscent of Pouilly-Fumé. But then Chablis is a wine which, when well made, can age for decades.

Chablis itself is very much the archetypal small French provincial town, with a handful of bars, a hotel finally receiving long-needed refurbishment, and a quiet stream beside which the Chablisiens can while away a dull

Chablis Wines

Grape	Chardonnay.
Soil	Chalky on Kimmeridgean or Portlandian clay.
Appellations	Chablis Grand Cru (AOC 1938, 5,400hl of white). Chablis ler Cru (AOC 1938, 40,200hl of white made from Chardonnay). Chablis (AOC 1938, 80,200hl of white from Chardonnay). Le Petit Chablis (AOC 1944, 5,100hl of light, fruity white).
Recommended producers	Domaine Servin; William Fèvre; Domaine Dauvissat; Domaine Raveneau; Domaine Pinson; Domaine Michel; Henri Laroche.

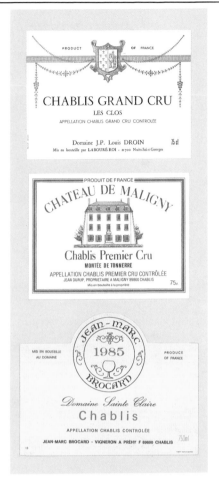

CHABLIS GRAND CRU
LES CLOS
APPELLATION CHABLIS GRAND CRU CONTROLEE

Domaine J.P. Louis DROIN 75 cl
Mis en bouteille par LABOURÉ-ROI - 21700 Nuits-St-Georges

PRODUIT DE FRANCE
CHÂTEAU DE MALIGNY
Chablis Premier Cru
MONTÉE DE TONNERRE
APPELLATION CHABLIS PREMIER CRU CONTRÔLÉE
JEAN DURUP, PROPRIETAIRE A MALIGNY 89800 CHABLIS
Mis en bouteille à la propriété 75 cl

JEAN-MARC 1985 BROCARD
MIS EN BOUTEILLE AU DOMAINE — PRODUCE OF FRANCE
Domaine Sainte Claire
Chablis
APPELLATION CHABLIS CONTROLÉE
JEAN-MARC BROCARD - VIGNERON A PRÉHY F 89800 CHABLIS 750ml

moment, but then he returned to his theme. "Vaudésir, now, that's different. More your silent, calm, beautiful woman. Needs patience, that one." Indicating the last two vineyards, my companion went on: "Les Preuses . . . Well, that's a wine which really fills the mouth, even when it's young, whilst the Bougros, to its left, is subtler, more perfumed."

In the face of such a beguiling description, it is surprising to realise that, thirty years ago, growing vines was just not an economic proposition here. The problem in Chablis is simply stated: this is one of the most inhospitable places in the world to make wine. Every year, frost threatens to kill the whole harvest, and if, as in 1985, the damage is less than was originally feared, the losses and the dead vines are invariably experienced even in the best vineyards.

In the days referred to by the old winegrower, there were no proven ways of combatting the frost and, besides, the wine fetched such low prices that no one could afford to take up the fight. Today, the picture has changed radically. The vineyards are now liberally served with such devices as water pipes, which spray a fine film of protective water over the vines, oil burners and special windmills. None of these methods is wholly effective, as was discovered in 1985, but they allow wine to be made in reasonable quantities every year. And, thanks to the international thirst for Chardonnay, prices have risen to such an extent that there can now be very little reason for a Chablisien to complain of poverty.

Today, however, he has other areas of complaint. The quiet town of Chablis has for some years seethed with controversy. The argument rages over the fundamental question of what makes Chablis taste like Chablis. According to one group, the radicals, it is the climate and the grape variety; according to the others, the reactionaries, it is the special Kimmeridgean clay soil which

afternoon fishing. Only the occasional "*Vin à Emporter*" sign, and the steep, long, vine-covered hill which overlooks the town let visitors know that this is the place in which to find one of the world's truly great white wines.

That hill, though, is the source of the very best Chablis of all, the *Grands Crus*, each with its own evocative and rather mysterious name. I shall always remember, on my first visit to Chablis, having these vineyards pointed out one by one by an old grower from his courtyard. "On the far right", he explained, "there's the Blanchots which tends to be a little lighter than some of the others, but with a more pronounced, more floral bouquet. Then, across that little track, there's Les Clos. That's the one which keeps best – and which needs to be kept." As I strained my eyes to separate one small parcel of land from the next, the old man directed my attention to a walled section within Les Clos: That, he explained was the "Clos des Hospices", an 8ha exclusivity of Chablis' biggest merchant, Moreau et Fils.

To the left of Les Clos, he continued, there was Valmur. The wines here were always particularly fat in flavour. As for the Grenouilles . . . "That, monsieur, is Chablis. Pour a glass in a restaurant and you'll have people sitting at the next table with their tongues hanging out, the perfume is so strong. It's an opera singer of a wine". The effort of description seemed to have worn the old man out for a

Below: *Frost is always a major hazard in Chablis. These oil burners can help to combat the effects of the cold temperatures in the vineyards.*

lies beneath the best vineyards. Until recently, vines planted on Portlandian clay were deemed ineligible to qualify for Chablis and Chablis *Premier Cru* status, and their wine had to be sold as Petit Chablis. But then the modernists won a famous victory, a large chunk of Petit Chablis vineyard was upgraded to Chablis and some of the *Premier Cru* vineyards were expanded for good measure. Only the (100 per cent Kimmeridgean) *Grands Crus* remained untouched. Needless to say, feelings ran high and matters have become politicized. Just to confuse matters, the chief reactionary is a radical politician called William Fèvre, while the modernists tend, in other respects, to be conservative.

It is unlikely that these questions will ever be successfully resolved, but even if they are, the ever-argumentative Chablisiens will be able to get their teeth into another controversy: should they, or should they not, use oak barrels for their wine? One group, supporters of stainless steel, claims that Chablis should be really crisp, and that oak is for fatter wines like Meursault; the other side scoffs that these people just want to avoid buying expensive barrels. Both sets of growers make good wine, but the very best producers, it must be said, do tend to favour the use of casks. Indeed, the most traditional, and the best winemaker in Chablis, François Raveneau, still uses the half-barrels which were once the only means of storing wine here, the cellars being too small for the full sized 225-litre casks used elsewhere in Burgundy.

Following all of these disputes, styles of Chablis vary enormously, even when the wine comes from the same vineyard, and the diversity might be even greater but for the fact that over a third of the annual harvest is handled by the dynamic La Chablisienne co-operative. Wines from this establishment are generally well-made, if sometimes infuriatingly labelled as though they were made and

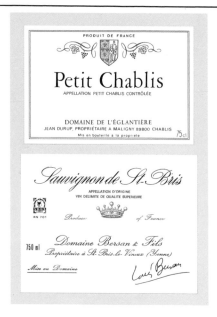

bottled by individual co-operative members. In this small region, many of the members inevitably share surnames with well known growers who make and bottle their own wine; care is therefore called for when buying. Réné Dauvissat, for example, is a first rate, domaine-bottling grower; Jean-Claude, Lionel and Michel Dauvissat are all members of the co-op.

This kind of complication, prices which leap upwards at any excuse, the new plantations, a spate of warm vintages, and a fast-developing taste for "soft", atypical Chablis have all combined to make Chablis a tricky

Below: *Huge tanks of white burgundy awaiting bottling and subsequent remuage. The Caves de Bailly are amongst the most impressive of all sparkling wine cellars.*

wine to buy. As a rule, it is best to buy plain Chablis from one of a small number of growers, preferably paying the extra for a *Premier Cru* from the Montmains, Fourchaume, Mont de Milieu or Montée de Tonnerre vineyards, and ideally lashing out on a *Grand Cru*. Petit Chablis is only worth buying if cheap.

Not all the wine from this northern corner of Burgundy is Chablis, however. The appropriately named village of St-Bris-le-Vineux grows the only Sauvignon in Burgundy, selling 500,000 bottles a year as VDQS Sauvignon de St-Bris and, in the process, giving quite a few people in Sancerre a lesson in how

Above: *The little-known village of Irancy, close to Chablis, and the source of good, unusual rosé. The rare César grape is used here – and almost nowhere else – to good effect in this case.*

to handle the Loire's best dry wine variety. Sauvignon de St-Bris is rarely as fleshy as good Sancerre, but it can be deliciously gooseberryish. A little good Aligoté is made here too, while at Bailly-sur-Yonne high quality Crémant de Bourgogne is produced in vast chalk caves referred to locally as the "*cathédrale du vin*". Nearby, at Irancy, a worthwhile rosé is made, with a flavour which depends entirely on the amount of the local César grape which has been used to complement the Pinot Noir. Within the town of Auxerre itself, an unusual Vin Gris is still being made at the Clos de la Chainette.

Below: *Deep in the cellars of the Cave de Bailly's "Cathédrale du Vin" a remueur does his daily task of turning the bottles. This is one of the most tedious jobs known to man.*

The first surprise to anyone used to buying white burgundy is that, despite the famous names of many white wine-making villages in the Côte d'Or, only about 20 per cent of the production here is white. Indeed, there are only two villages, Meursault and Puligny-Montrachet, which actually produce more white than red. Even Chassagne-Montrachet, known to most people as a white wine, comes from a commune which, each year, produces a little more Pinot Noir than Chardonnay.

Driving south from Dijon, it is hard to imagine that the busy suburb of Chenove was once an industrious winegrowing village, at the heart of what was then known as the Côte Dijonnaise. All that remains now is the appellation of Marsannay and a huge 13th century stone press. That press was capable of crushing enough grapes for the equivalent of 18,000 bottles of wine at a time; it would make short shrift of Marsannay's current annual crop of 10,000 bottles of red, but might take a little longer to handle the quarter of a million bottles of rosé. This style, "invented" in 1919 by Joseph Clair of the Domaine Clair-Daü, has proved very successful, though its sister-appellation "Clairet de Marsannay" is rather less so. The rosé is, however, really good, raspberryish Pinot Noir.

From Marsannay southward, one moves into the resolutely "red" territory of the Côte de Nuits but, when Fixin was given its appellation in 1938, it was permitted to make white as well as its tough, tannic red. I have never come across a grower who has taken advantage of this permission, even though Fixin Blanc might actually prove to be easier to sell than Fixin Rouge.

Gevrey-Chambertin makes no white, but in Morey St-Denis, the great Jean-Marie Ponsot, one of that village's best wine makers, produces 3,000 bottles of Chardonnay, almost all from his *Premier Cru* Monts Lui-

sants vineyard. This plot, which takes its name from the way a set of small hills glow in the sun, seems to be well suited to growing white grapes and produces a nuttily rich wine, not unlike Meursault. As another curiosity, Jacques Seysses makes a small amount of rosé Morey St-Denis at his Domaine Dujac, which has more flavour than the dilute 1982 wine some of his neighbours sold as red.

White grapes have always been grown at Chambolle-Musigny too, and their presence was recognised when the AOC for red and white was granted in 1936. Alongside the Pinot Noir, there is a scant half-hectare of Pinot Blanc and Chardonnay, some of which traditionally finds it way into the red *Grand Cru* Musigny and Petits Musigny, but never into the commune's other *Grand Cru*, Bonnes Mares. This Tuscan form of wine-making is supposed to make the red wine more delicate than it might otherwise be.

Below: *Plastic picking baskets full of the freshly picked grapes which will become Corton-Charlemagne. These belong to the domaine Bonneau de Martray, one of this vineyard's owners.*

Left: *Vineyards high in the savage hills of the Hautes Côtes de Nuits where, in cooler years, grapes rarely ripen sufficiently to make really good wine.*

Only the equivalent of around 1,250 bottles of white wine are made. When bottled separately, it is said to smell of violets, to taste of almonds, and to be worth buying only in years when the summer has not been too warm.

Still heading south, one comes to the *Grand Cru* walled vineyard of Clos de Vougeot, once Burgundy's nearest equivalent to a Bordeaux château. Until the early 1800s, two fifths of all of the wine made in the Clos was white, but the success of the red led to an uprooting of the white vines. In 1855, these accounted for only a fifth of the vineyard and now the amount of white made is negligible. The only producer of white Vougeot now is l'Héritier Guyot, whose wine, made in the aptly named *Premier Cru* Vigne Blanche or Clos Blanche is rather powerful and lacking in subtlety. But maybe that is how our ancestors liked it.

White Nuits St-Georges is just as rare (5,000 bottles a year) as white Morey and Clos de Vougeot, but there are a few rows of Chardonnay planted in the Clos Arlots which produce wine which is mostly drunk by its makers, as well as a real white oddity produced by the Domaine Gouges in the La Perrière vineyard. This wine has a curious history: back in 1934, Henri Gouges discovered that a section of the Pinot Noir vines in the Clos de Porrets vineyard he had just bought had grown white grapes. Gouges took grafts from these vines, transferring them to La Perrière. The wine they made has an unusual rich flavour quite unlike any other white Burgundy. With only 1,000-3,000 bottles being made each year, and given the wine's popularity amongst blind tasting pranksters, your best chance to taste it might be at the Taillevent restaurant in Paris, where there are usually a few bottles in stock.

Monts de la Côte d'Or

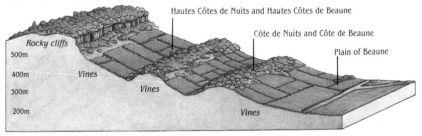

Above: *This diagram shows the topography of the vineyards in the Côte d'Or. The area is divided into three parts: the plain of Beaune, the Côte de Nuits and* *Côte de Beaune, which make the greatest wines and whose best vineyards face due east, and the Hautes Côtes in the lee of the chalky upland plateau.*

Above: *Burgundy vineyards, in this case in the Puligny-Montrachet area, long before they have taken on the green of summer or the burnished gold of autumn.*

Before leaving the Côte de Nuits, however, a few bottles of white can be found in the regional appellations of Côte de Nuits-Villages and Hautes Côtes de Nuits. Of the 420,000 bottles of wine made under the former appellation in the villages of Brochon, Fixin, Corgoloin and Comblanchien, only 25,000 are white, made from the Chardonnay and Pinot Blanc. With rare exceptions, they have every reason to remain obscure.

Hautes Côtes de Nuits is an appellation created in 1961 to cover wines made up in the hills above the villages which produce the higher quality wines of the Côte de Nuits. The whites (10 per cent of the crop) are rarely worth bothering with, and certainly not worth keeping.

Moving into the Côte de Beaune, the part of the Côte d'Or associated with white wine, one makes a disappointing start at Ladoix-Serrigny where only 25,000 out of total 250,000 bottles are white. Some of the soil here, particularly in the vineyards of Les Fautrières and Grechons, is ideal for growing Chardonnay, but the style is little known and most is sold and drunk locally. On the other hand, there are growers here who ought to know how to make white wine, since a small

section of the *Grand Cru* Corton-Charlemagne falls within the confines of the commune of Ladoix-Serrigny. That particular wine is, however, inevitably more readily associated with Aloxe-Corton. That village also produces a basic Aloxe-Corton Blanc, but only about 6,500 bottles of it, few of which reach the outside world. One which has on occasion is Daniel Senard's which, almost uniquely, is made from the Pinot Gris and is thus more comparable to Alsatian Tokay than Burgundian Chardonnay.

Among the plethora of *Grand Cru* Corton appellations the only vineyard which produces exclusively white wine is the Corton-Charlemagne itself. According to local folklore, the Emperor Charlemagne, who owned red wine vineyards here in the early 9th century AD, planted white grapes as a response to his wife's nagging complaints about the undignified wine stains which bespattered his beard! Whatever the truth of the story, the white grapes which were growing in the Charlemagne vineyard in the last century were Aligoté, and were thus ill-suited to making great wine. It was not until the great-great-grandfather of the Beaune *négociant*, Louis Latour, noticed this anomaly that Chardonnay was planted and the imperial reputation restored.

This potentially great, but sometimes disappointing, wine can take many years to open out, and can then last for as long as any white burgundy. When young though,

Corton-Charlemagne invariably shows poorly against the *Grand Cru* wines from Puligny and Chassagne-Montrachet, all of which seem far richer and more biscuity even when still in barrel. A very little white Corton is made, and this too can take a long time to mature to a satisfactory degree.

Part of the Charlemagne vineyard comes within the confines of Pernand-Vergelesses, a pretty little village tucked away almost behind the Corton hill. This village also makes 100,000 bottles of an underrated white wine of its own, as well as some of the best Aligoté in Burgundy.

Across the Route Nationale, Chorey-lès-Beaune produces just 1,600 bottles of white, none of which gets the chance to travel. The growers of Savigny-lès-Beaune have a little more Chardonnay with which to wash down their fish, but 75,000 bottles do not go very far either. There is also a little Pinot Blanc still planted here, which may account for the slightly leaner character of this village's white.

Following the same pattern, a fortieth of the vineyards of Beaune itself are planted in Chardonnay, the most familiar examples of which are the Beaune du Château from Bouchard Père et Fils and the Clos des Mouches from Joseph Drouhin. Both have curiosity value, but a bottle of Pernand-Vergelesses is probably the better option. The same can be said of white Côte de Beaune, a tiny (60,000 bottle) appellation covering vineyards just beyond those of Beaune itself.

Côte d'Or Wines

Grapes	Chardonnay and a little Aligoté; very occasionally Pinot Blanc and Pinot Beurot (white), and Pinot Noir (red).
Soil	Bathonian limestone and clay; the soil varies greatly.
Appellations	Marsannay la Côte (AOC 1965, 2,400hl of red, white and rosé). Fixin (AOC 1938, 3,400hl of red and rosé and 60hl of white). Morey St-Denis (AOC 1936, 30hl of white). Chambolle-Musigny (AOC 1936, 20hl of white). Vougeot (AOC 1936, 110hl of white). Nuits St-Georges (AOC 1972, 20hl of white). Côte de Nuits-Villages (AOC 1964, 82hl of white). Hautes Côtes de Nuits (AOC 1961, 1,900hl of white and very little rosé.) Ladoix (AOC 1970, 200hl of white). Aloxe-Corton and Pernand- Vergelesses (AOC 1938-1970, 1,030hl of white). Savigny (AOC 1970, 600hl of white.) Chorey-lès-Beaune (AOC 1970, 20hl of white). Beaune (AOC 1972, 125hl of white). Monthélie (AOC 1970, 100hl of white). Auxey-Duresses (AOC 1970, 1,400hl of white). St-Romain (AOC 1970, 1,500hl of white). Meursault (AOC 1970, 20,200hl of white). Puligny-Montrachet (AOC 1970, 11,900hl of white). Montrachet, Bâtard-Montrachet, Chevalier-Montrachet, Bienvenues-Bâtard-Montrachet, Criots-Bâtard-Montrachet (AOC 1937-1939, 1,450hl of white). Chassagne-Montrachet (AOC 1970, 7,750hl of white). Santenay (AOC 1970, 300hl of white). St-Aubin (AOC 1970, 1,850hl of white). Hautes Côtes de Beaune (AOC 1937-1961, 1,000hl of white).
Recommended producers	(Puligny-Montrachet) Domaine Leflaive; (Meursault) Domaine des Comtes Lafon; (St- Aubin) Domaine Thomas; (Pernand-Vergelesses) Domaine Rollin; (general) Leroy; Joseph Drouhin; Chartron and Trébuchet; Labouré Roi; Louis Latour; Domaine Sauzet; Michelot-Buisson; Louis Jadot; Antonin Rodet; Bouchard Père et Fils.

Above: *Burgundy's villages huddle in sheltered corners of land, out of the reach of the rigours of winter. Austere Norman churches generally set the style for the village as a whole.*

Pommard produces no white wine and Chardonnay grown in Volnay's Santenots vineyard is sold as Meursault, so the next white wine-making village one comes to is Monthélie. I have enjoyed young white Monthélie, but have never sampled a really old bottle, so I can neither confirm nor deny the Burgundian assertion that this is a wine which should not be kept because it maderizes too easily. Only 10,000 bottles are produced, so it cannot call for too much effort to drink them all up while still in their prime.

Literally across the Route Nationale from Monthélie, Meursault is unquestionably the most serious white wine village in the Côte d'Or, producing a third of the region's communal white wine – and virtually no red. The name is said to derive from *Muris Saltus*, the leap of the rat, though an alternative explanation refers to a Roman camp which was sited here. Whatever the explanation, Meursault not only produces the most immediately appealing of top class white Burgundy, wine with a mouth-coating butteriness and flavours of hazelnut and buttery toast, but it also perfectly demonstrates meaning of "*gout de terroir*".

Comparing the Perrières and the Charmes *Premiers Crus*, for example, one instantly smells and tastes the remarkable difference a few yards and a variation in soil type can make. When tasted young, the Charmes always has a far readier, riper flavour while the Perrières takes four or five years to open out into a finer, more complex wine. But these differences are just as discernable at a more modest level in village wines from specific "*lieux dits*" (named, non-*Premier Cru* vineyards), and there is no other commune which places such an importance on separate bottlings of wines such as these.

From a village outside Meursault, there is the separate appellation of Meursault-Blagny, some of whose wines seem comparable in style to Puligny-Montrachet, the commune within whose confines some of the Blagny vines are to be found. Puligny itself produces wines which seem leaner than most Meursault when young, but which, with time, develop even greater levels of complexity. The *Premier Crus* are generally reliable, my

own favourites being les Folatières, les Referts and les Combettes, while the *Grand Crus*, of which two are shared with Chassagne-Montrachet, are sublimely rich in flavour, at once floral, nutty and biscuity. Best of all is undoubtedly Le Montrachet itself, but comparisons to decide in which order to place the Bâtard, the Bienvenues-Bâtard, the Chevalier and the Chassagne Criots-Bâtard-Montrachets, would be far from odious. Given a choice, I think I would opt for the Bâtard.

Chassagne-Montrachet is, as has already been said, marginally more of a red wine village than a white one. Even so, the white wine, which seems to be more precisely full of fruit flavours, and perhaps slightly more floral than Puligny, is the commune's main attraction nowadays. Of the *Premiers Crus*, I would pick out the Morgeot, Clos Pitois, Clos St-Jean, Champs Gain and Chaumées as personal favourites.

Auxey-Duresses is an underrated appellation which produces wine which is like an earlier-maturing cross between Puligny and Meursault, at once biscuity and fat. One third of the wine here is white, the best coming from Les Duresses, la Chapelle and Reugne.

If Auxey-Duresses is little-known, St-Aubin is a really well-kept secret, many of whose wines were, until recently, sold as Bourgogne Blanc. Meursault lovers should try any of these wines, particularly the *Premier Cru* Les

Above: *Rough-stone walls surround almost all of Burgundy's best vineyards, with doorways allowing growers access to their few rows of vines. This gateway leads to Le Montrachet.*

Murgers des Dents de Chien (named after hound's tooth rocks in the vineyard) which has a nuttiness they are almost certain to find that they will appreciate.

Before coming to Santenay, at the southern end of the Côte d'Or, it is worth turning back and up into the hills where Orches, atop a savage cliff, produces a small amount of light, delicate rosé, and where St-Romain, at a similar altitude, makes a white which, in good years, can compete with Meursault. Only the very best examples improve with age, but even when drunk young, these can be deliciously rich. Hautes Côtes de Beaune white, produced from other villages high in the hills above the Côte de Beaune, can also provide good Chardonnay, and even, in a few cases, Pinot Blanc. One has, however to choose carefully, particularly in cooler years when ripening can be a problem.

And then one finally arrives at Santenay, where a small amount (30,000) bottles of white are produced, much of it drunk by visitors to the spa and casino. The one wine to try to rescue from this fate is the *Premier Cru* Clos Les Gravières.

In contrast to the Côte d'Or, with its cheek-by-jowl crowding of villages such as Meursault, Monthélie and Auxey-Duresses into a small geographical area, the five communes of the Côte Chalonnaise seem to stand in splendid isolation from one another. In theory at least, this separation ought to emphasise the individual character of their wines but, sadly, this is a region which has never quite discovered its own identity.

To start with, even the regional name seems questionable: despite official recognition as the Côte Chalonnaise, it is still referred to in a recently published French wine book as the "Mercurey Region". The communal appellations are more firmly established, though even here, in the 1920s, there were plans to encourage the sale of Rully by labelling it as Mercurey.

The *négociants* of Beaune, Nuits St-Georges and Mâcon can take some of the blame for this situation; they have traditionally treated this hinterland as a convenient source of better-than-average Bourgogne Blanc, or of communal wine which could be offered to favoured restaurants as a more affordable alternative to the wines of the Côte d'Or and Chablis. And there was a touch of class about ordering a bottle

Côte Chalonnaise Wines

Grapes	Pinot Noir, Aligoté, Chardonnay, Gamay.
Soil	Mainly limestone or calcareous clay.
Appellations	Rully (AOC 1939, 6,700hl of white). Mercurey (AOC 1936, 1,800hl of white). Givry (AOC 1946, 750hl of white). Montagny (AOC 1936, 6,650hl of white). Bourgogne-Aligoté-Bouzeron (AOC 1979, small quantity of white made from Aligoté grape).
Recommended producers	(Rully) Mme Niepce, Domaine du Chapître; Domaine Belleville; Domaine Jean Coulon; Domaine de la Folie. (Mercurey) P. de Launay, Bourgneuf Val d'Or; Domaine Marceau; Domaine du Prieuré; Domaine Saier. (Givry) Clos Salomon; Domaine Michel Derain; Domaine du Gardin; Domaine Thénard. (Montagny) Domaine Michel Goubard; Domaine Jouillot; Domaine A. P. de Villaine, Louis Latour; Cave des Vignerons de Buxy; Domaine Steinmaier; Antonin Rodet; Faiveley; Delorme; Bouchard.

Above: *Chardonnay grapes at the Buxy co-operative, close to Montagny in the Côte Chalonnaise. This is one of France's best co-operatives.*

Left: *The village of Rully produces good, still white wine, and a great deal of often excellent* Méthode Champenoise *fizz. The emphasis these days is turning away from the sparkling wines.*

BOURGOGNE ALIGOTÉ
APPELLATION BOURGOGNE ALIGOTÉ CONTRÔLÉE

MIS EN BOUTEILLES PAR
LES VINS GEORGES DUBŒUF   75 cl
71570 ROMANÈCHE-THORINS
PRODUCED AND BOTTLED IN FRANCE

of Mercurey or Montagny, rather than opting for the common-or-garden Mâcon Villages which would positively have denoted the cheapskate.

However, now that prices of Burgundy's better-known wines have leapt beyond the reach of most ordinary wine drinking mortals, the Côte Chalonnaise has suddenly, quite literally, become flavour of the month. The growers of this region are certainly more welcoming to visitors than some of their swollen-headed counterparts in the Côte d'Or, but whether this will survive their growing success is open to question.

The limestone soil widely found here suits the Chardonnay well, as does the high altitude of some of the vineyards and the surprisingly cool temperatures, cooler, for example, than in the more northerly Gevrey-Chambertin, but white grapes occupy a mere 20 per cent of the vineyards, with Aligoté almost as well represented as Chardonnay. As vines are replanted, however, an increase in white wine production can be expected.

The Côte Chalonnaise starts just beyond

Santenay, near the town of Chagny. This quiet collection of ancient and modern housing would probably pass completely unnoticed if it were not for the presence of the three-star Lameloise restaurant which, for many people, is one of the most reliable restaurants in France. Chagny itself is once said to have made notable wine of its own, but nowadays, one has to travel a few miles to the south to find a white wine of any note. After a winding drive, the village of Bouzeron appears where, by some trick of soil or climate, the producers have managed to make such good Aligoté that, since 1979 (and this is a privilege unique to this commune) they have been allowed to sell it as Bourgogne Aligoté de Bouzeron. Bouchard Père et Fils own a third of the vineyards and make a good example, but, given a choice, the Aligoté from the domaine of Aubert de Villaine is preferable. When he is not making Bourgogne Blanc and Aligoté here, de Villaine is usually to be found at the Domaine de la Romanée-Conti, of which he is co-owner. This combination of responsibilities, bringing together the annual production of both Burgundy's costliest and most affordable wines should serve as a useful retort to anyone who claims to restrict his or her drinking just to the top or bottom end of the price scale.

To many people, however, the Côte Chalonnaise proper begins at Rully, one of the sleepiest of villages in what, by any standards is a pretty comatose region. The village takes its name from Rubilium, its Gallo-Roman owner, but until recently the appellation existed more in text books than on labels

Above: *The vineyards of Montagny rise above the village. This sleepy commune is not only a good place to find white wine; the goat's milk cheese is very good too.*

because, although half of 800,000 bottles of wine produced here are white, a substantial proportion has been sold as (usually good) *Méthode Champenoise* Crémant de Bourgogne. Still white Rully is, however, better than the red and can have a delicious steely-buttery flavour, not unlike some Chablis.

Heading south, one arrives at Mercury, a more sizeable town boasting a Roman temple to the messenger of the gods from whom the commune takes its name. The largest appellation in the Côte Chalonnaise, Mercurey has benefitted from the skill and enthusiasm of a number of growers, most notably, Hughes de Suremain and Michel Juillot, and the presence of the well-thought-of *négociant* firm of Antonin Rodet. The Côte d'Or firms of Faiveley and Bouchard Aîné also have sizeable holdings here.

It used to be said that there were three types of Mercurey: for masters, for servants, and for washing horses' hooves. Whether this referred to the red or to the white is not quite certain, but if it were the latter, there must have been some very thirsty masters and servants, and some very dirty hooves; of the commune's annual production of 2.5 million bottles of wine, only 125,000 are white. Buy a bottle if you can; good, buttery, almondy-

toasty examples can outclass Chardonnay from even some very exalted Côte d'Or villages, as a group of distinguished growers from Puligny-Montrachet and Meursault ruefully discovered at a blind tasting organised recently in Burgundy. The outstanding wine, by the way, was a Château de Chamirey 1984.

The growers of Givry like to make much of the fact that Henri IV liked their wine best of all. This is open to question – and indeed argument by producers in at least one other region – but it does appear that his mistress, Gabrielle d'Estrées, had a vineyard here, so he certainly had a reason to visit what might otherwise be an easily overlooked village. Historically, the wines of Givry were thought to be equal to the finest of the Côte d'Or, but this reputation was, it must be said, established by the reds. Very little of the wine here (only 10 per cent of the 600,000 bottles produced) is white, though the Champ Poureau vineyard has a reputation for its Chardonnay, as does Domaine Joblot's Clos la Servoisine. I have never been dazzled by a white Givry but, thanks to their scarcity, I have not had the opportunity to taste very many.

The wine of Montagny, the southernmost appellation of the Côte Chalonnaise, is understandably named, given the 300-400m altitude hills on whose slopes the vines here are grown, so it comes as a surprise to learn that Montagny's wines used to be called Côte de Buxy after the nearby town. Encompassing the villages of Jully-les-Buxy, Mont-Laurent and St-Vallerin, Montagny produces

exclusively soft, spicy, if undemanding white wine, all of which enjoys the peculiar privilege of being able to declare itself a *Premier Cru* provided it has a strength of half a degree or more over the fixed 11° minimum. This casual use of a term which elsewhere refers exclusively to favoured vineyards seems curious and no doubt raises an eyebrow in the highly traditional offices of Louis Latour, the Beaune *négociant* who has done more than anyone else in Burgundy to create Montagny's reputation.

As part of an effort to promote the wines of their region, the producers of the Côte Cha-

lonnaise recently created a local answer to the Tastevinage in the form of an annual "Chanteflutage" tasting. Wines which satisfy the local judges are allowed to carry a special "Chantefluté" label. Sadly, however, too little effort has been made to promote this outside the region, so it would be surprising if it achieved very much.

Below: *A range of burgundies on show in the cellars of François Protheau, a* négociant *based in Mercurey, but selling wine from throughout Burgundy.*

The first mention of vinegrowing in the Mâconnais is by the 4th century Roman poet Ausonius, but it was the Cistercian monks who, in the 11th and 12th centuries, established the Mâconnais as a wine region. True recognition came a little later when, in 1660, a grower, Claude Brosse, travelled to Versailles (a 33 day journey in those days) with 2 casks of his wine. Arriving just as Mass was being said, he immediately kneeled but, being a head taller than the rest of the congregation, caught the attention of the king who thought he had remained sitting. The subsequent meeting and the monarch's tasting of the wine led to regular shipments of it to the court.

At that time, such shipments were not easily managed as all the wine had to be transported by boat up the river. Quite apart from the wine which had to be provided for thirsty boatmen, losses in transit were heavy, and it was not until 1854 and the opening of the railway that commercial transactions became easier.

The region itself, which follows the Saône southwards, consists of a strip of land around 45 by 15km in width, ranging in altitude from near river level to the savage Solutré cliffs near Pouilly Fuissé, over the edge of which primitive man forced hundreds of horses to plummet during some early religious ritual. Elsewhere, low hills and small valleys are so be-meadowed and generously dotted with goats and cows that it is easy to forget that this is a winegrowing region at all. In fact, before the arrival of phylloxera, there used to be three times more vines than there are today.

Above: *The Rock of Solutré in the Mâconnais, from which huge numbers of horses were forced to jump to their deaths by the ancient inhabitants here. Their descendants occupy themselves more peaceably by making fresh, white wine.*

Below: *High-tech winemaking – or the first signs of it – in the village of Fuissé, where newly picked Chardonnay grapes are being unloaded by suction on their way into the press.*

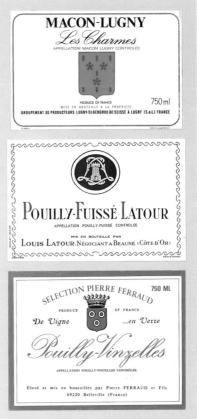

The climate can be ideal for grape growing, but it can cause problems too, as summers can be (too) warm and winters very cold indeed. One annual dread is the late frosts which can strike as late as 15 May.

The soil of the Mâconnais varies dramatically too, from the low acid, chalky soil of the best Chardonnay vineyards to the more acidic, sandier soil of the plots which favour more basic, younger-drinking wine. Despite the traditional predominance of black grapes, most of the region's land is better suited to Chardonnay – the existence of a village of that name suggests that the variety may have originated here – than for either Gamay or Pinot. Just over two thirds of the vines are now Chardonnay.

As a hangover from the days when wine made in the Mâconnais was difficult to sell, and when almost all vineyard owners relied on other forms of agriculture for survival, the co-operative movement is particularly strong, with 15 co-operative wineries handling around 85 per cent of each year's harvest. The co-operatives of the Mâconnais, many of which also produce good Crémant de Bourgogne, are some of the best equipped in France, and their best *"cuvées"* (each co-operative will make a great many) can be excellent. It is only a pity that the recent explosion of interest in, and prices for, white Burgundy of every kind, has allowed these co-operatives and their greedier members to get away with cutting quality corners on some of the less-than-best *cuvées*. This is not an area in which you should buy "blind". Not at today's prices anyway.

The most basic white wines of the region can be labelled as Mâcon Blanc or, more unusually, Pinot-Chardonnay-Mâcon, in recognition of the fact that small plantations of Pinot Blanc are still grown, and wines can be made from blends of both variety. The "Pinot-Chardonnay" often referred to in Italy, Australia and the USA, is, however, a mythical beast, the Chardonnay being quite unrelated to any of the Pinot family of vines.

In theory, a wine labelled Mâcon-Villages (an appellation which, incidentally, excludes red wine) should have more character than one merely called Mâcon Blanc; the designation Mâcon Supérieur can also be used for a slightly stronger wine, but few producers bother to do so. For the best wines at this level, however, one should climb one step further up the quality ladder and buy a wine whose label identifies the particular village where it was made.

The most famous of these villages – Lugny, Clessé, Prissé, Chardonnay and Viré – tried at one time to obtain their own appellations. Quite apart from the confusion the "Appellation Chardonnay Contrôlée" might have caused, a lack of individually identifiable character made such an application unacceptable, but there is no question that these communes can certainly produce wine which is better than most Mâcon-Villages. And in the case of a very few growers, the wines made here can leap way out of their class. At the 1987 International Challenge organised in London by WINE magazine, for instance, a Mâcon Clessé from the domaine Thevenet-Quintaine and a Mâcon Viré from the Domaine de Roally saw off a range of supposedly more prestigious wines from the Côte d'Or, and some from Pouilly-Fuissé.

First time visitors to the commune of Pouilly-Fuissé are almost always confused by a fork in the road and what seems to be a practical joke roadsign: one road leads to Pouilly, the other to Fuissé. In fact, the wine comes from no less than four villages – Pouilly, Fuissé, Vergisson and Chaintré – but the sign to follow is to Fuissé which proves to be an attractively Romanesque village overlooked by an immense church which is almost surrounded by vines.

Tasting Pouilly-Fuissé, it does not take long to realise that this is a very varied appellation indeed. On the one hand, the situation of the vineyard counts for a great deal but is not indicated on labels: Pouilly-Fuissé has no *Premiers Crus*. There are vines planted as high as 400m above sea level, and others at half that altitude; some are even planted on the same kind of Kimmeridgean clay as the best Chablis.

Even more important, though, is the way in which the wine is made. The Château de Fuissé, and Domaines Ferret and Leger Plumet all prove that this is a wine which can age beautifully, maintaining its southern richness, but developing a complexity of lemony-peachy-nutty-spicy flavours presumably undreamed of, or uncared about, by the growers who seem to be content with making a tank-matured, up-market Mâcon-Villages.

75 per cent of the wine is still sold to *négociants* who have not, until recently, had the courage to draw the line to establish sensible levels of price and quality. However, recently, the Pouilly-Fuissé price bubble has finally burst, to the relief of the wine-buying public.

Above: *An old grape press helps to direct the attention of passers-by to St-Véran and nearby Beaujolais communes.*

Promoted as Pouilly-Fuissé alternatives, the wines of Pouilly-Loché and Pouilly-Vinzelles from vineyards to the east of Fuissé do not seem to have high aspirations of quality. Most are made by the Loché co-operative and, whichever their source, sold as Pouilly-Vinzelles.

A bottle of St-Véran from the Lycée Agricole de Davayé or from the Beaujolais firm of Georges Duboeuf represents much better value. It is Duboeuf who, perhaps thanks to the fact that he was brought up in a Pouilly-Fuissé domaine, has done more than anyone else to promote this recent (1971) appella-

Mâconnais Wines

Grapes	Chardonnay, Gamay, Pinot Noir, Aligoté, Pinot Blanc.
Soil	Calcareous, or clay, sand siliceous.
Appellations	Mâcon Blanc and Supérieur (AOC 1937, 13,700hl of white, little rosé). Mâcon-Villages (AOC 1937, 134,000hl of white, little rosé). Pouilly-Fuissé (AOC 1936, 42,000hl of white). Pouilly-Loché and Pouilly-Vinzelles (AOC 1940, 4,000hl of white). St-Véran (AOC 1971, 24,500hl of white).
Recommended producers	(Pouilly-Fuissé) Domaine Corsin; Château de Fuissé; Domaine Ferret; Domaine Roger Luquet; Leger-Plumet; Gilles Noblet.(Mâcon) Domaine de la Condemine; Domaine Pierre Mahuet; Domaine de Roally; Domaine Jean Thévenet; Domaine de Chervin; Les Vignerons d'Igé. (St-Véran) Domaine Roger Tissier; Producteurs de Prissé.

tion. Although, usually spoken of as another Pouilly-Fuissé substitute, St-Véran was really created as a means of selling Beaujolais Blanc, a style which has traditionally sold badly and for which it serves as a kind of alternative label. Taking its name from the village of St-Verand, and dropping the final "d" in deference to another commune of the same name in the Beaujolais, the appellation includes vines grown in a crescent around Pouilly-Fuissé. English wine writer Oz Clarke believes that good St-Véran should smell of hot water bottles!

A small amount of light, refreshing Beaujolais Blanc from beyond the confines of St-Véran can still occasionally be found, thanks to the persistence of Louis Jadot and a small number of individual estates who have managed to keep this appellation alive.

Like Beaujolais Rosé, Mâcon Rosé is very rare (almost none is now produced) despite the suggestion made in 1967 by French writer Pierre Bréjoux in his *"Les Vins de Bourgogne"* that all of the Gamay in the Mâconnais be used to make pink wine, and the only red be made from Pinot Noir, planted in the best vineyards. My only taste of Mâcon Rosé did not leave me yearning to repeat the experience. Passetoutgrains Rosé. is, if anything, even harder to find.

Below: *The vines sweep down towards Château de Fuissé, unquestionably one of the very best producers of Pouilly-Fuissé. Many of the vines here are very old, and their wine, the Château's best, is labelled as "Vieilles Vignes".*

BORDEAUX

*H*ave you ever suddenly realised that you were doing the wrong thing, in the wrong place, and at the wrong time? Because that, putting it baldly, is the situation in which the white winemakers of the world's most famous red wine region found themselves after World War II. The whole world seemed to be clamouring for red wine, and these Bordelais were producing white.

A little more recently, when red wines began to fall our of favour, the pendulum may have appeared to have swung back in the white winemakers' favour. Once again, however, the Bordelais were out of luck; what the world wanted to drink was *dry* white wine – what they were making in Bordeaux was *moelleux*, or medium sweet. It would not have been so bad if they had been making the greatest semi-sweet wine in the world, but they were not. Nor did most of them prove any more adept at making dry wine: much of the wine being produced from Bordeaux's white grapes smelled of damp dishcloths and tasted only marginally better.

The problem lay partly in the principal grape variety which was being used, and partly in the way in which that variety was being handled. At its best, the Sémillon can make some of the most gloriously rich and honeyed wines in the world. These are, however, and are likely to remain, something of a minority interest. *Demi-sec* Sémillon, by contrast tends to be honeyed and quite devoid of freshness.

Ironically enough, that's just the kind of description which might do justice to some of the best-selling wines from Germany and Eastern Europe, but somehow the Riesling, or one of its various cousins and mimics, usually manages to evoke at least a hint of appealing grapiness which is wholly absent from the Sémillon, whose true vocation, like the Chenin Blanc of the Loire is, it seems, to make great sweet dessert wine.

In theory, therefore, if the world could be persuaded to switch its allegiance, or at least to take a slightly greater interest in this kind of fine sweet wine, the Bordelais would find life easier. But the difference would be slight. The conditions which allow producers to make sweet wines of the standard of good Ste-Croix-du-Mont and Loupiac, let alone Sauternes and Barsac, are found in few of the white vineyards of Bordeaux, and even where they do occur, they do so only intermittently rather than with regularity.

The only commercial answer for the Bordelais was to learn how to make better dry white wine. In the majority of the cases in some parts of Bordeaux, the growers have taken the easy way out and installed temperature-controlled stainless steel fermentation tanks and wall-to-wall Sauvignon Blanc. The wine produced by such a combination is streets ahead of the mediocre Sémillon wines and can be grassily fresh when young – a kind of poor man's Sancerre – but it is rarely characterful, rarely evocative of the region in which it was produced. The danger of making such wine is that it is open to increasingly stern competition from all the other grassily-fresh Sauvignons of which more and more are being made from New Zealand to New

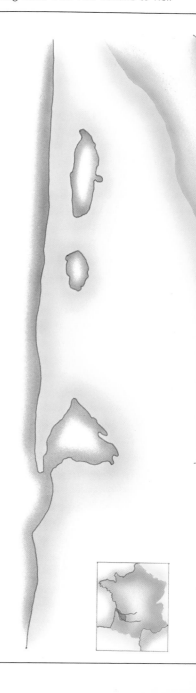

Grape Varieties

Red Cabernet Sauvignon, Cabernet Franc, Merlot, Malbec, Petit Verdot.
White Sémillon, Sauvignon Blanc, Muscadelle, Merlot Blanc, Colombard (both the latter in small quantities).

York State, not to mention in vineyards throughout France.

The other way to make dry white wine in Bordeaux calls for far greater interest and commitment on the part of the producer but, when done properly, it really pays off. It consists, very simply, of using the region's indigenous grape varieties to make wine which both bears the stamp of Bordeaux and appeals to an international market. All that is called for is an understanding of how to

Left: *Healthy, freshly picked grapes which will be used to make Domaine de Chevalier, a wine whose quality derives from the painstaking care of its owners.*

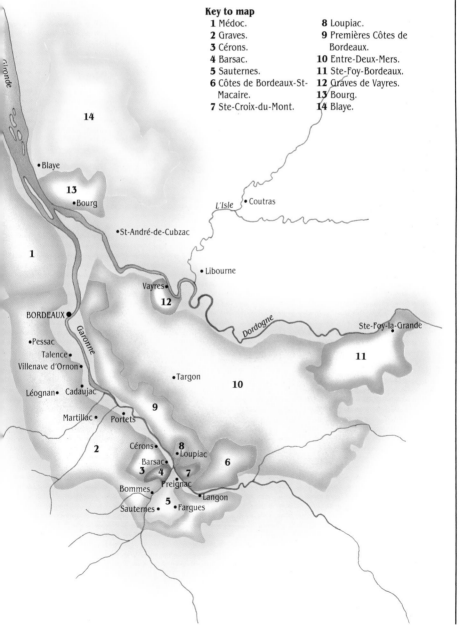

Key to map

1 Médoc.
2 Graves.
3 Cérons.
4 Barsac.
5 Sauternes.
6 Côtes de Bordeaux-St-Macaire.
7 Ste-Croix-du-Mont.
8 Loupiac.
9 Premières Côtes de Bordeaux.
10 Entre-Deux-Mers.
11 Ste-Foy-Bordeaux.
12 Graves de Vayres.
13 Bourg.
14 Blaye.

handle the Sémillon in a way which, ironically, the Australians of the Hunter Valley discovered for themselves a long time ago.

Four men can take the credit for helping their fellow winemakers to gain that understanding. First and foremost there is, inevitably, Professeur Emile Peynaud who transformed winemaking from a rustic form of agriculture to its present level of scientific sophistication (which in many cases initially simply meant instilling a bit of hygiene into the winery), followed by André Lurton and Pierre Coste who, between them, could be said to have "invented" new style cool-fermented white Bordeaux. Lastly there is the Danish-born Peter Vinding-Diers who, through studies of the different forms of natural yeast found in Bordeaux, has provided growers with the ability to control fermentation in a way never known before. Suddenly, as a growing number of Bordeaux white wines prove, it is possible to make wine that is at once fleshy and fresh, and even less than ideally sited châteaux can compete on increasingly level terms with white burgundy.

The "new" dry white Bordeaux producer will have learned when best to pick his grapes so as to obtain the best possible balance be-

Above: *Crushing the grapes in the vineyard is a traditional practice, seen less and less these days.*

Above: The Domaine de Chevalier produces one of the very greatest dry white wines in the world. However, only 9,600 or so bottles are made each year.

tween ripeness and the essential acidity the wine needs to keep it fresh. He will have taken a leaf out of the sweet winemakers' book and discovered the art of blending the ideal proportions of the more tangily acidic Sauvignon and Muscadelle with the Sémillon. And, increasingly, he will have found that fermenting his wine in oak barrels, as they do in Burgundy, can give his best wines a richness of flavour unobtainable in any other way. Many of these quite basic skills have been known at the best Graves properties for decades, as old bottles of Domaine de Chevalier prove quite conclusively, but their arrival amongst the humbler Bordeaux Blancs is nothing less than revolutionary.

Equally dramatic, in its quiet way, has been the progress made in the châteaux of Sauternes and Barsac, and in the sweet-wine-producing properties of their neighbouring communes. Here too, there was a great deal of room for improvement in all but the very

best wines. Often the problem lay in shoddy winemaking, in over-generous use of sulphur dioxide by producers who feared that, without a good dose of this valuable antiseptic, their wine might misbehave in the bottle. Cleaner wineries have done much to do away with the need for all that sulphur; if you cut down on the bacteria which go into the bottle, you cut down the need for bacteria-killing chemicals.

White Bordeaux has undergone a remarkable metamorphosis over the last decade or so, but there is still a great deal to be done, essentially now to establish (or re-establish) the identities of the region's various wines. Few people realise, for instance, that Bordeaux boasts no less than *eleven* separate semi-sweet and sweet appellations, not to mention six for dry white wine. The day when even the most avid wine buff can tell them apart and discuss their individual qualities is still some way off.

For people who like their wine regions to be neatly segregated, Bordeaux starts well: the great vineyard areas of the Médoc, Pomerol and St-Emilion are, to all intents and purposes, exclusively red wine districts with only the very occasional white wine being produced by the very occasional eccentric château. As one heads south however, life becomes far more confusing. The Graves makes both red *and* white.

The region is one in which I invariably become almost irredeemably lost, forever travelling in concentric circles around the châteaux I am trying to find. This is a pleasant enough experience in the gentle countryside which comprises most of the region; it is rather less fun when, as in the case of Château Haut-Brion, the vineyards are surrounded by burgeoning suburbia. Less than two decades ago, of the 2,600ha of vines under cultivation, just under 1,500 were planted in white grapes; today, while the overall area of vineyard remains almost unchanged, those white vineyards have been halved. So, one might suppose, the amount of white wine made each year must have fallen too. Far from it; there are now, at 11 million bottles, one-and-a-half times as many bottles of white Graves being produced each year as there used to be.

This apparent miracle was achieved by radically reducing the amount of sweet and semi-sweet wine and, quite simply, by instituting better vineyard management. André Lurton, whose name is associated with several good châteaux, including de Cruzeau, La Louvière and Couhins-Lurton has developed good, but neglected, vineyard land to the north of the Graves, while Pierre Coste has taken advantage of the cheaper land further south to make attractive, early-maturing wine.

My own favourite Graves is Domaine de Chevalier, whose 10,000 bottles of white wine are cask fermented and gently barrel-matured for 18 months. The proportion of Sauvignon is, at 70 per cent, fairly high, and one might expect this to be a short-lived wine; it is, however, nothing of the kind and should not even be opened until it is at least ten years old, by which time its peachy-spicy

Above: *Picking Sauvignon Blanc grapes at the Domaine de Chevalier. Machines have increasingly taken over harvesting, but not in the best properties.*

complexity should have begun to develop. This is also where to buy "difficult" vintages.

Laville-Haut-Brion, another classic slow-developer, contains around 60 per cent Sémillon and, with time, takes on a more determinedly honeyed character than Domaine de Chevalier. I prefer it to Haut-Brion Blanc which can, nevertheless, be a very impressive wine, both in its lemony-spicy youth, a stage during which I fear that most of the many bottles exported to the USA are drunk, and after a decade in bottle.

Of the other "greats", I would choose Malartic-Lagravière (a 100 per cent Sauvignon), de St-Pierre and, since barrel-fermentation was introduced, Smith-Haut-Lafitte, along with Rahoul, La Louvière and de Fieuzal. The Vin Sec du Château Coutet really

Bordeaux "Rive Droite" Wines

Grapes	Mainly Sémillon, Sauvignon, Muscadelle, Merlot Blanc, Colombard.
Soil	Clay and gravel in varying proportions.
Appellations	Côtes de Bourg (AOC 1941, 3,100hl of white). Blaye (AOC 1936, 10,750hl of white). Côtes de Blaye (AOC 1936, 10,200hl of white). Premières Côtes de Blaye (AOC 1936, 775hl of white). Bordeaux Côtes de Francs (AOC 1936, 220hl of white).
Recommended producers	(Côtes de Bourg) Cave Vinicole de Tauriac, Bourg-sur-Gironde. (Blaye) Château Barbé.

ought, by rights, to be sold as Bordeaux Blanc, like dry wine from Yquem and the other Sauternes and Barsac. By a quirk of location it is, however, eligible to call itself Graves; I have never liked it as much as other, fleshier Graves, or more typical dry wines from its Sauternes and Barsac neighbours.

Basic Graves Blanc is to be bought with care, while Graves Supérieures, in its dry, semi-sweet and sweet forms is no more reliable, though some dry examples sold under the name of the château can be worth buying. More obscure, and just to the north of Sauternes, the appellation of Cérons produces dry wine under its own name as Cérons Sec (or, more usually, as Graves), and some deliciously rich and old fashioned sweet wine which bears comparison with its more illustrious neighbours. The best of these comes

Below: *Claude Ricard of Domaine de Chevalier believes that the healthy state of his grapes is of crucial importance.*

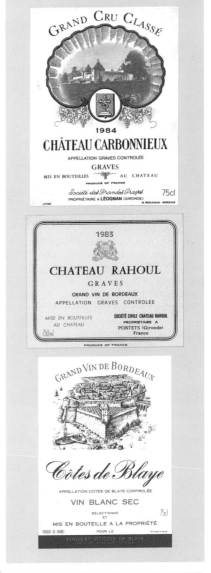

from the Grand Enclos du Château de Cérons, and from Château Archambeau.

Of the other sweet, would-be Sauternes alternatives, the most familiar are probably Loupiac and Ste-Croix-du-Mont. The first of these communes, situated just across the river from Barsac, takes pride in the fact that its vineyards were among the very first to be planted in Bordeaux. In a good vintage, and at properties such as Châteaux Loupiac-Gaudiet and Barbe-Morin, the wine can be attractively like a scaled-down Sauternes. Quality at other châteaux is less consistent, however; indeed Château de Ricaud, historically the "top name" in the commune and a great name to look for amongst old vintages, is only just beginning to recover from an extended period of mediocrity. Sales are not easy and production of dry white is growing.

To some people, Ste-Croix-du-Mont might just as well throw in its lot with Loupiac, producing a joint sweet appellation on their two neighbouring hills, in a similar association to the one which exists between Sauternes and Barsac on the other side of the Garonne. The producers of Ste-Croix-du-Mont would, however, disagree violently, believing that their slightly larger appellation (2.25 million bottles to Loupiac's 1.5 million) makes more than slightly better wine. The co-operative is quite reliable, but the best properties in Ste-Croix-du-Mont are probably Château Loubens, Château de Maille and Château Lousteau-Vieil. The pure Sauvignon Château de Tastes, which belongs to Bruno Prats, owner of Château Cos d'Estournel in St-Estèphe, may well be the very best of all, but only tiny quantities are made.

The Cadillac label now appears on unexceptional semi-sweet and sweet wine which would once have been sold as Premières Côtes de Bordeaux-Cadillac; Château Fayau is a name to look for. As for the Premières Côtes de Bordeaux appellation itself, this is in grave danger of becoming reds-only territory, particularly now that the wines from the best, southernmost, white grape vineyards are increasingly being sold as Cadillac.

There are three other sweet appellations, none of particular interest. Bordeaux Supérieur-Haut-Bénauge is situated in the heart of the Entre-Deux-Mers and uses that appellation for its growing proportion of dry white, while the Premières Côtes de Blaye makes a tiny amount of semi sweet and sweet white. Those who like the idea of Loupiac being a scaled-down Barsac, might care to try Côtes de Bordeaux St-Macaire, made just over the river from Langon; one of its producers described it as "scaled-down Loupiac".

Another traditional "poor man's Sauternes" is to be found at Ste-Foy-Bordeaux, on the left bank of Dordogne, but you should hurry; within a few years, dry Sauvignon Blanc is almost certain to have taken over here, as it will in Graves de Vayres on the left bank of the Dordogne, where the best wines have always been dry.

Fans of these fast-disappearing *moelleux* styles will need to make similarly speedy expeditions to Blaye and the Côtes de Blaye, both of which are going dry very quickly. The Blaye may be of slightly greater interest than some of these wines, since it legally contains both Folle Blanche and Frontignan as well as the more usual varieties.

Of all the Bordeaux appellations, Entre-Deux-Mers is perhaps the one which has undergone the most apparent sea change, transforming itself, in only a few years, from a dull *moelleux* in a clear glass bottle to a steely Sauvignon in a green one. Actually, despite the inexorable progress of the Sauvignon here, the permitted varieties include the Colombard, Ondenc, Ugni Blanc and Merlot Blanc, and there are traditionalists in the region who regret the likely disappearance of these and the ensuing development of a single, commercial, "Sauvignon-de-Bordeaux" style of wine.

If that were to happen, judging by their success so far (the appellation has grown by three quarters in a decade), most growers here are unlikely to complain too loudly. In any case, most see their wine as undemand-

Central Bordeaux Wines

Grapes	Mainly Sauvignon, Sémillon, Muscadelle and Merlot Blanc.
Soil	Clay and gravel in varying proportions.
Appellations	Entre-Deux-Mers (AOC 1937, 195,500hl of white). Entre-Deux-Mers-Haut-Bénauge (AOC 1937, small quantities of white). Bordeaux Haut-Bénauge (AOC 1936, 3,300hl of white). Premières Côtes de Bordeaux (AOC 1973, 32,100hl of white). Loupiac (AOC 1936, 10,500hl of white). Ste-Croix-du-Mont (AOC 1936, 18,000hl of white). Côtes de Bordeaux St-Macaire (AOC 1937, 1,650hl of white). Ste-Foy-Bordeaux (AOC 1937, 4,850hl of white). Graves de Vayres (AOC 1937, 14,750hl of white). Cadillac (AOC 1973, 1,600hl of white).
Recommended producers	(Cadillac) Château Fayau; (Ste-Croix-du-Mont) Château Barbe-Morin. (Loupiac) Château Loupiac-Gaudiet.

ing, reliably fresh stuff with which to wash down the fish caught in the *deux mers*, which are the Dordogne and Garonne rivers.

This gravelly-soil appellation, which exclusively covers dry white, includes wine of this style made in the Graves-de-Vayres, Premières Côtes de Bordeaux, Loupiac, Ste-Croix-du-Mont, Côtes de Bordeaux St-Macaire and Ste-Foy-Bordeaux. A few properties are eligible to use the smaller appellation of Entre-Deux-Mers-Haut-Bénauge, and one which does, Château de Toutigeac, produces one of the region's most reliable whites, some of which is also sold under the Château de Lagorce label. Otherwise look out for Châteaux Thieuley, Bonnet and Launay.

Nearby, but not as good as Entre-Deux-Mers, Bordeaux Supérieur-Côtes de Francs produces a very small amount of dry white, as does Côtes de Bourg, while Bourg-Bourgeais, though legally allowed to make dry, *demi-sec*

and sweet white, has more or less switched to producing red wine.

White wines which fall into none of the above appellations, nor those of Graves, Sauternes and Barsac, can only term themselves Bordeaux or Bordeaux Supérieur. Even the well-thought-of, and highly-paid-for, Pavillon Blanc from Château Margaux, is allowed no more prestigious an appellation than these. Such wines are rare, the only other one I would recommend being Château Sénéjac.

The same strict rules apply to rosé, deeper pink Clairet (from which the name claret derives) and *Méthode Champenoise*, which can call themselves Bordeaux Rosé, Bordeaux Clairet and Bordeaux Mousseux respectively.

Below: *Château Bonnet produces one of the very best of all Entre-Deux-Mers, thanks to the modern winemaking techniques of the Lurton family.*

Despite boasting vineyards which date from the days of the Roman occupation, the communes of Sauternes and Barsac (and those of Fargues, Bommes and Preignac which fall within these appellations) have only been making the style of wine for which they are now known for a relatively short while. Four hundred years ago, the "vins de Langon" as they were called (after the nearby town) were lighter, and drier, and needed to be beefed up with a decent shot of alcohol before the Dutch, who were the biggest customers for this style, thought they were worth drinking.

It did not take the Sauternais very long to realise that they ought to be able to make the more powerful kind of wine the Dutch liked, and in 1787 they were evidently getting it reasonably right, because Thomas Jefferson, then American ambassador to France, reckoned Sauternes to be the best white wine in France after Champagne and Hermitage Blanc from the Rhône.

But it was not until the mid-19th century, however, that the Sauternais discovered the key that led to their subsequent success: "noble rot". Stories about how that discovery was made vary from château to château. At Yquem, they say that it all happened because, in 1859, the harvest was delayed and the grapes were, for the first time, attacked by the peculiar fungus *Botrytis cinerea*, the "noble rot" which covered the surface of the fruit, concentrating the sweetness and the flavour within. Down the road, they say that it was thanks to a German named Focke who, in 1836, deliberately developed the fungus with which he was already familiar from his upbringing among the rot-susceptible vines of the Rhine.

Whichever story you accept, there is no question that the 1859 Yquem sufficiently excited the brother of the Tsar of Russia for him to offer a far higher price than this wine had ever previously commanded. From that vintage on, noble rot was "in", and Yquem was expensive.

But life is not that simple. The nearby river and the shape of the landscape help to encourage the damp mist which the *Botrytis* needs, while the autumn weather can remain

fine enough to permit a late harvest without floods of flavour-diluting rain. There are, however, years when the climate is just too good for the fungus to develop properly. Good years for red Bordeaux are often poor ones for Sauternes; and vice versa.

This unreliability of production, coupled with an abandonment of the fashion for sweet wine drinking which was so popular in the last century, mean that the Sauternais lead lives of even greater financial insecurity than do most of their colleagues in other regions. If they were to work together to promote their wines more vigorously, perhaps they might bring about a renaissance of interest in great sweet wine. As it is, most of the château owners seem to pursue their vocation in isolation from one another.

The village of Sauternes itself is tiny; blink twice and you could miss it completely. It claims 600 inhabitants, a town hall and rather a curious-looking church. There are a few concessions to tourism here, in the

Left: *Botrytis-affected grapes at Château Climens, greatest of all Barsac. Lucien Lurton owns this and the tiny Château Doisy-Dubroca in the same commune; at both properties, the wines are made with great care, though Climens produces over 4,000 cases against Doisy-Dubroca's 500.*

Above: *A view of Château Coutet, seen through the vines. Estates in Sauternes are much smaller than in the Médoc, and each vine may only produce enough wine to fill a few glasses.*

shape of an unassuming "Maison de Sauternes" and a restaurant or two but, beyond that, this could be just about any one of France's tens of thousands of *villages de campagne*, all of which eke out some kind of living from agriculture.

A little over a kilometre out of Sauternes, however, there is a driveway and a small stone pillar. Follow that driveway to the château at the end and you will have found your way to the one wine about which there can be no argument. In the Médoc, they debate whether Margaux is better than Latour – and whether Haut-Brion or Pétrus might not outclass the lot of them; and in Burgundy, the Domaine de la Romanée-Conti's Montrachet is compared with that from the Domaine Leflaive and several others, in order to decide on the greatest white burgundy of all. In Sau-

Bordeaux "Rive Gauche" Wines

Grapes	Sauvignon, Sémillon, Muscadelle.
Soil	Gravel in the Graves, with higher clay content elsewhere.
Appellations	Graves (AOC 1937, 50,600hl of white). Cérons (AOC 1936, 2,650hl of white). Barsac (AOC 1936, 15,100hl of white). Sauternes (AOC 1936, 33,000hl of white).
Recommended producers	(Cérons) Château de Cérons; Château de Calvimont. (Graves) Château Haut-Brion; Château La Mission-Haut-Brion; Domaine de Chevalier; Château La Louvière; Chateau de Fieuzal; Château Rahoul. (Sauternes) Château Raymond-Lafon; Château d'Yquem; Château Rieussec; Château Suduiraut.

ternes however, life is simpler: there is Yquem, and then there are the rest. Rieussec is often regarded as number-two-trying-harder now, since a huge injection of Lafite-Rothschild money, and there are a few other châteaux which are making great wine, but Yquem still stands pre-eminent.

The secret lies partly in Yquem's position – soil and microclimate are everything here – and partly in the Lur-Saluces family's ability to obtain a high enough price for their wine to ensure that they can make it in exactly the way they want. This is textbook Sauternes. Each harvest is picked in several painstaking stages, literally bunch by bunch, and grape by grape. If another few days are needed for the grapes on this or that vine to be covered by the fungus, then another few days they shall have. And if, in the meantime, a rainstorm tears all these fragile bunches from the vines, well that is the risk one takes.

For each vine at Yquem only one glass of wine is produced, as compared with twice that amount at some other Sauternes properties and nearly a bottle-full in a great Médoc.

Production figures like these are crucial to an understanding of Sauternes. Wine drinkers who think these wines too expensive re-

Below: Château d'Yquem, source of unquestionably one of the very greatest wines – red or white – in the world. And one of the rarest.

Above: *Château Filhot was built in the 19th century by the Lur-Saluces family who still own Château d'Yquem.*

fuse to buy them; the owners of the least financially secure châteaux have to cut corners, picking earlier, and with less care. Their wine drops in quality; the wine drinker thinks it overpriced; and so the vicious circle continues. And lest anyone doubt the seriousness of the situation, it should be remembered that, not so very long ago, one winemaking property here simply closed its doors. That property was Château Myrat, an estate whose wine was rated as being one of only 13 *Deuxièmes Crus* when the Sauternes was classified in 1855 (a few years, incidentally, before noble rot became a general feature of the region's wines). Today, that classification is neither more nor less valid than its red counterparts, except that it recognises only first and second growths.

Today, my top twenty would include a few names which were not listed in 1855, most notably Château Raymond-Lafon which belongs to the *régisseur* of Château d'Yquem and Château de Fargues which belongs to the de Lur-Saluces, owners of Yquem. Château Bastor-Lamontagne is making gloriously honeyed-apricotty-spicy wine too, as is Château Les Justices. Another unclassified oddity is Château Gilette where wines are kept in tank for up to twenty years before bottling. Opinions about the validity of this method vary, but it does at least guarantee a source of older Sauternes; far too much of this, potentially the longest-lived of all wines, is drunk decades before it should be.

Dry wine made in Sauternes can only call itself Bordeaux Blanc, even the illustrious "Ygrec" produced at Yquem. Such wines can be both interesting and enjoyable, often smelling as though they are going to taste sweet before proving to be bone dry; R de Rieussec is one of the best examples of the style. Inevitably, they are not cheap, but if their production and sale helps to enable their makers to continue to make good sweet wine, then they deserve support.

Buy Sauternes and Barsac from any of the châteaux listed in these pages but, unless you want to experience poor sweet winemaking at its worst, and unless you enjoy tickling your throat with sulphur dioxide, do *not* take the risk of buying the cheap "own-brand" Sauternes on sale throughout the world. If the region's best producers could take one step to improve the image of their wine, it would be to prevent such travesties from existing. They do as much harm as the "Spanish Sauternes" of 20 years ago.

The 1855 Classification of Sauternes and Barsac

Premier Cru Supérieur
Ch d'Yquem, *Sauternes*

Premiers Crus

Ch Climens, *Barsac*	Ch Lafaurie-Peyraguey, *Bommes*	Ch Sigalas-Rabaud, *Bommes*
Ch Clos Haut-Peyraguey, *Bommes*	Ch La Tour Blanche, *Bommes*	Ch Rieussec, *Sauternes (Fargues)*
Ch Coutet, *Barsac*	Ch de Rayne-Vigneau, *Bommes*	Ch Suduiraut, *Preignac*
Ch Guiraud, *Sauternes*	Ch Rabaud-Promis, *Bommes*	

Deuxièmes Crus

Ch d'Arche, *Sauternes*	Ch Filhot, *Sauternes*	Ch Nairac, *Barsac*
Ch Broustet, *Barsac*	Ch Lamothe, *Sauternes*	Ch Romer, *Preignac*
Ch Caillou, *Barsac*	Ch Lamothe-Guignard, *Sauternes*	Ch Romer-du-Hayot, *Preignac*
Ch Doisy-Daëne, *Barsac*	Ch de Malle, *Preignac*	Ch Suau, *Barsac*
Ch Doisy-Dubroca, *Barsac*	Ch Myrat, *Barsac*	
Ch Doisy-Védrines, *Barsac*		

CHAMPAGNE

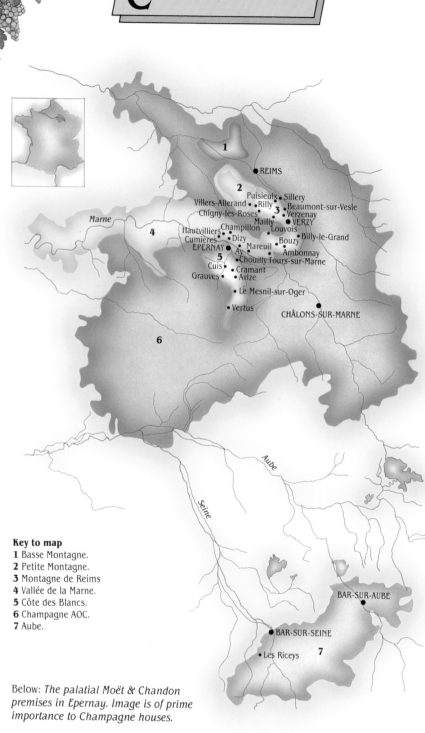

REIMS

Puisieulx • Sillery
Villers-Allerand • Rilly • Beaumont-sur-Vesle
Chigny-les-Roses • **3** Verzenay
Mailly • VERZY
Champillon • Louvois
Hautvilliers • Billy-le-Grand
Cumières • Dizy • Bouzy
EPERNAY • Mareuil • Ambonnay
5 Chouilly Tours-sur-Marne
Cuis • Ay
Cramant
Grauves • Avize

Le Mesnil-sur-Oger

• Vertus
CHÂLONS-SUR-MARNE

2

Marne

4

6

Aube

Seine

1

BAR-SUR-AUBE

BAR-SUR-SEINE

• Les Riceys **7**

Key to map
1 Basse Montagne.
2 Petite Montagne.
3 Montagne de Reims
4 Vallée de la Marne.
5 Côte des Blancs.
6 Champagne AOC.
7 Aube.

Below: *The palatial Moët & Chandon
premises in Epernay. Image is of prime
importance to Champagne houses.*

Above: *Champagne vineyards at Charly sur Marne. Surprisingly to many visitors, other forms of agriculture abound here and vines are only planted in sites which are best suited to their cultivation.*

Whether or not Dom Pérignon, the Benedictine monk who managed the cellars and vineyards of the Abbey of Hautvillers, actually invented today's style of Champagne is very much open to question; claimants to the honour include sparkling wine makers in several other regions of France, not to mention Spain. One thing remains certain, however, Dom Pérignon took a far more scientific attitude to the whole business of his region's wine than had ever been taken before.

During his time at the abbey, from 1668 to 1715, he became interested in the way in which bottles of the wine he had blended for his fellow monks tended to explode during the Spring following the harvest. Given the very rough-and-ready way in which the wines would have been made and bottled, complete with readily re-fermentable yeast and sugar, the effect of the warm weather after the chill of winter must have been almost inevitable; the monks ought to have given thanks for the bottles which miraculously remained intact.

Dom Pérignon, evidently decided to try to control this problem, importing thicker, stronger bottles from England and replacing the traditional hemp-wrapped wooden bottle stoppers which were still in use, with corks imported by fellow monks who had dis-

covered their efficacy in Spain. Perhaps more importantly still, Dom Pérignon seems to have developed the press which permitted him to make white, rather than pale pink, wine from the region's black grapes, and the skill of blending wines from different vineyards, and the production of a single "Cuvée" (or blend). Dom Grossard, Dom Pérignon's 19th century successor at Hautvillers, wrote that he could "tell at once which grapes were from which vineyards and would say, 'This one must be married with the wine of that one', and never once did he make a mistake".

The Pérignon fizz, if we still had a bottle in its original state, would almost certainly have had a heavy, gritty sediment made up of all the dead yeast cells which had set off the second, bubble-producing fermentation in the first place. For years, no-one could devise a way effectively to separate the yeast from the wine without losing most of the sparkle. Filtering was out of the question; a process known as *transvasage* – literally decanting

Right: *As in Chablis, frost costs Champagne producers many sleepless nights during the winter months. These oil burners help to solve the problem in all but the most severe cold snaps.*

the wine into another bottle – was little better, and the only method which met with any great favour was the storage and sale of the bottles bottom-up or *cul-en-l'air*.

People who bought their Champagne in this way had to learn the knack of *dégorgement à la volée*: removing the cork swiftly and in such a way that the yeast which had settled in the neck of the bottle could fall out without taking too much wine with it in the process.

It was a young widow who had, against all the advice, just taken on her dead husband's Champagne house, who discovered a way of removing the yeast from these unpredictable *cul-en-l'air* bottles in her own cellars. Veuve Clicquot's invention, devised following prolonged experiments with an upturned kitchen table drilled with varying shapes and sizes of holes, involved special racks in which the wine bottles could be placed, neck down-wards and in which, by *remuage* (deftly turning the bottles a few degrees every day) the yeast could be reliably shifted down on to the cork. While Madame Clicquot's personal role in the creation of what would become the A-shaped *pupitre* racks still in use today is unquestionable, it was her *chef de caves*, Antoine Müller, who perfected the angle of the holes and of the racks. And it was Müller

Champagne Wines

Soil	Chalk with occasional sandy topsoil.
Grapes	*Chardonnay* The variety from which all good white Burgundy is made, and all *blanc de blancs* Champagne. It is also an essential component in most Champagne blends, alongside the Pinot Noir and Pinot Meunier. Covering 24 per cent of the region's vines, much of them in the Côte des Blancs close to Epernay, where it benefits from the chalky soil and is the only permitted grape. *Pinot Noir* Covering 28 per cent of the vineyard area, and particularly concentrated on the Montagne de Reims. The earliest-ripening variety in the region, this Burgundian grape does best on these south and south-west facing slopes. Care has to be taken when picking these grapes, not to break their skins and thus allow the pigment to dye the juice. Even so, Pinot Noir Champagne can be a little more pink in colour than *blanc de blancs*. *Pinot Meunier* The black sheep of Champagne, and the variety few producers care to admit to having or using – despite the acknowledged fact that it accounts for 48 per cent of the region's vines and a rather higher percentage of its wine. Forbidden from any of the Grands and Premiers Crus vineyards, it provides a generous crop per acre – which accounts for its continued domination.
Maximum Yield (all varieties)	13,000kg grapes/ha or 85hl/ha (150kg grapes can make a maximum of 1hl)
Ageing	Non-vintage Champagne must spend at least 12 months on its yeast before *dégorgement*. Vintage Champagne must, however, spend 36 months on its yeast before it is disgorged.
Age	Non-vintage Champagne is a blend of several years' wines. Vintage Champagne must contain at least 80 per cent of wine from the particularly good vintage which appears on the label, though the remaining 20 per cent can come from various other, non-declared years.

who subsequently founded the house of Müller-Ruinart and employed a young man called Jacques Bollinger to open up a market for his Champagne in Germany. It was thus scarcely surprising that Veuve Clicquot's "secret" method was soon adopted by many of her competitors.

From the invention of the *pupitre* it was a simple step at the end of the 19th century for Armand Walfart to conceive of *dégorgement*: a procedure of chilling the neck of the bottle in freezing brine before removing the stopper and allowing the yeast to fly out under pressure, leaving the clear wine behind.

The process has been modernised very extensively since then, with beer caps replacing corks for this initial stage, and with machines called *giropalettes* increasingly replacing the highly skilled *remueurs* whose job it had been to turn all those bottles. Now, a further development has been made which could make Madame Clicquot's work seem quite unnecessary: special, easily removable, permeable capsules, called *microbilles*, could permit the yeast to do its bubble-creating job in the bottle without there being any need to handle the bottles at all. It will be several years – if ever – before this process

becomes legal for use in the making of Champagne, but the very fact that it is currently being tested by at least one major Champagne house proves how seriously the producers take the need to reduce their high production costs.

But the turning of a still wine into a sparkling one, by means of a secondary fermentation in the bottle – which in essence defines the Champagne method wherever it is used – is only part of the Champagne story. And to understand just why Champagne genuinely does taste different, and potentially better than other wines made in the same way, one has to return to the vineyard.

As elsewhere, there is in Champagne a crucial marriage of grape and soil. Here, however, the mixture is particularly odd. On the one hand, despite the fact that this is France's most northerly winegrowing region, and one of the least climatically hospitable, the Champenois persist in growing mostly

Below: *Birds can be a major pest in vineyards: here, netting is being used to keep starlings away from Pinot Noir grapes on which they would happily feed.*

sun-loving black grapes to make their white wine. Of the two black varieties, one, the Pinot Meunier, is planted almost nowhere else, and the other, Burgundy's Pinot Noir, is notoriously difficult to handle. The third variety, the white Chardonnay, is easier to deal with, but even so would need warmer weather to produce truly rich-flavoured wine with any regularity at all – as a taste of a cool vintage Coteaux Champenois, the region's attempt at still white, amply proves.

The secret of the flavour of Champagne lies in the way in which the three varieties react to the chalk on which they are grown, and the subtle variations in quality and flavour derived from vineyards in specifically well-sited communes. The Côte des Blancs, for example, which includes the villages of Cramant, Vertus, Chouilly, Avize and Le Mesnil-sur-Oger is perfectly suited to the Chardonnay and produces the best Blanc de Blancs; the Montagne de Reims, by contrast, which includes such villages as Ambonnay, Bouzy, Mailly, Sillery, Verzy, and Chigny-lès-Roses is planted with both black and white grapes with some of its communes – Bouzy for instance – growing almost no Chardonnay at all.

Right: *Harvesting Pinot Noir grapes. The value of grapes throughout Champagne is established annually according to a strict financial hierarchy.*

Below: *The 36,000l stainless steel tanks in which the wines of Champagne Palmer undergo their first fermentation. The temperature of the wine in these tanks can be very carefully controlled.*

In Champagne, as nowhere else in France, there is an established financial hierarchy which sets the value of the grapes harvested in these communes, each of which has a rating of somewhere between 75-100 per cent. Every year, following discussions between the growers and the Champagne houses, under the auspices of the local *Comité Interprofessionnel*, a price is fixed per kilo of grapes grown in a 100 per cent vineyard. So, a grower with 1,000 kilos of grapes from a 80 per cent commune will be paid 20 per cent less than his neighbour whose vines are rated at 100 per cent. The system does not operate quite as simply as that, however, because as the Pinot Noir and Chardonnay have become more popular, these two grapes have commanded a premium beyond the intrinsic value of the vineyard in which they are grown; a kilo of Chardonnay from a 90 per cent vineyard is worth more than a kilo of Pinot Meunier from the same plot. In a continual attempt to rationalise the situation, a large number of vineyards have been upgraded following the uprooting of the Pinot Meunier and its replacement by Chardonnay; some communes now have two percentage ratings, one per grape variety.

Above: *The skill of the blender lies in creating a balanced* cuvée *from the different wine stocks at his disposal.*

Almost all of the Champagne houses and individual growers claim to make their wine from grapes rated at an average of at least 90 per cent, and most will give precise proportions for each of the grape varieties they use. In real terms this is usually nonsense, because every year highly-skilled blenders have to use the wine at their disposal to re-plicate the house style of Non-Vintage wine. Last year, Maison X may well have used the 43 per cent Chardonnay they claim, but if that variety is less available this year due to frost damage, or if the blender finds that the desired flavour of wine is best achieved with only 38 per cent, then that will be the figure used on that occasion.

More important than the specific compo-nents, though, is the stock of mature wine a blender has at his command (some houses have better stocks of old wine than others) and how long he can leave the Champagne in contact with its yeast. The legal minimum for Non Vintage Champagne is 12 months, while Vintage has to spend 36 months between initial bottling and *dégorgement*, but here too each Champagne house has, within those limits, the option of being as generous or as mean as it likes with its yeast contact. A cheap supermarket fizz may thus have been rushed on to the market after only 12 months and a day on its yeast, while prestigious houses such as Krug leave theirs for a period of over five years.

Lastly, and of crucial importance, comes the *dosage*, the blend of cane sugar wine and sometimes brandy which is added to the Champagne bottles following *dégorgement* to fill the space left in the bottle by the dis-gorged yeast, and to take the edge off the bone dry and rather acidic flavour of the wine. Even the driest of Brut Champagnes has been sweetened in this way – only the very rare but modish Brut Zéro and Brut Sauvage brand are marketed without it – but the style and sugar content of the *dosage* can vary widely. Some houses, such as Mumm, favour a rich, softening *dosage*; others such as Pommery prefer a more neutral one. One fact

Above: *A rare view of the yeasty deposit sitting in the neck of the bottle. Usually, at this stage, the bottle is "corked" with a crown cap identical to the ones used for beer bottles.*

Right: Dégorgement – *the all-important removal of the dead yeast from the neck of a bottle of Champagne, prior to its* dosage *and final recorking.*

every honest Champagne blender would admit is that a "sophisticated" *dosage* can hide a multitude of sins like, in the words of one Champenois, "skilfully applied make-up on the face of a very plain woman".

Historically, the role of the *dosage* was even more crucial than it is today. Different countries demanded different levels of sweetness; William Thackeray, the author of *Vanity Fair*, chauvinistically reckoned the wine he found in England to be "the best Champagne I know . . . the most doctored, the most brandied, the most barley-sugared . . .", but it was the English who were among the first to demand a move away from the

Champagne Sweetness Scale

Brut Zéro	Also, called Brut Sauvage, Brut Intégral and Brut Non Dosé. Made with no *dosage* at all: bone dry and too acidic for most tastes. Enjoyed a brief boom of popularity in the USA in the early 1980s.
Brut	The standard dry style. 0-15gms cane sugar/litre can be added; some houses' Brut is much drier than others.
Extra Sec	Confusingly named. The sweetness can be between 12-20gms sugar/litre, quite a wide variation. Less popular as a style than one might expect.
Sec	4 per cent is acknowledged to be the "perceptible level" of sweetness in any wine; *dosage* can take Sec Champagne to between 3-5 per cent or 17-23gms/litre.
Demi Sec	There is between 33-50gms added sugar per litre here so the flavour is easily as sweet as most people would want. Traditionally popular in Asti Spumanti-loving Italy.
Doux	Very sweet (more than 50gms/litre of sugar) and very rare nowadays. A throwback to the days of "pudding Champagnes" on Victorian dinner tables.

"pudding Champagne" style favoured by the Imperial court of Russia. Even today, when sweeter Champagnes are rare and difficult to sell, some houses reflect their long-learned skills by producing "Extra-Dry" and "Rich" Champagne of a higher quality than their more basic Brut.

It is the skill of the blender and the range of wines from which he can work, which, according to the Champagne houses, provide them with the edge over individual growers' own domaines. Few would deny that this is often the case, but some well-situated growers have proved that ownership of a really first class vineyard can provide its own advantages. There is little question that, in some vintages, the major houses have found it difficult to buy the quality of grapes they have needed. Proof of this could be found in the "green", unripe flavour of some of the non-vintage wine which has found its way on to the market bearing some very distinguished names on its labels. Shortage of those good quality grapes can result in the inclusion of fruit from the more recently planted vineyards, and in the use of the *taille*, or second pressing, rather than just the *cuvée* first pressing. Many houses like to stress that they never use the *vin de taille*, claiming that they only sell it in bulk. In some cases, that will be true, but in others, well, let us just say that the proof is in the tasting, and there have been some very coarse-tasting big-name Champagnes around. But then of course, there is nothing to say that the individual grower may not pull precisely the same stunt.

Whatever the style of Champagne you prefer – and Champagne is very much a matter of personal taste – you may still have to choose between a non-vintage, a vintage and perhaps a Prestige Cuvée (see the Champagne Wines fact box for an explanation of non-vintage and vintage Champagne). There are those in the region who regard non-vintage Champagne as the truest, most traditional version of the wine. Krug very evidently holds this view, pricing its NV Grande Cuvée at the same level as its Vintage. Others disagree, creating instead a hierarchy of styles and prices, ranging from a Non-Vintage to a Vintage Prestige Cuvée set (in theory at least) right at the top of the quality pyramid. Confusingly, as with port (the only other fine wine with "declared" vintages), different houses choose to declare in different years, sometimes surprising people by their decisions.

Today's wine drinkers tend to take the existence of such "super-quality" wines as Moët & Chandon's Dom Pérignon and Roederer's Cristal so much for granted that it is easy to forget that these brands (for that is, after all, what they are) are relatively recent creations. Moët started the trend with the 1921 vintage of Dom Pérignon, sold in 1937 after much hesitation. Roederer could, however, be said to have pipped them to the post, selling a large consignment of Cristal to South America in 1919. Since this was Champagne which had originally been intended for the Tsar of Russia who, for one reason and another had been unable to pay for the wine of which his court was the sole purchaser, and since it was a particularly sweet blend which proved unsaleable to anyone else, this can hardly be termed a commercial sale. It was not until the 1945 vintage came on the market that Dom Pérignon really had a competitor.

It would be reassuring to be able to say that these two highly expensive Champagnes, much loved by rock singers and movie stars are overpriced and of disappointing quality. In fact, blind tastings have proved both to be among the very best Champagne one can buy. On the other hand, buying a prestige *cuvée* from one of the many houses which now offer them is no guarantee of buying a really top-class wine. Some houses' non-vintage easily outrank their competitors' so-called prestige wines.

Champagne Bottle Sizes

Decoding The Label

Every Champagne label reveals the identity of its producer to those who know how, and where to look. Unfortunately, the following list can only point you in the right direction for further research; the list which would permit you to decode the identification number which follows each of these prefixes, and which, by its very nature, changes constantly, can only be consulted by appointment by people in the region itself.

RM

Récoltant-Manipulant An individual estate (there are nearly 5,000) which grows its own grapes and sells its own Champagne which it has either vinified itself or had vinified by a co-operative. Growers own 86 per cent of the vineyards in Champagne.

NM

Négociant-Manipulant A producer who makes Champagne partly or wholly from grapes which he has had to buy in. In practice this means all of the *Grandes Marques* and other major houses, though some grow far more of their own grapes than others. There are 120 of these, though just 10 control 50 per cent of the market.

CM

Coopératives de Manipulation Co-operatives which make wine from their members' grapes and either market the finished wine in bottle under a wide range of labels, or sell it *sur lattes* (literally "on the laths" i.e. from their storage cellars) to the Grandes Marques who carry out the *dosage* themselves to create a flavour as similar to their own wines as possible. There are 146 of these.

MA

Marque Auxiliaire A brand name belonging to a buyer who has bought his Champagne from an RM, NM or CM. There are a great number of these around, ranging from a supermarket's "own label" to fizz labelled "Pierre Dupont" or some such.

Above: *Packaging is crucially important to Champagne – from the shape of the bottle to the colour and style of the gold, or silver or bronze, capsule which conceals the cork.*

Right: *Mumm's "standard" and its "prestige" Champagnes. Many experts would agree that Mumm's more humbly labelled Blanc de Blancs is a better wine than its "prestige" Réné Lalou.*

Left: *The range of Champagne bottles: (left to right) the Split (20cl), the Pint (40cl), the Bottle (75cl), the Magnum (2 bottles) the Jeroboam (4 bottles), the Rehoboam (6 bottles), the Methusalah (8 bottles), the Salmanazar (12 bottles), the Balthasar (16 bottles) and the Nebuchadnezzar (20 bottles).*

The Major Champagne Houses

Champagne House	Address	Founded	Production
Ayala	Ay	1860	1m bottles
Billecart-Salmon	Mareuil-sur-Ay	1818	450,000 bottles
Bollinger	Ay	1829	1.4m bottles, 70 per cent from Bollinger's own 142ha
Canard-Duchêne	Rilly-la-Montagne	1868	3m bottles, 4 per cent from the company's own 15ha
Charles Heidsieck	Reims	1808	3.5m bottles
Heidsieck & Co Monopole	Reims	1785	1.8m bottles, 33 per cent from own 110ha
Henriot	Reims	1808	1.5m bottles
Krug	Reims	1843	500,000 bottles, 30 per cent from own vineyards
Lanson	Reims	1760	5m bottles, 35 per cent from own 210ha
Laurent Perrier	Tours-sur-Marne	1812	6.5m bottles, 10 per cent from own 80ha
Mercier	Epernay	1858	6m bottles, 20 per cent from own vineyards, much of the rest from Moët & Chandon, Mercier's parent company
Moët & Chandon	Epernay	1743	18-26.5m bottles, 20 per cent from own 876ha (2 per cent of the entire region)
Mumm	Reims	1827	9.5m bottles, 25 per cent from own 220ha
Joseph Perrier	Châlons-sur-Marne	1825	650,000 bottles, 30 per cent from own 20ha
Perrier-Jouët	Epernay	1811	3m bottles, 40-45 per cent from own 108ha
Philipponnat	Mareuil-sur-Ay	1912	450,000 bottles, 20 per cent from own 12ha
Piper Heidsieck	Reims	1785	4.8m bottles
Pol Roger	Epernay	1849	1.3m bottles, 40 per cent from own 70ha
Pommery & Gréno	Reims	1836	6.5m bottles, 50 per cent (including all Vintage) from own 300ha
Louis Roederer	Reims	1760	2.5m bottles, 80 per cent from own 180ha
Ruinart	Reims	1729	1.3m bottles, 20 per cent from Moët & Chandon's 876ha
Taittinger	Reims	1734	4m bottles, 50 per cent from own 250ha
Veuve-Clicquot-Ponsardin	Reims	1772	7m bottles, 33 per cent from own 265ha

House Style/Notes	Prestige Cuvée	Other Best Wines	Average Yeast Contact
Heavy Pinot influence – old fashioned	Blanc de Blancs Millesimé	Carte Blanche Demi Sec	2.5 years
Heavy Chardonnay influence	Billecart Cuvée	–	(not given)
"Serious", rich, high Pinot Noir influence. One of the very best, but not universally liked	Bollinger R.D.	Vieilles Vignes	3 years
Belongs to Veuve Clicquot; often heavily discounted; modest Non-Vintage – high Pinot content in NV	Charles VII	–	(not given)
Recently bought by Rémy-Martin. "Commercial" but improving. High Pinot content	Cuvée Champagne Charlie	–	(not given)
Belongs to Seagram. Fast improving quality following replanting. High Pinot content	Diamant Bleu	–	3 years
Bias towards Chardonnay. Now merged with Moët and Chandon and Veuve Clicquot	Réserve du Baron Philippe de Rothschild	Blanc de Blancs	(not given)
Belongs to Rémy Martin but still family-run. Arguably the finest of all Champagne. Supports the unfashionable Pinot Meunier and makes the best Non-Vintage of all	Grande Cuvée (though Krug claim to have no prestige cuvée as such)	Clos du Mesnil, Rosé	6 years
Belongs to the giant BSN food and beer corporation. Soft, highly commercial, 50/50 Pinot and Chardonnay NV	Noble Cuvée	–	2.5 years
Full, clean, unusually rich NV	Cuvée Grande Siècle	Rosé	(not given)
Commercial, heavy *dosage*, high Pinot content	Réserve de l'Empereur	–	2.5 years
By far the biggest house in Champagne, 25 per cent of annual exports. Very commercial, can be variable Pinot-dominated NV, but Dom Pérignon is great	Dom Pérignon	–	2-3 years
Belongs to Canadian liquor giant Seagram and is linked to Heidsieck & Co Monopole. Commercial, "soft" NV Cordon Rouge	Président Réné Lalou	Crémant de Cramant	3 years
Light, fresh, often undistinguished NV, but exceptional rosé and pure Chardonnay prestige cuvée	Cuvée du Cent-Cinquantenaire	–	3 years
Light and flowery – heavy Pinot Noir influence. Good Vintage wines	Belle Epoque	–	2-3 years
Good, small house, belonging to Gosset. Rich, with softer than usual mousse	Clos des Goisses	–	2-3 years
Unexciting when young, the Non-Vintage wines are sometimes worth keeping	Florenz Louis	Brut Sauvage	2.5-4 years
Winston Churchill's favourite. One of the very best. Fresh yeasty NV	Cuvée Sir Winston Churchill	–	3-4 years
Climbing back up to its previous position amongst the best in Champagne, but wines need to be cellared before drinking. Very dry, usually discreet *dosage*	Louise Pommery	–	3.5-4 years
One of the very best. Rich, full-flavoured with a high Pinot content	Cristal	–	3.5-4 years
High quality, often underestimated house. High Chardonnay influence	Dom Ruinart	–	3 years
A very good, small, family-owned house. Strong Pinot influence	Comtes de Champagne	–	3 years
Particularly popular in Britain. Very full, Pinot Noir-influenced flavour	La Grande Dame	–	"At least 3 years"

Recommended Lesser-Known Champagne Producers

House	Address/Remarks	House	Address/Remarks
Barancourt	Bouzy Wines worth keeping	Jacquesson	Dizy Generally great, particularly R.D.
Besserat de Bellefon	Reims Good Crémant	Jeanmaire	Epernay
Boizel	Epernay	Lechère	Paris
F. Bonnet & Fils	Oger Good Blanc de Blancs	Legras	Chouilly Great Blanc de Blancs
Bricout & Koch	Avize Good quality range	Abel Lepitre	Reims Good Prince A. de Bourbon-Parme
De Castellane	Epernay Good Vintage Commodore	Marne & Champagne	Epernay Sells 10m bottles per year under more
De Cazenove	Avize		than 250 different
A. Charbaut	Epernay Good Crémant		labels, including A. Rothschild
Collery	Ay Good Cuvée Herbillon Pinot Noir	Montaudon	Reims Good Vintage wine
Deutz	Ay Good range	Napoléon	Vertus Good Vintage
André Drappier	Bar-sur-Aube Good Carte d'Or	Bruno Paillard	Reims Good Vintage
Duval-Leroy	Vertus Good inexpensive range	Ployez-Jacquemart	Ludes Good Cuvée Liesse d'Hardonville
H. Germain	Rilly-la-Montagne Good Blanc de Blancs	Théophile Roederer Sacotte	Reims Epernay Good Blanc de Blancs
Gosset	Ay Good range – the oldest house in Champagne	J. de Telmont	Epernay Good range
Georges Goulet	Reims Good range	De Saint-Marceaux Salon	Reims Avize Truly great Blanc de Blancs
Alfred Gratien	Epernay Very traditional, very good range	De Venoge	Epernay Good Vintage des Princes
Ivernel	Ay Good Cuvée du Roi François Ier		

hampagne is unique amongst the world's quality rosés in being legally made from a blend of red and white wine. This "addition method" is, however, not the only way in which rosé Champagne is produced and there are traditionalists who would argue that the only "real" way to achieve really high quality is to make what the Champenois call "Rosé de Noirs" and what is known elsewhere as the "maceration method" or, in California, as "skin contact".

As the name implies, this involves using 100 per cent black grapes, usually Pinot Noir. There are two methods of doing this. The first is the one now used in Burgundy by red wine makers in years of high production when they feel that they are likely to make light-bodied wine. To remedy the situation, they effect a *saignée* (literally a "bleeding") of the vatful

Right: *Pinot Noir, the grapes from which Rosé de Noirs Champagne is usually made.*

Rosé Champagne

The Wine

Rosé Champagne, whichever method is used, must be made 100 per cent from grapes grown within the Champagne region.

Non-Vintage

Rules of bottle-ageing as for white Champagne; at least 12 months.

Vintage

As for white: at least 36 months' bottle ageing.

Rosé de Noirs

The Champenois' name for wine made by the maceration method: the process of allowing the pigment in the skin of the black Pinot grapes to dye the juice pink.

This is in contrast to the addition method: the process of blending red and white wine to make pink Champagne.

Recommended Rosés

Laurent Perrier; Pommery "Louise Pommery"; Louis Roederer; Krug; Bollinger; Perrier-Jouët; Philiponnat; Pol Roger; Piper Heidsieck; Veuve Clicquot, Lanson; Alfred Gratien; Besserat de Bellefon; Billecart-Salmon Crémant des Moines; Deutz Vintage; Dom Ruinart; Gosset; Charles Heidsieck; Taittinger Comtes de Champagne; Moët & Chandon Vintage; Gosset; André Jacquart; Jeanmaire; Montaudon.

---

of fermenting crushed grapes within the first 24 hours of fermentation, drawing off a certain amount of pale pink wine which has begun to pick up colour through the skin contact enjoyed by the juice. The essential difference between the *saignées* practised by the Burgundians and the Champenois is that the former want to concentrate the colour and flavour of their remaining red wine, while the latter are intent only on producing exactly the colour of pink wine they want.

The other method of making rosé from black grapes is to leave them overnight in the press before the wine is extracted. Although, as some proponents of Rosé de Noirs have discovered to their embarassment, it can be impossibly difficult to determine the way in which any given Rosé Champagne has been made, it is probably fair to say that the 100 per cent Pinot wines can have a more intensely raspberryish character. Both maceration methods may also, by their nature, allow less consistency of colour than the addition method which permits the blender a far greater degree of control.

Coteaux Champenois

An appellation since 1974, these still white wines are Champagne's very expensive answer to Burgundy and are worth sampling once, if for no other reason than to learn why this region has concentrated its attention on selling wine with bubbles.

Of the three styles produced, despite the northerly nature of the vineyards, the most successful is probably the red which falls outside the scope of this book. The rosé is extremely rare, though the best, when found, will probably come from the Montagne de Reims. The white can be light and pleasantly floral but with a level of acidity which leaves this taster yearning for a glass of Chablis at perhaps two thirds of the price. The most easily found white is Laurent Perrier.

When Coteaux Champenois is made solely from grapes harvested in one specific *Grand* or *Premier Cru* vineyard, the village name – principally Avize, Bouzy and Ambonnay – may feature on the label. The maximum permit-

ted yield is 13,000kg per ha, as for Champagne. Each year, the INAO decides on the proportion allowed to Champagne and Coteaux Champenois.

Rosé de Riceys

This is a non-sparkling rosé which gained *Appellation Contrôlée* status in 1971, but whose existence is of almost academic interest since less than 100,000 bottles are made each year. If you find one of those when in Champagne, it should be an attractive "pellure d'onion" (onion-skin) colour and ought to smell and taste pleasantly raspberryish. Wines have to be made from Pinot Noir grapes harvested at Riceys and in vineyards delimited for the production of Champagne. The maximum yield is 85hl/ha; maximum alcohol content is set at 10°.

Key to map
1 Alsace.

Note: There is only one appellation here – that of Alsace. The wines are primarily distinguished by their grape varieties. Total white wine production in 1986 was 1,127,500hl.

The Alsaciens are one of the most self-possessed people in France, proud of their own very particular identity. But although they are in no doubt at all about who they are, the rest of the world remains really rather confused. In 1860, the Alsaciens owed their allegiance to the Emperor of Germany; the following year they suddenly became French, but were only allowed nine years to become used to their new condition because, from 1870 until the postwar peace settlement of 1918, Alsace once again became part of Germany.

And then, of course, came 1940 and the turn of the whole of France to experience German rule. Given that persistent uncertainty as to whose side they should be on, which language to use when saying good

morning, it is hardly surprising that the Alsaciens built up a pride in their own regional identity. If, in a moment of bureaucratic lunacy, the European Community decided to annexe Alsace to Switzerland, Luxembourg or Liechtenstein, the region's populace would probably smile their impish smile, continue to speak their own dialect (an odd mixture of Gallic and German) and make their own rather peculiar wine.

The wine-producing region itself is shaped like a long, and very thin, sausage, stretching 70 miles from Wasselonne, level with Strasbourg in the north, to Thann in the south. It ranges between half a mile and three miles in width, in an almost unbroken band running along the foothills of the Vosges, from quaint oak-timbered village to village. Unlike most

Above: *Setting up the wiring for one year old vines for Hugel at Riquewihr. New plantation in Alsace has been extensive in recent years – often in areas once thought unsuitable for fine wine-making. Hugel is a traditionalist firm, preferring the "old" land for its vineyards.*

of France's other wine regions, however, Alsace produces wines which are known by the grape variety from which they are made, rather than the village in which those grapes were grown. This tends to obscure both the fact that certain villages are unquestionably better suited to some grape varieties than to others, and that in any case Alsace is effectively divided into two parts, the better-situated Haut-Rhin to the south which is protected by the Vosges mountains, and the Bas-Rhin which is the source of much of the region's more basic wines. There has always been a certain measure of rivalry between these two sub-regions which once produced equal amounts of wine before the Haut-Rhin finally began to take precedence over its more northerly neighbour.

No-one can agree on precisely when the vine was introduced to Alsace. Fossils of vines and seeds dating back before 3,000 B.C. have been found but these, it seems, were *Vitis sylvestris* – eating rather than drinking grapes – and it is thought that *Vitis vinifera*, the winemaking variety, was not grown until the Romans arrived. Though probable, it is not even certain that the new form of agriculture started then because the first records of vinous viticulture date from 200 A.D. This means that winemaking certainly started later in Alsace then elsewhere, but the Alsaciens were quick to catch up and, by the end of the ninth century, there were no less than 119 villages whose inhabitants tended vines and made wine. By the 12th century, the Alsaciens had learned to accept that theirs was a region which was better suited to the production of white wine than red and, in the middle ages, wines were exported eastwards to Germany and up to the Nordic countries, thanks partly to the region's situation at the crossroads of western Europe – Strasbourg was the biggest port on the Rhine – and partly to the international communications enjoyed by the region's 300 winemaking abbeys.

Between the 15th and 17th centuries, quality began to improve too, following the arrival of grapes such as the Riesling, Gewürztraminer and Pinot Gris, now thought of as the "noble varieties", and producers in the best-sited villages created their own forerunner of *Appellation Contrôlée* legislation in an attempt to promote the use of these varieties. The wine growers' association of Riquewihr, for example, founded in 1520, laid down rules for harvest dates (as late and ripe as possible) and the grape varieties which the villagers could grow. In 1575, there was a decree which differentiated between the "noble" varieties and the rest; four years later a grower was obliged to pull up his plantation of Elbling (a grape still grown to little good effect in Germany). In 1644 and 1674 subsequent decrees restricted the producers still further.

As the quality improved, so did the region's prosperity. Towns were built, privileges conferred, growers became landowners and founded the firms of merchants which

Right: *The Trimbach winery, overlooked by vines, is typical of the timbered style of building in Alsace.*

Alsace Grands Crus Vineyards

Lieux dits (vineyards)	In the commune(s) of
Altenberg de Bergbieten	Bergbieten
Altenberg de Bergheim	Bergheim
Brand	Turckheim
Eichberg	Eguisheim
Geisberg	Ribeauvillé
Gloeckelberg	Rodern and Saint-Hippolyte
Goldert	Gueberschwihr
Hatschbourg	Hattstatt and Voeglinshoffen
Hengst	Wintzenheim
Kanzlerberg	Bergheim
Kastelberg	Andlau
Kessler	Guebwiller
Kirchberg de Barr	Barr
Kirchberg de Ribeauvillé	Ribeauvillé
Kitterlé	Guebwiller
Moenchberg	Andlau (67) and Eichhoffen
Ollwiller	Wuenheim
Rangen	Thann (68) and Vieux-Thann
Rosacker	Hunawihr
Saering	Guebwiller
Schlossberg	Kaysersberg and Kientzheim
Sommerberg	Niedermorschwihr and Katzenthal
Sonnelglanz	Beblenheim
Spiegel	Bergholtz and Guebwiller
Wiebelsberg	Andlau

An Alsace *Grand Cru* must:
● Satisfy all the conditions of ordinary AOC Alsace
● Be made from Riesling, Gewürztraminer, Pinot Gris (Tokay) or Muscat grapes, 100 per cent single variety
● Contain (for Pinot Gris and Gewürztraminer) 187g/l minimum of natural sugar, and have a minimum of 11° after fermentation or (for Riesling and Muscat) contain 170g/l natural sugar and 10° minimum alcohol after fermentation.
● Come from a vineyard producing no more than 70hl per ha of vines in production (though this is the basic yield, and in some years may be increased by a small percentage, like ordinary AOC Alsace)
● Come from the same vintage
● Come from one of the vineyards above

They used Alsace as a cheap source for base wine from which to make their sparkling Sekt, bought at rock-bottom prices, positively discouraging any moves towards higher quality, and individuality. Across the Rhine, the winegrowers of the Mosel and Rhine saw no reason to offer a helping hand to would-be competitors.

After 1945, the response from the French was little better than it had been 30 years earlier, but the situation was worse. Entire villages, such as Ammerschwihr, Bennwihr and Sigolsheim had been shelled and fought over to near or total destruction, the cellars were almost empty of the best older wine, and there was no market for the new harvest. Growers who had supplied their grapes to local merchants or to co-operatives to be made into wine which they in turn sold to those merchants, found the whole system constipated. The only solution was for the co-operatives to compete with merchants on their own terms, making, bottling and selling their own wines.

The earliest co-operatives had been founded just after the turn of the century, but it was not until the post-war crisis that they really began to come into their own. Since then, they have increased their influence annually, a trend which is easily explained in a region whose 9,000 producers have, according to recent figures, an average of only around one and a half hectares apiece. In the Grand Cru Kaefferkopf vineyard alone, over 220 individuals share 60ha of vines, of which several five or six hectare plots belong to merchants. Even when vines are planted in vineyards of this prestige, four hectares is the bare minimum size for a parcel of vines which is intended to keep a small family; over two thirds of Alsace's growers do not even have a single hectare to their name and are thus obliged to derive a major part of their income from other forms of agriculture and crop cultivation.

Most of the co-operatives have fully exploited their position, investing in modern equipment, advising their members on how and where they should plant and building up strong marketing operations. The biggest and best merchants have modernised too, though many would admit that they have lived through difficult times in recent years as sources dried up with the growth of the co-operatives and of individual estates.

These estates complicate the overall picture because many of them combine small merchant operations with the running of their own domaines. So René and Marie-Thérèse Muré, for instance, have their own 15ha Clos St-Landelin vineyard in Rouffach which produces first class wine they sell under that label, and two businesses, called Muré and Muré-Ehrhardt, under whose names they sell a further 400,000 bottles of wine a year.

The name of a producer's wine is particularly significant in Alsace where one of the legacies of those years of making basic wine for the Germans has been the most generous

still produce some of the region's best wine. The Dopff family (known today through the firms of Dopff au Moulin and Dopff & Irion) set down roots here in 1574 while Trimbach and Hugel started business in 1626 and 1637 respectively.

As in other regions, the revolution in 1790 brought about further changes in the make-up of the region, breaking up the large estates owned by the church and wealthier nobility and sowing the seeds for the present-day patchwork of tiny, individually-owned parcels of vines.

In 1837 these vineyards covered some 24,000ha, twice as large an area as there is now, but this was to be the high-point of the region's vinous success. The Thirty Years' War cost Alsace dearly, both financially and in lives lost by the young soldiers who had left their vineyards to fight. Then, in 1871, with annexation by Germany came the introduction of grape varieties whose only value lay in the huge yields they could produce. Phylloxera only made matters worse, encouraging the plantation of high-yield vines to make up for the lost production. From then until the early 1950's Alsace seemed to be on a desperate and inexorable slide towards lower and lower quality.

The historical kick-about of the 19th and 20th centuries affected more than just the language the Alsaciens spoke. As Johnny Hugel, one of the region's best merchants remarked, "To change nationality is not only to change flags, it is also to enter into a different economic space. They move the customs offices, you lose all of your customers and you are subjected to another set of viticultural rules . . . After the 1914-1918 war, when the region was returned to French rule, we didn't have a single customer in Paris." Under the Germans, life was little better.

Notable Alsace Villages – Haut-Rhin

Village	Vineyard Area	Grape Varieties	Best Vineyards	Good Producers
Ammerschwihr	348ha	Gewürztraminer, Riesling	Kaefferkopf Kuehn	Sick-Dreyer, Ehrhardt, Adam, Schneider
Beblenheim	197ha	Riesling	Sonnenglanz	Bott-Geyl, Co-operative Beblenheim
Bennwihr	274ha	Muscat	Rebgarten	Co-operative Bennwihr
Bergheim	243ha	Gewürztraminer, Riesling	Altenberg, Kautzlerberg	Marcel Deiss, Gustave and Jérome Lorentz
Eguisheim	252ha	Gewürztraminer	Eichberg, Pfersigberg	Co-operative Eguisheim, Marc & Leon Beyer, Freudenreich, Stoffel
Guebwiller	122ha	Tokay, Gewürztraminer, Riesling	Kitterlé, Sarig	Schlumberger
Hunawihr	222ha	Sylvaner, Gewürztraminer, Riesling	Rosacker, Clos Ste Hune, Mullforst	Co-operative Hunawihr, Mittnacht, Mader
Katzenthal	160ha	Gewürztraminer, Muscat	—	Ecklé
Kayserberg	54ha	Riesling, Gewürztraminer, Tokay, Sylvaner	—	Don Weinbach
Kientzheim	53ha	Tokay, Gewürztraminer, Riesling	Schlossberg	Blanck, Kientzheim-Kayserheim Co-operative
Mittelwihr	202ha	Guwürztraminer, Muscat, Riesling, Tokay	Mandelberg (also called "Côte des Amandiers")	Preiss-Henny, Burghoffer, Edgar and Patrick Schaller, Co-operative Mittelwihr
Orschwihr	244ha	Gewürztraminer, Riesling	Bollenberg, Affenberg, Pfingstberg	Paul Reinhart, Lucien Albrecht
Pfaffenheim	272ha	Pinot Blanc	Schneckenberg, Bergweingarten	Co-operative Pfaffenheim, Riefle

permitted yields of any quality-wine-producing region in France, and one of the lowest required natural alcohol levels – despite a climate which turns the Chablisiens to the south-west green with envy. Generous yields made for ungenerous wines. Thankfully, estates, *négociants* and co-operatives alike often achieve more modest targets, particularly when making wines they are going to label as "Cuvée Personnelle", "Réserve Spéciale" or some other such quality designation of the producer's own devising.

Where a wine comes from one of the recently designated (the process is still continuing) *Grand Cru* vineyards, you can at least be sure that it has been subject to stricter requirements than a plain Alsace, but even here nothing is quite certain since there are those in the region who have decided to ignore the *Grands Crus* entirely. As I say, the Alsaciens know who they are and what they are doing – so whether they are making gloriously rich, or flat and over-sulphured wines (which, sadly, is sometimes the case), they persist in going their own independent way.

Notable Alsace Villages – Haut-Rhin

Village	Vineyard Area	Grape Varieties	Best Vineyards	Good Producers
Ribeauvillé	255ha	Riesling, Muscat, Gewürztraminer	Kirchberg, Geisberg, Zahnacker, Clos Schlossberg	Trimbach, Bott Frères, Robert Faller, Metz Frères, Co-operative Ribeauvillé
Riquewihr	272ha	Tokay, Muscat, Riesling, Gewürztraminer	Schoenenberg, Sporen	Rene Schmidt, Hugel, Dopff au Moulin, Preiss-Zimmer, Dopff & Irion
Rorschwihr	110ha	Muscat, Gewürztraminer	–	Rolly-Gassmann, Engel Fernand
Rouffach	162ha	Gewürztraminer, Riesling	Clos St Landelin	Muré
Saint Hippolyte	220ha	Pinot Noir, Pinot Blanc	–	GAEC St Fulrade
Sigolsheim	322ha	Gewürztraminer	Mambourg, Altenbourg, Vogelgarten	Pierre Sparr, Ringenbach-Moser, Co-operative Sigolsheim
Thann	180ha	Riesling	Rangen	Zind-Humbrecht
Turckheim	179ha	Tokay, Pinot Noir, Riesling, Gewürztraminer	Eichberg, Brand (including Jesbal, Weingarten, Kirchthal, Steinglitz, Schneckenberg)	Charles Schleret, Zind-Humbrecht, Co-operative Turckheim
Voegtlinshoffen	126ha	Muscat	Hatschburg	Theo Cattin
Westhalten	234ha	Riesling, Gewürztraminer, Pinot Blanc, Sylvaner	Strangenberg, Zinnkoepflé, Bollenberg,	Co-operative Westhalten, Heim
Wettolsheim	330ha	Riesling, Muscat	Steingrubler	Wunsch & Mann, Victor Peluzzi, Antoine Gaschy
Wintzenheim	64ha	Riesling, Gewürztraminer, Pinot Blanc, Muscat	Hengst	Zind-Humbrecht, Jos Meyer
Zellenberg	118ha	Gewürztraminer, Riesling	Schlossberg	GAEC Marcel, Rentz Alphonse Fux, Becker

Notable Alsace Villages – Bas-Rhin

Village	Vineyard Area	Grape Varieties	Best Vineyards	Good Producers
Andlau	95ha	Riesling	Wiebelsberg, Moenchberg, Kastelberg	André and Fernand Gresser
Barr	88ha	Gewürztraminer, Sylvaner Clos, Riesling, Tokay, Muscat	Freiberg, Gaensbroennel, Kirchberg	Klipfel, Willm, Charles Wantz, Clos Zisser
Dambach-la-Ville	384ha	Sylvaner, Riesling, Tokay, Pinot Noir	Scherwiller	Willy Gisselbrecht, Louis Gisselbrecht, Hauller
Heiligenstein	128ha	Klevener de Heiligenstein	–	Charles Wantz, Louis Klipfel
Marlenheim	56ha	Pinot Noir	–	Laugel, Mosbach
Mittelbergheim	171ha	Sylvaner, Gewürztraminer, Riesling, Pinot Blanc	Zotzenberg, Brandluft, Wibelsberg Clos Ste-Odile	E. Boeckel, Seltz
Obernai	65ha	Gewürztraminer, Tokay, Pinot Noir		Co-operative Obernai

Alsace is unusual in that it produces wines that are known by the grape varieties from which they are made, rather than the villages in which the grapes are grown. Varietal names are important, and so these pages examine in detail these grape varieties, and the nature of the wines they produce. The figures in brackets indicate the percentage of the total production each variety accounts for, and the area under cultivation (in hectares).

Chasselas (3%/375ha)

Acreage of this variety dropped by more than 50 per cent between 1969 and 1982 and the way things are going, it may well have disappeared completely before very long. All of which would be sad, if the Chasselas were not such a fundamentally dull variety. Only the Swiss seem to have mastered its use (they call it Fendant), but even they find it difficult to make a case for its continued survival in Alsace. With low natural acidity, most Chasselas used to go into Edelzwicker blends, or be sold locally in bars as the *vin de café*. It is now barred from use in the best vineyards.

Klevner de Heiligenstein (0.1%/13ha)

If there were any logic, this would be the Clevner or Klevner described below. But it is not; it is a wine made from the Savagnin Rosé, an Italian variety related to the Gewürztraminer, much grown in the Jura, and imported into Alsace in the 18th century.

Pinot Auxerrois (8%/1,000ha)

Not, as you might reasonably suppose, another kind of Pinot, nor, think some experts, even an import from Auxerre in northern Burgundy, this is a wholly unrelated variety which is still grown in Lorraine and almost nowhere else. The Alsaciens rarely trouble to mention it, usually treating the Auxerrois as a useful component in Edelzwicker. Nowadays, as that label becomes more scarce, this handily frost-resistant, high-acid, high-alcohol variety is more often blended with the better Pinot Blanc and sold under the name of that variety, or as Clevner or Klevner.

Above: *Ripe Pinot Blanc grapes. These are used to make dry wines rather than late-harvest sweet ones.*

Pinot Blanc/Klevner/Clevner (17%/2,000ha)

In many ways the rising star of Alsace, the Pinot Blanc makes the wine you should give to people who do not think they like Alsace. Related to both the Pinot Noir and Pinot Gris (the leaves are identical) this variety can produce appley-fresh wine which seems to combine qualities of Chablis and Alsace.

Unfortunately, until quite recently, the Pinot Blanc only used to go into Edelzwicker blends with the Chasselas, so the Alsaciens have yet to come to terms with it having a vinous character of its own. They make this clear with ludicrously complicated and confusing legislation which permits the blends of the Pinot Blanc, Pinot Gris, Pinot Auxerrois and Chardonnay with white wine made from the Pinot Noir, to be sold as Pinot Blanc, Klevner or Clevner.

New planting of the Pinot Blanc itself increased its vineyard area by well over 50 per cent between 1969 and 1979, and more examples are to be expected on the market as the legal laxity allows it to become an easily made, but classier-sounding, replacement for the Edelzwicker, and as its use in sparkling Crémant d'Alsace encourages even further expansion of its vineyards.

Pinot Noir (4.5%/500ha)

Having doubled its acreage between 1969 and 1979, this variety is rapidly becoming a significant feature of the region's vineyards. Once a handy means to make rosé (for which 90 per cent was used) and red wine for mostly local consumption, Burgundy's great red wine grape now seems to represent the same challenge here as it does to the winegrowers of California and Australia. When I visited the firm of Hugel, its *directeur*, Johnny Hugel, was eager to show off all his wines, but it was the 1983 Pinot Noir which was his undoubted pride and joy.

Above: *Pinot Noir grapes, ripe and ready for picking.*

The least interesting Pinot Noir, red or rosé (the two are often almost indistinguishable), is like a watered-down Côte de Beaune burgundy; unassumingly pleasant raspberry juice. The best, however, though still light, are of near Burgundian quality themselves. Everything depends on the quality of the vintage and the yield produced. Unfortunately, and perhaps inevitably, given the price people are ready to pay for a Bourgogne Rouge, Alsace Pinot Noir can be more expensive than it ought to be.

Pinot Gris, Tokay d'Alsace (4.5%/500ha)
According to most wine writers, the Riesling is unquestionably "king" of the Alsace varieties; according to many of the region's producers, the crown sits more appropriately atop this curious mutation of the Pinot Noir.

Below: *The small town of Riquewihr is overlooked by the slope of its vineyards, and by the ranges of hills which surround it on all sides.*

Its another of those confusingly named varieties; the Burgundians would know it as the Pinot Beurot or Burot, in the Loire and Switzerland they call it Malvoisie and in Germany and Austria, it is the Rülander. In the 17th century, the Alsaciens in their apparent desperation to call every grape "Clevner" referred to it as "Grauklevner", but by that time, in theory at least, they already knew it as Tokay.

The grape is quite different from the one used to make Tokay in Hungary but there is a Hungarian connection: the name is supposed to derive from the victory over the Turks at Tokaji in Hungary enjoyed in 1565 by Baron Lazare de Schwendi of Alsace, and the 4,000 vats of Tokaji wine that general brought back with him. The story may explain the name, but the flavour is still open to question, as it is not clear how the good Baron came to bring back the Pinot Gris from

Above: Harvesting is still very much a family affair among the small estates in Alsace.

Hungary (where it may have originally been taken by the Emperor Charles IV two hundred years earlier) rather than the Furmint, the variety still used for Hungarian Tokay.

In 1980 Europe's bureaucrats bowed to pressure from beyond the Iron Curtain and resolved to put an end to the confusion once and for all by forbidding the use of the name Tokay in Alsace. Needless to say, few Alsaciens have taken any notice of the ban!

If the Pinot Gris changes its name at every turn, it has a similar facility for altering its appearance. Sometimes the skin is blue-black, sometimes pale pink and often a shade between the two. There is often very little aroma to wines made from the Pinot

Right: The Pinot Gris, or Tokay, clearly showing its dark skin. The juice of this variety can have a pink tinge too, when it is first pressed.

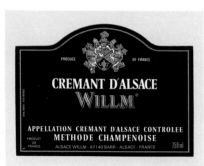

Alsace Wines: Decoding the Label

This box explains what the various terms and descriptions that appear on the labels of Alsace wines mean. Under AOC (Appellation d'Origine Contrôlée) regulations, to qualify for a particular grade on the AOC quality ladder a wine must achieve a specified minimum alcohol content, be produced only from permitted grape varieties, and in quantities that do not exceed a prescribed maximum yield per hectare. The basic requirements for the various Alsace AOC grades are detailed below.

Appellation Alsace Contrôlée (+ the name of the grape variety or Edelzwicker)
This is what you will find on the labels of bottles of basic quality Alsace wine. Unlike the other major French wine areas, the appellation for the entire region is simply "Alsace", and this is normally used in conjunction with the name of the grape used in the winemaking. Permitted varieties are Chasselas, Pinot Gris (Tokay), Pinot Blanc (Klevner), Auxerrois Blanc, Gewürztraminer, Riesling, Sylvaner, Muscat, and Pinot Noir. Edelzwicker ("noble mixture") means that a blend of different grapes, normally Pinot Blanc, Sylvaner and Chasselas, has been used. The minimum strength allowed is 8.5°. Annual production is in the order of 120 million bottles.

Appellation Alsace Contrôlée (+ "Cuvée Speciale", "Réserve Personnelle", or some similar description)
Such descriptions are used by producers for their better wines. While they are indicative of wines of a higher quality, they have no basis in Appellation Law.

Appellation Alsace Contrôlée Grand Cru
Grand Cru Alsace must come entirely from a single grape variety from one of the officially designated *Grand Cru* vineyards (see box on page 86). All labels must display the name of the grape variety, the vineyard from which it comes, and the vintage. Permitted grapes are Riesling and Muscat (minimum strength, 10°), and Tokay and Gewürztraminer (minimum strength, 11°). The maximum yield is set at 70hl/ha, although this figure can be raised in good vintages.

Appellation Alsace Contrôlée Vendange Tardive
"Vendange Tardive" means late harvest; it signifies that in good years the grapes have been left to ripen longer on the vine before picking, so heightening their individual sugar content. Permitted grapes are Riesling and Muscat (minimum strength, 12.6°), and Tokay and Gewürztraminer (minimum strength, 14°). The maximum yield is 60hl/ha, although again this can be raised in good vintages.

Appellation Alsace Contrôlée Sélection de Grains Nobles
"Sélection de Grains Nobles" wines are made in exceptional years from individual late-picked grapes of outstanding ripeness, which have been affected by botrytis or "noble rot". Permitted varieties are as for Vendange Tardive wines but the minimum strengths rise to 14.6° for Riesling and Muscat, and 16° for Tokay and Gewürztraminer. The maximum yield is 70hl/ha, although this may be raised in good years. These are very rare wines; since 1865 only 11 vintages have been exceptional enough for Sélection de Grains Nobles wines to be produced.

Crémant d'Alsace
Granted AOC status in 1976, the sparkling wines of Alsace must be made according to the Méthode Champenoise from Pinot Blanc, Auxerrois Blanc, Tokay, Chardonnay, Riesling or Pinot Noir grapes. For the Auxerrois and Pinot Blanc, 100 litres of juice are permissible per 150 kilos of grapes. Annual production is around 5.5 million bottles.

Gris – this is its one failing – but the flavour can be at once oily, smoky and honeyed, with a richness unequalled by any other Alsacien variety. The producers themselves call it "the Sultan" and believe it to be the perfect complement to the region's Foie Gras.

Muscat (4%/500ha)
Although the Muscat is usually referred to as if it were a single grape variety (and that is certainly the way in which its name appears on labels), there are in fact two different kinds of Muscat, grown in Alsace, the Muscat d'Alsace, also known as the Muscat Blanc à Petits Grains and, in southern France, as the Muscat de Frontignan; and the Muscat Ottonel. The former variety, widely grown on the Mediterranean coast, makes deliciously

grapey, dry wines in Alsace but misses the warm, dry climate it enjoys elsewhere. Rot and mildew are particular problems, neither of which affect the finer, earlier ripening Muscat Ottonel, which explains the latter variety's increasing cultivation in Alsace since its development by the nurseryman Moreau-Robert in the mid-19th century.

The Muscat Ottonel has proven very successful, increasing its presence in Alsace, almost the only French region where it is grown, from only 200ha in 1968 to over 1,000ha today. But the variety has its own problems: in some years, 1978 and 1980 for instance, it produced almost no wine at all, and even when the harvest is successful, the wines tend to be short of the depth of flavour which the Muscat d'Alsace can provide. It is now generally agreed that a blend of two thirds Ottonel, to one third d'Alsace is about right; in villages where the newcomer had more or less taken over, new plantations of Muscat d'Alsace are taking place to restore the balance.

The Muscat d'Alsace likes damp, non-sandy soils; while the Muscat Ottonel does best in more fertile earth, disliking calcareous soil.

Above: *Lovely pink-skinned, maturing Gewürztraminer grapes.*

Gewürztraminer (22%/2,500ha)

Until relatively recently, Alsace producers made and sold wine under the labels of both Traminer and Gewürztraminer, the latter being more highly prized for its spicy, "gewürz", character. Now the Alsaciens have restricted themselves simply to Gewürztraminer, increasing the amount planted enormously over the last 20 years to the point at which it now competes with the Sylvaner for the honour of being the most widely grown variety in the region.

This pink-skinned grape which smells and tastes exactly like the wine it makes, has the smell and flavour of smoke, parma violets, lychees and tropical fruits of every kind, with an added grapiness which can be very like that of the Muscat. It is essentially the most

perfumed of grapes, and it has a peculiarly oily texture; both features help to explain the reverse of the coin which is that, unless carefully handled, the Gewürztraminer's overt character can make for some very blowsy wines, lacking freshness and acidity. The final quality and style depend on the soil in which the vines are planted (the variety likes heavy clay and limestone), and the amount made.

Yields can vary from 40hl/ha to more than the permitted maximum of 100hl/ha but these figures can be cut back by the variety's susceptibility to disease and frost damage. Despite being harvested earlier than its other neighbours in Alsace, it consistently produces wines which are more alcoholic and with a lower acidity.

When picked late, in a *Vendange Tardive* and *Sélection de Grains Nobles* style, the "Gewürz" (as the grape is known) can make wine with a potential natural strength of 20°.

Riesling (18%/2,000ha)

Mostly planted in the Haut-Rhin, but with a growing acreage in the Bas-Rhin where it is gradually supplanting the Sylvaner, the Riesling is a hardy vine which, though particularly liking slate, can flourish in various kinds of soil, putting up with meagre, infertile dirt which the Gewürztraminer might disdain.

Also called the "Gentil-Aromatique", the Alsacien Riesling was recorded in the region, under the name "Rissling", in the late 15th century. Over the following five hundred years, it gained in popularity but only began to achieve anything like its present importance following the last war. It is the same

Below: *Freshly-picked Riesling grapes, still in their traditional wooden buckets, arrive at the Trimbach winery to be crushed and fermented.*

Above: *Riesling grapes revealing the occasional hint of botrytis.*

Above: *The Sylvaner, one of Alsace's dull but reliable varieties.*

variety as is grown by the Germans across the Rhine, but the style is very different. Here, with the exception of the rare *Vendange Tardive* and *Sélection de Grains Nobles*, the wines are bone dry with a steeliness rarely found in even the most "trocken" (dry) of Trocken wines from the Mosel. There is the grapiness of its German neighbours, but little of their overtly floral character. It is essentially, unlike those German versions, wine to be enjoyed with food.

In ripe years, and when grown on limestone, the Riesling makes wine which lasts well, taking on the peculiarly attractive "petrolly" character which marks its mature wines wherever they are made. Alsace producers promote the ageing of their wine by not releasing it until it is 18 months old, a year later than is the custom in Germany. Best villages: Ammerschwihr, Dambach-la-Ville, Husseren-les-Châteaux, Hunawihr, Kaysersberg, Mittelwihr, Orschwihr, Ribeauvillé, Thann, Wolxheim.

Sylvaner (22%/2,500ha)
Dull in Germany, the Sylvaner (or Silvaner) contrives to be dull and acidic in Alsace, unless it is very skilfully handled. The Alsaciens are probably better at making Sylvaner than anybody else; at least they manage to communicate some of their region's spiciness to it, but not very much. The variety may have started its days in Transylvania (which may account for Dracula's taste for the stronger flavour of human blood), arriving in Alsace sometime in the 19th century and now occupying around half the vineyards of the Bas-Rhin. Resistance to disease and a potential for high yields are the Sylvaner's greatest qualities and, when well made, the wine can be refreshing provided it is drunk young.

Goldriesling, Knipperle, Müller-Thurgau
Less than 5% of Alsace is now planted with these varieties which are not classed as "noble" and are consequently being phased out of vineyard cultivation.

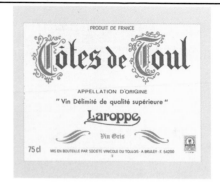

*T*he winegrowers of Lorraine are intensely proud of their region and its wines. So, you might say, are producers throughout the rest of France, but history has arguably dealt Lorraine a less generous hand than many other regions. Indeed, a quarter of a century ago, it seemed as if this prettily isolated region might give up trying to make wine at all and concentrate its attention on the fruit trees which have often proved to be a safer bet.

The history books refer so readily to Alsace-Lorraine that it is easy to suppose that these two regions are in fact one. But, as the winemakers of Lorraine themselves would stress, they are in fact intrinsically separate, both in their climate and in the style of their wines. Despite their northerly situation, some 70 miles to the north-west of the Alsace vineyards, and a climate which dictates a late October harvest if grapes with

even a modestly acceptable level of sugar are to be picked, the vineyards of Lorraine have a long-established tradition and were producing wine of some repute as early as the 6th century. While there are few outside the region who would argue that these VDQS wines ought to be promoted to full *Appellation* status, they do still have the potential to fill more than one hole in the market.

If, for instance, the world suddenly decided that it had become tired of white wine and wanted to turn back to pink, Côtes de Toul would be well placed to answer the call. The current tiny area of 50ha, smaller

Below: The vineyards of the Laroppe family in the Côtes de Toul. These Pinot Noir vines need warm summers to ripen properly this far north, but they can certainly make good rosé.

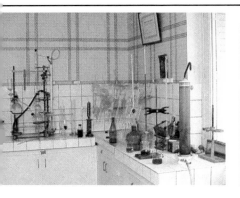

Above: *Laboratories are an essential part of any modern winery, particularly in regions like Côtes de Toul where there are fewer local wine chemists.*

Above: *500 hectolitre stainless steel tanks of the kind which are used throughout France, but especially in regions like this producing white and rosé wine.*

than that of Château Léoville-Poyferré in Bordeaux, could at any time be expanded to ten times that size and, although the permitted yield of this VDQS is, at 60hl/ha, over a third less generous than that allowed to *Appellation Contrôlée* Alsace, this would still represent a large amount of wine. The only problem is that, in other than warm vintages,

these can be wines with far more acidity than flavour, and agreeable to drink only when taken very cold and with very spicy sausage. When well made, however, and from a warmer year, these can be wines to serve to a Pinot Noir fan who is missing the wild raspberry flavour of that variety (which must make up at least 85 per cent of the blend). Better as an aperitif than as an accompaniment to food perhaps, but pleasant wine all the same.

Vin de Moselle, from 15 villages which sit along the banks of the Moselle itself, is another wine which varies enormously in style and quality. Given the cool climate, it is perhaps not surprising that although producers try hard to make full-blooded reds, they generally manage to achieve the same kind of darkish rosé found in Alsace and in Germany. Even so, the Pinot flavour can be appealingly raspberryish. As for the whites, everything depends on the grape varieties which are used; Gewürztraminer can produce attractive wine but, like the other red and white varieties, it is dependent on the rare warmer vintages to make anything better than basic country wine.

Lorraine Wines

Côtes de Toul
VDQS: 1951
Production: 50ha/260,000 bottles
Grapes: Aligoté, Aubin, Auxerrois, Gamay, Pinot Meunier, Pinot Noir
Minimum strength: (white and rosé [Vin Gris] wines) 8.5°
Maximum yield: (white and rosé [Vin Gris] wines) 60hl/ha

Vins de Moselle
VDQS: 1951
Production: very limited
Grapes: (for whites) Auxerrois Blanc, Sylvaner (max 30%), Riesling, Gewürztraminer, Meunier Blanc and Pinot Blanc (for reds and Gris) Pinot Noir, Gamay, Auxerrois Gris, Meunier Gris
Best vintages: All of these wines should be drunk as young as possible

*L*OIRE

O f all France's wine region, the Loire is
one of the most immediately attractive, and one of the most immediately
identifiable as *French*. This is picture book
farming country, with green meadows and
rivers of every size, often absurdly ornate
châteaux, and stolidly sensible greystone
villages dotting the landscape.

Although it is believed that the vineyards
of the Loire were cultivated by the Romans,
few records have been found of winemaking
at that time, and the region's oldest important wine artifact is a 2nd Century press now
on show in the Tours wine museum. Until the
middle of the 12th Century, the wines rarely
travelled very far, but the ascent of the Plan-
tagenets to the English throne brought an
overseas market and, with it, a fixing of the
prices for the wines of Saumur, Anjou and
Touraine. Soon, the expansion of commerce
along the river led to the wines becoming
popular in Paris. Similarly, the expulsion of
religious dissidents caused migration to
countries to the east, which in turn created
an awareness of and liking for wines such as
Sancerre in those countries.

If France has a single identifiable "White,
Pink and Sparkling" wine region, it has to be

Right: *The magnificent cathedral of Blois,
overlooking the Loire.*

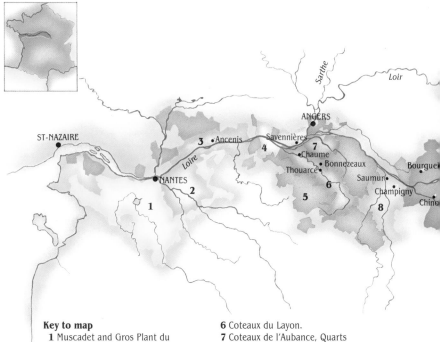

Key to map

1 Muscadet and Gros Plant du
  Pays Nantais.
2 Muscadet de Sèvre-et-Maine.
3 Muscadet des Coteaux de la
  Loire and Coteaux d'Ancenis.
4 Anjou Coteaux de la Loire,
  and Savennières.
5 Anjou-Saumur.
6 Coteaux du Layon.
7 Coteaux de l'Aubance, Quarts
  de Chaume, and Bonnezeaux.
8 Saumur.
9 Touraine.
10 Vouvray and Montlouis.
11 Coteaux du Loir and
   Jasnières.
12 Coteaux du Vendômois.

the Loire. Of course there are some very good reds made here but, given the frequently unkind climate in this part of the world, one of France's very northernmost wine regions, the quality of the red wine produced is far from reliable.

So, it is names such as Muscadet, Sancerre and Vouvray, not to mention Anjou Rosé and sparkling Saumur, for which the region is best known. But these offer only the smallest hint of the range of styles produced in the vineyards which bestride France's longest river as it follows its 1,000km course from the continental climate of Burgundy in the east to the sea at St-Nazaire.

Above all, the Loire is a land of variety. Grapes such as Pinot Noir, Gamay, Cabernets Sauvignon and Franc, Malbec, Chenin Blanc and Noir, Sauvignon Blanc, Chardonnay and a host of other, less memorable varieties, are all grown. The soil can be schistous, which stores the heat and produces full bodied, rich wine, or chalky which makes for the drier, steelier flavour of wines like Sancerre and Pouilly Fumé.

Styles range from the driest in France to some of the very sweetest, and from still to sparkling and *pétillant*. No other region can offer this wide a selection; sadly however, standards of winemaking are just as varied and the international white wine boom has given every opportunity for greedy and non-quality-conscious producers to do their worst as they cash in.

Even referring to the Loire as a single region can, however, lead to more confusion than understanding; it is far more sensible to divide the valley into its constituent parts, heading along the river, from the Atlantic towards Burgundy. As the map shows, the four main areas to consider are: Nantes, Anjou-Saumur, Touraine, and the Central region around Pouilly-sur-Loire.

Grape Varieties

White

Chenin Blanc (also known as Pineau de la Loire), Sauvignon, Chardonnay, Pinot Gris (also known as Malvoisie, Pinot Beurot and Tokay d'Alsace), Pineau Menu, Muscadet (also known as Melon de Bourgogne), Gros Plant (also called Folle Blanche or Picpoul), Romorantin.

Rosé

Gamay Noir à Jus Blanc, Cabernet Franc, Cabernet Sauvignon, Malbec (also known as Cot), Pinot Noir, Pineau Meunier, Groslot (also known as Grolleau), Pineau d'Aunis (also known as Chenin Noir).

13 Cheverny.
14 Valençay.
15 Vins de l'Orléanais.
16 Reuilly.
17 Quincy.
18 Menetou-Salon.
19 Sancerre.
20 Pouilly-sur-Loire.
21 Coteaux du Giennois.

GROS-PLANT
DU PAYS NANTAIS
APPELLATION D'ORIGINE VIN DÉLIMITÉ DE QUALITÉ SUPÉRIEURE
ANDRÉ VINET
VALLET (L.-A.)

*M*uscadet is France's white answer to Beaujolais: wine made to be enjoyed young, and without too much time being spent analysing the precise nuances of its flavour. As if to emphasise the link between the regions, autumnal wine buyers are now being offered Muscadet Nouveau or Primeur, as well as the internationally renowned Beaujolais Nouveau.

Like Beaujolais, Muscadet used unashamedly to be beefed up by the addition of wine from Algeria, and like Beaujolais today, its quality can vary from dull to delicious. Some of this variability can be blamed on the grape from which all Muscadet is made, a relation of the Gamay Blanc known locally as "le Muscadet" but officially termed the "Melon de Bourgogne". As its name implies, this is a variety which was imported (expelled might be a better term) from the vineyards of Burgundy.

Although tasting young Muscadet alongside young Chardonnay from Chablis or Mâcon reveals no similarities, well-made older Muscadet can taste rather like old white burgundy; inferior old white burgundy, but old burgundy nevertheless. Drink within 18 months of the harvest should be the rule.

Bottles merely labelled "Muscadet" are the most likely to be dull; Muscadet des Coteaux de la Loire is better and fuller, but there is very little made – just 5 per cent of the total production. According to the textbooks, the best Muscadet is labelled Muscadet de Sèvre et Maine and is grown on the stony-clad soil of a small region, south of the

Above: *A rare photograph of the "sur lie" process at work in a special glass-fronted barrel in the cellars of Chéreau Carré. The yeasty lees are clearly visible lying in the bottom of the cask.*

Loire and to the east of Nantes. The text books often forget to mention that this "best" region accounts for no less than 85 per cent of the annual crop.

A (somewhat) surer way of finding higher quality Muscadet is to look for one whose label states that it has been bottled "*sur lie*". This traditional local process of leaving the wine in contact with its yeasty lees between first pressing and bottling in the spring following the harvest can give Muscadet a deliciously rich, yeasty flavour and, in theory at

Pays Nantais Wines

Grapes	(White) Melon de Bourgogne, Chenin Blanc, Pinot Gris, Chardonnay, Sauvignon, Gros Plant. (Red) Cabernet Sauvignon, Cabernet Franc, Gamay Noir à Jus Blanc, Pinot Noir, Pineau d'Aunis.
Soil	Mostly schistous, and covered with small flinty pebbles.
Appellations	Muscadet (AOC 1937, 40,000hl of dry white). Muscadet des Coteaux de la Loire (AOC 1936, 150hl). Muscadet de Sèvre et Maine (AOC 1936, 450,000hl).
VDQS wines	Coteaux d'Ancenis (VDQS 1973, 9,775hl of red, white and rosé). Fiefs Vendéens (VDQS 1985, 20,000hl of mainly rosé and red). Gros Plant du Pays Nantais (VDQS 1954, 90,000hl of white).
Recommended producers	Domaine des Herbauges (Pierre et Luc Choblet); Hermine d'Or (Jean Douillard); Château de la Tour (Vincent Guoy); Domaine des Genaudières (Augustin Athimon); Domaine des Vignes (René Bossard et Fils) Domaine de la Borne (Lucien Pauvert); Château de Cléray (Sauvion et Fils); Domaine des Hauts Pemions (Joseph Drouard); Domaine de l'Hyvernière (Mme Veuve Marcel Sautejeu); Domaine de la Juiverie (Maurice et Olivier Bonneteau); Domaine de la Landreau-Village (Drouet Frères); Domaine des Mortières Gobin (Robert Brosseau); Moulin de la Bidière (Gaston Maillard); (Joseph Babin) Jean Forget "La Gautronnière", Joseph Hallereau, GIE Louis Metaireau); Château de Paget (M. Bonneau); Château de la Ragotière (Les Frères Couillaud); Clos des Roches-Gaudinières (Michel Chiron); Domaine des Sensonnières (Georges Ripoche); Domaine de la Tourmaline (Gadais Frères); Château La Touche (André Vinet).

least, a slight natural sparkle. Here again, sadly, actual practice and the textbooks can part company, since a large proportion of so-called *"sur lie"* is not truly eligible for the term because its producers filter and assemble their wines, thus denying them any legitimate right to the *"sur lie"* appellation. As for the "natural sparkle", let us just say that the region has long provided a ready market for bottled carbon dioxide.

The finest Muscadet is usually made at individual estates, some of whose wines are

Below: *Harvest time at the Château de Chasseloir. Sadly, horses are now being replaced by tractors.*

sold by one or other of the larger firms of merchants, two of which, Sauvion et Fils and Donatien Bahuaud, have done much in recent years to raise the overall quality of Muscadet. Although different communes certainly can give their wines individual characteristics (Vertou, Vallet, Clisson, Loroux Bottereau and St-Fiacre produce the best) and vintage variation can be enormous (warm years leading to flabbiness, cool ones to "green" acidity), good winemaking remains the most important factor of all.

Apart from Muscadet, the Pays Nantais has little to offer beyond light, white and bone dry wine to drink very well chilled with seafood. Gros Plant, made from the grape of the same name, is one of the few wines to make Burgundy's Aligoté seem even remotely classy. To its credit one must say, however, that Gros Plant is much cheaper than Muscadet, and of at least as high a quality as many of the more "commercial" wines sold under that appellation — as was proved by recent trials of a merchant charged with substituting Gros Plant for Muscadet. In future years, however, the situation may change as current experiments are beginning to prove that the Gros Plant's true role in life is as a base wine for *Méthode Champenoise*.

Coteaux d'Ancenis is a relatively recent (1973) VDQS, producing white wine from the Chenin Blanc, Pinot Gris, and a little rosé from the Cabernet France and Gamay. Both are inexpensive and enjoyable enough with a plate of fish. Fiefs Vendéens, an even newer (1985) VDQS may, however, be a more interesting wine in the long term since its white wine (which can be made from Chenin Blanc, Sauvignon and Chardonnay) can be both refreshing and quite characterful, as is the case with Domaine Coirier's "Blanc de Pissotte".

S ay the word "Anjou" to most wine drinkers and there is a fair chance that you will conjure up the vision, and flavour, of one of the world's very worst pink wines. What Liebfraumilch is to the Rhine, Anjou Rosé has been to the Loire: sweet, commercial, and often very badly made wine. Say "Saumur" and those same wine drinkers' minds will turn to the bottles of sparkling wine which feature so reliably at weddings whose hosts cannot quite run to Champagne. The region of Anjou and Saumur is indeed the source of vast quantities of pink and sparkling white wine but, fortunately, much of that wine can be of much higher quality than is often supposed and, more importantly, the region also produces some far less well known and far more characterful wines that are worth seeking out.

The vineyards here date back to the third century AD; and by the eighth century, vines had become economically vital to the region. As elsewhere, both vineyards and winemaking were in the hands of the church and, in 769 AD, it was to the Abbey of St-Aubindes-Vignes in Anjou that the emperor Charlemagne gave a vineyard. An important overseas market opened up with the accession of the Count of Anjou, Henry Plantagenet, to the English throne in 1154, and over the following centuries, the wines of the region gained such a high reputation for their quality that, in 1331, Philippe IV of France, in order to maintain that quality, forbade wine from other regions from entering the Anjou-Saumur area.

Between the early 16th and the end of the 17th centuries when war prevented cross-Channel trade, the Dutch succeeded the English as importers of sweet Anjou, and it was their influence which led to the development of Anjou's very highest quality sweet wines. At the time, the wines of the region were divided into two categories: *vins pour Paris* – the dregs – and *vins pour la mer* – the good exportable stuff. Even today, it

Above: *The Château de Montreuil-Bellay was mostly built in the 14th century; among the original features which remain are a chapel and a well which is over 300m deep. This is one of the Loire's most impressive wine châteaux.*

Below: *The vineyards of the Loire compete for space with all manner of other forms of agriculture, many of which are far more remunerative than the difficult business of vinegrowing.*

seems easier to find the poorest quality Anjou on the shelves of France's supermarkets than in their counterparts overseas in other parts of the world.

Anjou's least inspiring wine, Anjou Rosé, made from Cabernet Franc, Sauvignon, Gamay, Pineau d'Aunis, Cot (Malbec) and Groslot, is a relatively modern invention (it was unknown a century ago) which allowed winemakers to take usually undistinguished black grapes and to vinify them as if they were making semi-sweet white wine. There *are* a few decent Rosés d'Anjou around, but they are few and far between. Very occasionally, a semi-sparkling ("*Pétillant*") version may also be found, but subjecting wine of this quality to the Champagne process is expensive and really rather pointless. Hence the rarity.

Fans of drier pink wine would be better advised to try Rosé de Loire which has to contain a minimum of 30 per cent Cabernets Sauvignon and Franc. Even so, the semi-sweet Cabernet d'Anjou and the slightly lighter Cabernet de Saumur can be a far better bet. Both wines are, as their names suggest, wholly made from Cabernet grapes and, when well made, good and richly blackcurranty. The one failing encountered in these wines, though, is the often carelessly excessive use of sulphur dioxide by their makers. Given five or six years in bottle, the throat-tickling sulphur would probably be less troublesome but that is of little comfort since, like all rosé, pink Loires should be drunk within a year of the harvest.

The white wines of Anjou are of a far higher standard (thank goodness) than most of the rosé. Made purely from Chenin Blanc grapes or from a mixture of Chenin Blanc, Sauvignon and Chardonnay (with these two varieties representing only 20 per cent of the blend), they can be dry or *demi-sec*, though the former style is usually the most successful. Sparkling, and a small amount of *pétillant* Anjou are also produced, both pleasant, neither exceptional.

Well-made examples of the still wines can age beautifully too, as anyone who has tasted older vintages from the Moulin Touchais will have appreciated. This quirky company has a cellar containing around a million bottles of apricot and floral-flavoured wine, none of which is sold until it is at least 10 years old, and surprising numbers of which are a great deal older.

The appellation of Anjou Coteaux de la Loire allows its producers less leeway than plain Anjou: only the Chenin Blanc can be used. At their least impressive, these dry or *demi-sec* wines can be very similar to those of Vouvray, with either a honeyed cloying character or an unripe appley sharpness, but well-made examples in good vintages, from the better communes – La Possonnière, St-Georges-sur-Loire, Ingrandes, Champtocé, Bouchemaine and Savennières – can provide a rare opportunity to taste just how successfully the Chenin Blanc can be used for these varying styles of wine.

Nearby, and a step or two up the ladder of quality Coteaux du Layon produces white wines from the Chenin in bone dry, *demi-sec* and sumptuously sweet versions, depending on the commune and on the quality of the vintage. Of the villages which face each other across the river Layon, Rochefort-sur-Loire, Faye, St-Aubin-de-Luigné and Beaulieu, on the right, and Rablay and St-Lambert-du-Lattay on the left bank, all make wine of acknowledged quality and are consequently allowed to tack their names on to the Coteaux du Layon appellation.

The right bank communes unquestionably make the better wines and one of these, Rochefort-sur-Loire, is the source of the

Anjou and Saumur Wines

Grapes	(White) Chenin Blanc, Chardonnay, Sauvignon, Pinot Blanc, Pinot Meunier. (Red) Cabernet Franc, Cabernet Sauvignon, Pineau d'Aunis, Gamay, Cot, Groslot, Pinot Noir.
Soil	Dark clay – siliceous soils. Saumur vineyards are situated on chalky slopes and Layon on chalky-sand.
Appellations	Anjou and Rosé d'Anjou (AOC 1957, 560hl of white, rosé, and red. Can be *pétillant* or still). Anjou Coteaux de la Loire (AOC 1946, 1,500hl of white). Anjou Mousseux (AOC 1957, rosé and white wine. All made *Méthode Champenoise*). Bonnezeaux Grand Cru (AOC 1951, dry to sweet white). Cabernet d'Anjou and Cabernet d'Anjou-Val-De-Loire (AOC 1964, 90,200hl of rosé). Cabernet de Saumur (AOC 1962, 900hl of rosé). Coteaux de l'Aubance (AOC 1950, dry, white). Coteaux de Saumur (AOC 1962, 90hl of dry to sweet white). Coteaux du Layon (AOC 1950, dry and sweet white). Coteaux du Layon Villages (AOC 1950, as above, 41,000hl). Coteaux du Layon Chaume (AOC 1950, produces a superior quality wine to the above). Crémant de Loire (AOC 1975, 30,000hl of sparkling white and rosé). Quarts de Chaume (AOC 1954, 750hl of strong dry and velvety dry-sweet white). Rosé de Loire (AOC 1974, 18,800hl of dry rosé). Saumur Mousseux (AOC 1976, 75,200hl of sparkling white and rosé, light and fresh wine. All made *Méthode Champenoise*). Saumur Pétillant (AOC 1976, minute production of white *Méthode Champenoise*). Savennières (AOC 1952, 1,700hl of elegant dry to sweet white).
VDQS wines	Vins du Haut Poitou (VDQS 1970, 20,500hl of red, rosé and white sparkling and still wine). Vins du Thouarsais (VDQS 1966, 650hl of fruity dry red, white and rosé).
Recommended producers	(Bonnezeaux) Château de Fesles; Château de Gauliers. (Cabernet d'Anjou) Château de Tigne; Domaine des Maurières. (Coteaux de l'Aubance) Domaine des Rochettes; Richou-Rousseau. (Coteaux du Layon) Aubert Frères; Château des Rochettes; Clos de Sainte Catherine. (Coteaux du Layon Villages) Domaine de la Motte; Château de la Guimonière; La Pierre Blanche; Château de Chamboureau; Château Montbenault; Domaine de la Bizolière. (Savennières) La Coulée-de-Serrant; La Roche-aux-Moines; Château de la Roche. (Haut Poitou) Cave Coopérative du Haut Poitou.

Above: *A typically picturesque landscape with vineyards in the white wine producing region of the Loire valley around Anjou. This part of the Loire produces both dry and* demi-sec *wines, as well as fine sweet wines such as Quarts de Chaume and Bonnezeaux.*

great sweet Coteaux du Layon Chaume which is named after the village of Chaume, as well as of the even greater Quarts de Chaume.

Taking its name from the quarter of each year's harvest demanded as the "*droit de seigneur*" by the local aristocracy, and with one of the lowest permitted yields (22hl/ha) of any appellation in France, Quarts de Chaume has everything it needs to make truly great wine: a unique microclimate which both protects it from wind blowing from any direction and which ensures perfect ripening conditions. Even in an unpromising year, the Chenin Blanc vines which slope gently down from the village of Chaume to the banks of the river Layon can, with the help of a little noble rot, produce 100,000 bottles of concentrated apricotty-rich and floral wine which, thanks to its backbone of acidity, can easily improve over 10-20 years.

Quarts de Chaumes has one neighbouring competitor, however: produced in ridiculously small quantities by a small number of growers, good Bonnezeaux can rival Quarts de Chaume in its rich sweetness, but differs in having a slightly spicy character rather than the latter wine's pleasant hint of bitterness. Perhaps I have been unlucky, but I have been disappointed by Bonnezeaux more often than by Quarts de Chaume; as elsewhere, the producer's name printed at the foot of the label is as crucial as the appellation itself. Good Bonnezeaux should be kept for at least 5-10 years before opening.

Back amongst the drier styles, Savennières is, to many people, the archetypal wine of the Loire, challenging producers to make the most of the Chenin Blanc, both as a dry and as a *demi-sec*. Once vinified sweet, these are not "easy" wines; they can have a high acidity which has an almost bitter-lime twist to it but which, in ripe years, blends perfectly with the honeyed flavour of the wine. In cooler, wetter years, however, that acidity never quite marries in. So it is perhaps hardly surprising that of the 15 growers who produce Savennières, less than five survive solely from their winemaking.

Greater than Savennières itself, however, are the two *grands crus*, Savennières Coulée-de-Serrant and Savennières Roche-aux-Moines. Both of these rich, dry wines are, in a way, reminiscent of the dry wines made by producers in Sauternes, combining intense flavours of ripe fruit and flowers with a bone-dry acidity. Of the two wines, however, the greatest is undoubtedly the Coulée-de-Serrant, a tiny seven-hectare appellation belonging to a single owner, Mme Joly.

Saumur, once seen as a wine of the same prestige as Vouvray, has suffered during the last century from the enthusiasm of the sparkling wine producers to put bubbles into what would otherwise be perfectly pleasant dry wine. But it is easy to understand their motives: naturally acidic wine made from grapes grown on chalk provides the perfect raw material for fizz. And if some Saumur Mousseux is not very distinguished, neither is the base wine from which it is made.

The major difference between sparkling and still Saumur (apart from the bubbles) lies in the grape varieties from which they are made; the fizz can contain white-vinified black grapes and up to 20 per cent Sauvignon and Chardonnay as well as the Chenin. The first Mousseux was made here in 1811 by Jean Ackerman, a man who had worked in Champagne and who created a style which, for many years, before the advent of strong *Appellation Contrôlée* legislation, used to be sold successfully as Champagne. Nowadays links with the world's greatest sparkling wine region remain strong, with Taittinger and Bollinger respectively owning the Saumur houses of Bouvet-Ladubay and Langlois-Château and with the association between Alfred Gratien in Champagne and Gratien & Meyer in Saumur.

While no Saumur Mousseux can hope to compete with a high quality Champagne – the grape mix precludes the richness and complexity of flavour afforded by the Pinots and the Chardonnay – much is of a higher quality than most other alternatives to Champagne. The one criticism is of a tendency to heaviness and lack of zing to be experienced in some of the less well-made wines from Saumur.

Produced from the Chenin Blanc, wines bearing the appellation Coteaux de Saumur are rare sweet and very sweet versions of wines which, if dry or *demi-sec*, would be sold as Saumur. The appellation has fallen into obscurity since the days when a winemaker known as "Père Cristal", a friend of both Edward VII and Clemenceau produced a wine in the Clos des Murs which was the most expensive in the Loire. The peculiarity of the Clos, which can still be visited today, was a set of eleven 100m long walls all of which contained holes through which the vines were trained so as to benefit from the sun. There are, however, few producers who are really exploiting the potential of the appellation at present and most of the honeyed, floral wine is drunk locally.

Another *demi-sec* white, the Coteaux de l'Aubance is made from the Chenin Blanc in a set of communes which also produce a great deal of uninspired rosé. The soil here is very similar to that of Layon, but, although sharing many of that appellation's characteristic honeyed and floral flavours, the wines tend to be lighter in style.

Above: Remuage *in Saumur is precisely the same as it is in Champagne, with each bottle being turned daily to shift its deposit down on to the cap. Machines are now replacing men, however.*

Left: *The calm river Loire as it passes by Saumur. Much of the wine produced here will be turned into* Méthode Champenoise *fizz, but the inhabitants still relish the non-sparkling white and rosé, little of which ever seems to travel far from French shores.*

Two promising VDQS appellations are produced to the south of Saumur, the Vin du Haut-Poitou whose good rosé, Chardonnay and Sauvignon wines are well made by the Loire's biggest and most modern co-operative, and the Vin du Thouarsais which produces Cabernet rosés and Chenin Blanc whites. At best, Vin du Thouarsais white can be compared to the wines of Anjou.

Sparkling Loire Wines

Grapes	(White) Chenin Blanc (also known as Pineau de la Loire), Chardonnay, Pineau Menu, Gros Plant, Aligoté, Tresallier, Arbois. (Red) Cabernet Franc, Cabernet Sauvignon, Pineau d'Aunis, Gamay, Cot, Groslot.
Appellations	Anjou Mousseux (AOC 1957, mainly rosé or white. All made *Méthode Champenoise*). Crémant de Loire (AOC 1975, 30,500hl of white and rosé). Saumur Mousseux (AOC 1976, 75,200hl of light, fresh white and rosé, made *Méthode Champenoise*). Saumur Pétillant (AOC 1939, small proportion of white wine made *Méthode Champenoise*). Touraine Mousseux (AOC 1939, white and rosé. All made *Méthode Champenoise*). Touraine Pétillant (AOC 1939, as above but bottled as still wine). Montlouis Mousseux (AOC 1938, 26,300hl of dry-sweet white, made *Méthode Champenoise*). Montlouis Pétillant (AOC 1938, as above but bottled as still wine). Vouvray (AOC 1936, dry-sweet white). Vouvray Mousseux (AOC 1936, dry-sweet white, made *Méthode Champenoise*). Vouvray Pétillant (AOC as above, little made).
VDQS wines	Chéverny (VDQS 1973, 14,000hl of red, rosé and white, still and sparkling). St-Pourçain-sur-Sioule (VDQS 1951, red, white and rosé; only 3-5 per cent of total production is Mousseux). Vins du Haut Poitou (VDQS 1970, 20,500hl of red, rosé and white).
Recommended producers	(Vouvray) Domaine Huet; Marc Brédif; Château Moncontour; Clos Baudoin. (Saumur) Gratien & Meyer. (Haut Poitou) Cave Coopérative du Haut-Poitou

If one had just a single day to devote to the Loire, Touraine would have to be the region to visit. This is not the source of the Loire's very best dry white wines – some of the finest Touraines are red – but it is unquestionably the most beautiful section of the wide river's winding progress to the sea. According to local legend, it was in Touraine that St Martin discovered the art of pruning when he noticed that vines, whose fruit had been partly eaten by his donkey, produced a smaller, better, crop of fruit than plants which were allowed to grow as they pleased. With or without St Martin's help, winemaking became, over the centuries, the major form of agriculture in the region, taking its place alongside cereal cultivation and various kinds of fruit growing.

Phylloxera, an exodus of manpower, and the lack of prestige of the Touraine appellation which accounts for over a third of the region's production, have, however, all conspired to reduce the size of the Touraine *vignoble* to only a little over a tenth of its pre-phylloxera size. Driving through Touraine now is as good an introduction to "polyculture" as any agricultural student might ever need; vines, strawberries, wheat and asparagus (a local speciality) all grow almost alongside each other. And the variety of crops is matched by the variety of wines and winemakers – from the winery attached to the Château de Chenonceaux, to the cellars and even homes at Vouvray which are quite literally carved into the sides of chalky cliffs, as shown in the picture above.

The Touraine appellation itself owes much of its present success to the efforts of the small 25 year-old co-operative of Oisly et Thésée which under the direction of Jacques Choquet has operated the rare (for co-operatives) policy of subjecting all of its mem-

Above: *Visitors find it hard to believe that people actually live in caves in the Loire, but it is true. Many of these caves are almost luxurious inside.*

bers' wines and grapes to a stringent quality test. The Sauvignon is first class, as are the rosé blend, and limited early production of pure Chardonnay.

There are three other regional Touraine appellations, all of which can make better wine than much plain AOC Touraine. Touraine-Azay-le-Rideau, the size of Vouvray, produces pure Chenin white, thought by its makers to be worth ageing for three or four years; the rosé is made mainly from the Groslot, with up to 40 per cent Gamay and Cot. Touraine-Amboise's rosé can include some Cabernet Franc, while its Vouvray-like whites are 100 per cent Chenin. Touraine-Mesland produces a Chardonnay-Chenin white which can be good value; its rosé uses Cabernet Franc, Gamay and Cot.

Wines labelled Touraine Mousseux and Touraine Pétillant are occasionally to be found in France, and are likely to be pleasantly undemanding, but the focus of sparkling wine production in the region is unquestionably Vouvray.

Bourgueil, better known as a red appellation, also makes a little attractive rosé from the Cabernet Franc and Sauvignon (maximum 20 per cent), as does the nearby appellation of St-Nicolas-de-Bourgueil, while Chinon, another principally red wine commune, makes 5 per cent of its production as white or rosé. The Cabernet-based dry rosé is of some interest, while the white Chenin has an unusually attractive, spicy and floral bouquet. This was, it seems, one of Rabelais' favourite drinks.

Touraine Wines

Grapes	(White) Chenin Blanc, Pinot Meunier, Sauvignon, Chardonnay. (Red/Rosé) Gamay, Cabernet Franc, Cabernet Sauvignon, Malbec, Pinot Gris, Pinot Noir, Pineau d'Aunis, Groslot.
Soil	Chalk rock forms the sub-structure with a clay and sand mixture on top.
Appellations	Touraine (AOC 1939, 263,000hl of fruity red, white and rosé). Touraine-Amboise (AOC 1955, 3,550hl of red, white and rosé). Touraine- Azay-le-Rideau (AOC 1977, 1,380hl of dry white and rosé). Touraine-Mesland (AOC 1962, 2,500hl of red, dry rosé and white). Touraine Mousseux (AOC 1939, red, rosé and white sparkling wine, all made *Méthode Champenoise*). Touraine Pétillant (AOC 1939, as above, but bottled as still wine and drunk locally). Bourgeuil (AOC 1937, red and dry and crisp rosé). Chinon (AOC 1937, 538,000hl of dry white, red and rosé). Coteaux du Loir (AOC 1948, 1,500hl of white and rosé, the whites can be *pétillant*). Jasnières (AOC 1937, 500hl of dry white). Montlouis (AOC 1938, 5,250hl of dry to sweet white, can be sparkling, light wine with less acidity than nearby Vouvray). Montlouis Mousseux (AOC 1938, as above, made *Méthode Champenoise*). Montlouis Pétillant (AOC 1938, as above but bottled as semi-sparkling wine. Very little made). St-Nicolas-de-Bourgueil (AOC 1937, 15,000hl of red and rosé). Vouvray (AOC 1936, dry to sweet white – can be sparkling). Vouvray Mousseux (AOC 1936, as above but made *Méthode Champenoise*). Vouvray Pétillant (AOC 1936, as above, but very little is made and most is drunk locally).
VDQS wines	Cheverny (VDQS 1973, 14,000hl of red, rosé and white). Coteaux du Vendômois (VDQS 1968, 1,500hl of red, white and rosé). Valençay (VDQS 1970, 3,000hl of red, white and rosé).
Recommended producers	(Touraine-Amboise) Hubert Denay; Dutertre et Fils. (Touraine-Azay-le-Rideau) Château de l'Anlee; Gaston Pavy. (Touraine-Mesland) Domaine Girault-Artois; Philippe Brossillou. (Vouvray) Domaine Huet; Clos Baudoin; Marc Brédif; Château Moncontour; Jean Bertrand; Domaine Allias. (Cheverny) Chai des Vignerons; Confrérie des Vignerons de Oisly et Thésée.

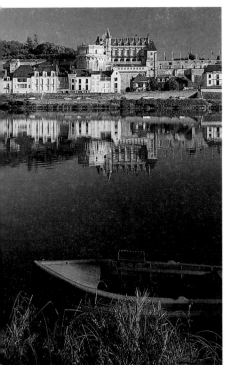

Left: *The still water of Amboise in Touraine, a region where vinegrowing has to compete with a wide range of other types of agriculture.*

Coteaux du Loir is a small appellation in great danger of being engulfed by an ever-encroaching orchard of fruit trees. The Chenin-based white would be missed as it has (in its dry and *demi-sec* forms) some affinity with Vouvray; the Groslot-based rosé is so insignificant in numbers and flavour that its disappearance might go unnoticed.

Like Savennières, Jasnières is one of those "difficult" Chenin Blanc wines: difficult to make well and, for some people, difficult to grow to love. The problem is the level of acidity which, even in warm years, can be almost aggressively high and, in cool ones, mouth-scrapingly vicious. Given a few years of good cellaring, well-made examples from ripe vintages can develop marvellous spicy-peach smells and flavours which outclass all but the very best Vouvray. Watch out however for poor, over-sulphured Jasnières from cold wet years.

Vouvray is a puzzle. One of the finest wines I ever drank was a 1934 sweet Vouvray, bought for a few pounds and drunk with a picnic of cheese on the bank of the Loire (the producer had warned me that the wine might not survive a car journey to Britain). On the other hand, there are few wines I have enjoyed less than a set of mouth-scouring dry Vouvrays from a cool vintage, and a sickly, Liebfraumilch-like *demi-sec* served to me in a restaurant in Tours.

The problem lies in the absolute need of the Chenin Blanc to have just the right kind of weather – a warm enough summer to ripen the grapes, in the case of the dry wine, and a humid enough autumn to encourage the noble rot which can produce the truly great sweet Vouvray. And it also lies in the skill of the winemaker in handling this tricky variety.

Below: *A cross section of the soil of the Coteaux de Touraine. The slatey upper slope is ideal for red wine; when the subsoil is chalky, white is good too. The chalkier lower slope is good for Chenin.*

It is hardly surprising that so many producers opt out completely and turn their attention to making sparking wine instead. The *Méthode Champenoise* fizz, made from the Chenin Blanc, can be agreeably mouthfilling and appley, but it will never have the character of the still wine at its best.

Good, dry Vouvray, from a ripe year, should be at once appley and creamy. Monsieur Huet is one of the very few producers who seems to be able to achieve this; just as he is one of the small number who can make the *demi-sec* better than the sickly honeyed stuff it can be. Balance between sweetness and acidity is all, and these can be very wobbly wines indeed.

Coteaux de Touraine Soils

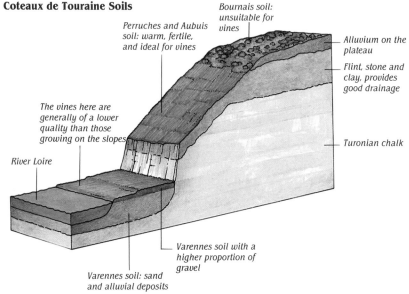

Perruches and Aubuis soil: *warm, fertile, and ideal for vines*

Bournais soil: *unsuitable for vines*

Alluvium on the plateau

Flint, stone and clay, provides good drainage

The vines here are *generally of a lower quality than those growing on the slopes*

Turonian chalk

River Loire

Varennes soil with a higher proportion of gravel

Varennes soil: *sand and alluvial deposits*

Left: *The Loire has unquestionably one of Europe's finest collections of great buildings. This château is in Vouvray, overlooking the Loire. Vouvray wine, made from the Chenin Blanc, can range from very dry to sweet.*

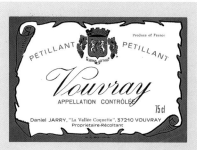

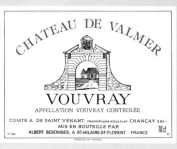

Made from grapes grown on the opposite (southern) bank of the Loire to Vouvray, and once sold under that name, the wines of Montlouis have never achieved international recognition. Dry Montlouis, though sharing the same characteristic Chenin Blanc, floral, almond and honey flavour as Vouvray, tends to be a little lighter and less acidic in style. Montlouis is also ready to drink rather earlier than Vouvray and is said to have a shorter lifespan. Even so, sweet examples from warm vintages – and Montlouis needs very warm years to make those sweet styles – can age absolutely beautifully.

Sadly the lack of appellation for the still wines of Montlouis has led to a greater emphasis on making *Pétillant* and *Méthode Champenoise* wine; over 3.5 million bottles are made in this way each year, as compared with only 700,000 bottles of non-sparkling.

Of the VDQS areas in this region, white Cheverny has the distinction of being made from Sauvignon, Chenin Blanc and the unusual Romorantin grapes, while the rosé is made from Pineau d'Aunis. Both wines are light and quite floral, and can be dry or *demi-sec*, still or mousseux. Valençay can be made of all kinds of grapes, including the Arbois and Chardonnay, but is of little interest. Coteaux du Vendômois wines are more worth tasting, the unfashionable Pineau de la Loire being used to produce a rather fuller rosé.

Sweet Loire Wines

Grapes	(White) Chenin Blanc, Pinot Gris, Sauvignon, Menu Pineau (synonym for Arbois). (Red) Gamay, plus (but rarely) other red varieties of Touraine.
Appellations	Bonnezeaux Grand Cru (AOC 1951, medium dry- sweet white). Coteaux de Saumur (AOC 1962, 90hl of medium dry-sweet white). Coteaux du Layon (AOC 1950, sweet white). Quarts de Chaume (AOC 1954, 750hl of dry-sweet white). Touraine (AOC 1939, dry-sweet white and rosé). Montlouis (AOC 1938, 5250hl of dry-sweet white, including sweet liqueur wine). Vouvray (AOC 1936, dry-sweet and sparkling white made from Chenin Blanc. Grapes left on vine as long as possible to ensure maximum *pourriture noble*).
Recommended producers	(Bonnezeaux Grand Cru) Château de Fesles; Château de Gauliers. (Coteaux du Layon) Aubert Frères; Château des Rochettes, Clos de Sainte Catherine. (Montlouis) Jean Pierre Leblois. (Vouvray) Domaine Huet; Clos Baudoin.

rance's most famous wine-loving monarch, Henri IV, planted a tree which still survives in the village of Chavignol, close to Sancerre, declaring that the wine of that commune (wine now sold as Sancerre) was the best he had drunk, and that if everyone in the kingdom were to drink it, there would be an end to religious wars. One should not, however, jump to the conclusion that Henri was referring to the kind of Sancerre we know today, because at the time he was tasting it – indeed until the last century – most of Sancerre was red, while the white was made from the uninspiring Chasselas grape.

Nowadays, the Chasselas has been more or less banished, along with a large proportion of the Pinot Noir, the remainder of which is still used to make red and pink Sancerre. Anyone interested in tasting the kind of white wine Henri IV might have drunk, will have to make do with the rarely exported Pouilly-sur-Loire; today this heartland of the Loire is essentially Sauvignon Blanc territory. And if Vouvray, Bonnezeaux and Quarts de Chaume are the finest sweet wines of the Loire, Sancerre and Pouilly-Fumé must be the region's best dry whites. At their best, these wines express precisely what the Sauvignon Blanc can achieve, combining flavours of gooseberry, blackcurrant leaf, asparagus and, it has to be said, aromas of cat's pee.

Given half a chance, Sancerre would be a Burgundian appellation, or even a set of Burgundian appellations, allowing each of 14 villages the chance to establish its own reputation based on the variation of types of chalky soil. Even without those appellations, the names of such villages as Chavignol (source also of famous small goat cheeses known as Crottins de Chavignol), Bué, Champtin, Sury-en-Vaux, Reigny and Ménétréol are proudly printed on their labels by growers based in those communes.

The best vines are planted on south-facing slopes which are, on occasion, almost as steep as some of the most steeply sloping vineyards of the Rhône. Looking at these slopes, it is easy to understand how the farmers here came to choose to breed the goats which still produce the cheese which, for a Sancerrois, is the ideal accompaniment to his wine. Elsewhere, however, there has been some expansion of the vineyards which may, in turn, have brought about a certain lowering of the quality of some Sancerre.

At its best, Sancerre can be richer, more unashamedly fruity, than Pouilly-Fumé, but all too often, and particularly in warmer vintages, its less well-made wines can be a bit *too* rich and even rather flabby. Unfortunately, as in Chablis, the Burgundian neighbour whose vines are planted in the same Kimmeridgian chalk subsoil as they are in all of the vineyards of this part of the Loire, the departure from the traditional "biting" style of Sancerre has met with some commercial success, particularly in the USA, among wine drinkers who claim to like dry wine but balk at the crispy acidity which is the mark of truly typical Sancerre.

Rosé Sancerre can be a delicious opportunity to taste the wild raspberry-plummy Pinot Noir outside its native Burgundian vineyards. Sadly, however, its discovery by chic Parisian restaurants, and the realisation that this is a style which is well suited to light Nouvelle Cuisine dishes, has helped to raise its price to a level at which it has long ceased to offer value for money.

If it were not confusing enough to have to remember that Pouilly-Fuissé is the one from Burgundy and Pouilly-Fumé from the Loire, the village of Pouilly-sur-Loire complicates matters still further by making two wholly different wines: Pouilly Blanc Fumé (also called Pouilly-Fumé), which is made from the Sauvignon grape, and Pouilly-sur-Loire, made from the Chasselas. If it were not for the wine, there would be little reason to

Right: Sancerre and the country which surrounds it, is undoubtedly one of the most beautiful parts of France. The best slopes are all planted in vines and plantation has been extended in recent years, but other forms of agriculture still survive, particularly dairy farming; the goats from Chavignol produce a very famous cheese.

come here; the town is dull and featureless, benefitting only from its riverside location, but enjoying none of the picturesque charm of Sancerre.

Pouilly-sur-Loire makes no greater a case for the Chasselas grape than has been achieved in Switzerland or Alsace, the variety's other traditional homes. At its best, the wine can be refreshing and acidic and occasionally reminiscent of a (very) scaled-down Pouilly-Fumé, thanks to the growers' propensity for passing their Chasselas over the lees of their Pouilly-Fumé. It cannot, however, be said that the Chasselas is taking up space which might better be used for growing a better variety: the 55 per cent of the total Pouilly vineyard from which Pouilly-sur-Loire comes is, in any case, reckoned to be unsuitable for growing Sauvignon.

Pouilly-Fumé itself is said to owe its name either to the smoky flavour associated with the wine, or, to the smoky dust which flies off the grapes as they are picked. I prefer the first explanation because smoke and a flinty-steeliness are certainly characteristics which allow you to identify a good Pouilly from a Sancerre. The flinty flavour of Pouilly-Fumé is attributable to the lighter clay content of the soil here. These are wines which can outlast dry Sauvignon produced anywhere else in the world, but which should still be drunk within three or four years of the harvest, as they do not age well beyond this period.

Like Sancerre, Pouilly-Fumé has been debased by its recent success, but there is the crucial difference that whereas in Sancerre winemaking is in the hands of a large number of individual growers and a co-

operative, here, one man, Patrick de Ladoucette at the Château du Nozet (apparently Napoleon's favourite white wine) sells 60 per cent of the total production. I have not always been as impressed by the Ladoucette wines as their reputation would have led me to hope, but the Baron de L, Prestige Cuvée, produced only in the very best years and sold in a fancy bottle at a very fancy price, is truly perfect Pouilly-Fumé. When buying growers' Pouilly, look out for "Les Loges" or "Les Berthiers" on the label; these are the appellation's best communes.

Producing wine very similar in style to both Pouilly-Fumé and Sancerre, and with vines planted in soil almost identical to that of both those communes, Reuilly is nevertheless very much the poor relation. The problem lies in the readiness of growers to turn their attention to other, more reliable crops. The recent success of the commune's better known neighbours will, one hopes, convince the winemakers of Reuilly to replant some of those vineyards. In the meantime, do try to find a bottle of Reuilly rosé; made from the Pinot Gris, known here as the Pinot Beurot, and the Pinot Noir, this is one of the best rosés in the Loire.

Menetou-Salon is in a similar position to Reuilly, producing wines almost literally in the shadow of Sancerre on the same kind of soil, known locally as "*terre blanche*", as that commune. Ironically, given their respective reputations today, Menetou-Salon was accorded its appellation in 1953, six years before Sancerre and nine years before

Reuilly. Good examples can readily outclass many an ordinary Pouilly-Fumé or Sancerre but they do not bear comparison with the best wines from either of those communes. Drunk young, the whites are agreeable examples of the Sauvignon; the rosés, made from Pinot Noir, by contrast, are rarely of particular interest.

Central Vineyards Wines

Grapes	Sauvignon, Pinot Noir, Chasselas, Pinot Gris, Gamay, Chenin Blanc, Gamay Noir à Jus Blanc, Chardonnay, Tresallier, Aligoté, Pinot Meunier, Cabernet Franc.
Soil	Heavy in lime content, with varying amounts of gravelly top soil and clay and sand.
Appellations	Pouilly-Fumé (AOC 1937, 22,500hl of dry white). Menetou-Salon (AOC 1953, 400hl of red, white and rosé). Pouilly-sur-Loire (AOC 1937, as Pouilly-Fumé, with addition of Chasselas grape). Quincy (AOC 1936, 3,375hl of dry white). Reuilly (AOC 1962, 375hl of red, rosé and white). Sancerre (AOC 1936- white, 1959-red/rosé. 56,250hl of red, rosé and dry white).
VDQS wines	Châteaumeillant (VDQS 1965, 4,500hl of red and rosé). Coteaux du Giennois (VDQS 1954, 3,750hl of red, dry rosé and white). Côtes Roannaises (VDQS 1955, 3,750hl of red and dry rosé). Côtes d'Auvergne (VDQS 1977, mainly red and rosé). Côtes Du Forez (VDQS 1956, red and dry rosé). St-Pourçain-sur-Sioule (VDQS 1951, red, dry rosé and white). Vins d'Orléans (VDQS 1951, 5,250hl of red, rosé and dry white).
Recommended producers	(Pouilly-Fumé) Maison Blondelet; Chatelain; Domaine Saint-Michel; Serge Dagueneau; Rene Michit et fils, Château de Tracey. (Menetou-Salou) Domaine de Chatenoy; Jean-Paul Gilbert; Domaine Henri Pelle. (Quincy) Pierre et Jean Mardon; Bernard Pichard; Raymond Pipet; Pierre Ragon. (Reuilly) Robert Cordier; Henri Beurdin; Claude Lafond. (Côtes Roannaises) Maurice Lutz. (Sancerre) Ladoucette.

Quincy, the oldest appellation in the region, from vines grown on the banks of the river Cher, is a wine which deserves a place in any tasting of typical Sauvignon. Though not often of any enormous complexity of flavour, Quincy's pure gooseberry and asparagus flavour can be a great deal finer than those of either Reuilly or Menetou-Salon, while its

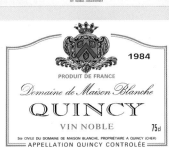

Above: *The Château du Nozet, one of the truly fairytale Loire castles, and the source of good Pouilly-Fumé. This was apparently Napoleon's favourite wine.*

price is still significantly lower than Sancerre or Pouilly-Fumé.

At an even lower price level, there are a number of VDQS wines dotted around at the eastern end of the Loire valley. None is really comparable with the better appellations of the area, but all are of interest to visitors (few are exported). Côtes de Gien, covering only 30 of a possible 2,000 hectares, makes light rosé from the Gamay and Pinot Noir and similarly light whites from the Sauvignon and Chenin. Slightly more wine is made under the Châteaumeillant designation, but only red and rosé wines and predominantly from Gamay. The *vin gris* rosé is particularly good – if you can find it. Vin de l'Orléanais is worth tasting: it includes a very rare, very pale, pink wine made from the Pinot Meunier. As for the Côtes Roannaises and Côtes du Forez, the southernmost vineyards of the Loire – which explains their frequent inclusion in books on the Rhône – both make rosé from the Gamay which can, in ripe years, be pleasantly fresh. Before, leaving this southern corner of the Loire, however, it is also worth tasting St-Pourçain, a white Sauvignon/Chardonnay which also usually includes a varying dollop of the unusual, if rather acidic, Tresallier. Rosé St-Pourçain is a Gamay/Pinot Noir blend which is rarely seen.

Tucked away in the Massif Central, in skiing, rather than wine country, Côtes d'Auvergne and its five "*crus*", Chateaugay, Chanturgues, Madargues and Corent, use Gamay and Pinot Noir to produce good rosé and pure Chardonnay for light, tangy, whites.

Key to map
1 Côtes du Jura.
2 Arbois.
3 Château-Chalon.
4 L'Etoile.

I always think of the Jura as producing the white equivalent of Cahors – wines which, centuries ago, were amongst the most highly regarded in France but which have since gone out of fashion. These wines are now enjoying a renaissance of popularity within their own borders, but elsewhere, outside the most specialist restaurant, you would be lucky to find a single bottle of Vin Jaune or Vin de Paille, the Jura's most famous wines.

They are, however, worth the search because, like Cahors, these can be some of the most characterful wines in France, wines which you may well dislike the moment you taste them, but which, with time, can win over the most ardent converts.

There is something wonderfully medieval about the Jura. Dôle, its capital, which lies about 20 miles north-west of Arbois, has the tiny, winding streets of Alsace but little of the tourist glitz; this is very much the old market town, strategically placed in the heart of a mountainous region in that part of eastern France which seems to be as close to Germany and Switzerland as it is to the rest of France. Though less sheltered than Alsace, the climate here is pleasantly warm – at least in the summer, and sometimes in the autumn. The winters, however, tend to be

bitterly cold; this can be a very difficult place to grow vines and, just as importantly, to persuade grapes to ripen.

As the atmosphere of the region would suggest, the wines of the Jura have a history which is amongst the oldest in France. Pliny Junior recommended them in his *Natural History* and, for centuries, indeed until as recently as the late 19th century when the region's vines covered some 16,000ha, they competed successfully as a form of currency in preference to the more customary salt from the nearby salt-springs at Salins, Lons-le-Saunier and Grozon.

Until 1032, the Comté (or county) was attached to Burgundy, its neighbour to the west, but in that year it gained its independence, falling in the 15th century under the rule of the great dukes of the Occident and developing in importance to such an extent that Dôle was given a parliament, a university and a Chamber of Commerce.

Towards the end of the 19th century, with the arrival of the phylloxera beetle in France's most southerly vineyards, Jura wines enjoyed a brief moment of increased popularity and an expansion of the region's vineyards to nearly 20,000ha. Inevitably, however, the pest eventually reached the Jura, leaving in its wake a region which, even when it came to

Above: *The countryside of the Jura is, paradoxically, at once savage and gentle. This view is of vineyards above Poligny; the small parcels of land are very typical of the region.*

Below: *Separating Trousseau grapes from their stalks. The juice from these grapes could become Arbois Rouge, Rosé or, most likely, Gris de Gris.*

replant with resistant American rootstock, supported less than 8,000ha of vines, a figure which dropped to just over 6,000 in the wake of the First World War, and 2,000ha (only 1,300 of them AOC) at the beginning of the 1980s.

Although the Jura produces a very varied range of wines, it has become internationally known for just one, the almost legendary Vin Jaune of Château-Chalon, which could best be described as France's unfortified answer to Fino sherry. It is one of the very few wines in the world which is allowed – indeed encouraged – to oxidise, gaining rather than suffering through the process, thanks to the protection provided by a film of yeast which develops on the surface of the wine, just as it does in the *bodegas* of Jerez, the sherry-producing region of Spain.

It was this very rare phenomenon which was to fascinate Louis Pasteur who, born in the region, returned here to experiment on ways to prevent wine from going bad. Pasteur's understanding of the importance of hygiene in winemaking, and of the antiseptic potential of sulphur dioxide, radically altered the way in which wine is produced throughout the world. However, it was another Juracien, a local merchant called Henri Maire, who rescued his region from what seemed to be permanent obscurity. Maire concentrated on neither the traditional Vin Jaune, nor the curious, raisiny-sweet, straw-mat-dried Vin de Paille, both of which are of too eccentric a style and of far too limited a production ever to form the mainstay of an ambitious merchant. Instead, he introduced the market to the red; light, dry white; and, most particularly, the pale Vin Gris rosé, all three wines which Arbois had been making for centuries.

White Arbois, like many other Jura whites, owes its character to the Savagnin grape with its curious, nutty, almondy flavours, while the rosé and Vin Gris offer the chance to taste the redcurrant and berryish spice of the Trousseau and Poulsard. Defining regional styles is, however, made more difficult by the use of such other varieties as the Chardonnay, Pinot Noir and Pinot Blanc. This is the case, for example, of white Côtes du Jura which can be made purely from Chardonnay or Savagnin, or a blend of the two. Even so, this appellation is generally better regarded than Arbois itself and Arbois Pupillin, that wine's equivalent of a superior "Villages" appellation. The one link between these Jura wines is the 24-36 months cask-ageing which gives them all a rich, ready-to-drink character which can make their age very hard to guess in a comparative tasting.

For the true essence of the Jura, however, it is to the Vins de Paille and the Vins Jaunes that one must look. Both these wonderfully old-fashioned wines are made throughout the region but for the very best Vin Jaune, one has to buy Château-Chalon. The difference between the wine of this appellation and Vin Jaune made elsewhere in the Jura is not unlike that which separates Manzanilla from

Below: *Harvesters in the vineyards of Henri Maire in Arbois. M. Maire's wines are not necessarily the best made here, but he was almost single-handed in reviving the appellation.*

The Structure of the Wine Industry

Producers	Over 20,000 growers work some 5,300ha, each having an average of 500-1,000m^2.
Co-operatives	Strong in the major towns, and supported by 5,000 of the growers.
Négociants	Unlike many other regions, here, the merchants buy grapes rather than wine.
Particuliers	A growing band of estate-bottling individual producers.

Fino sherry. The Château-Chalon wines, of which only 50,000 bottles are made each year, have a delicacy and a richness which combine flavours of grilled nut, spice and fresh biting acidity. But whichever commune it comes from, the rules which dictate the way in which Vin Jaune is produced remain the same. It has to be made exclusively from the Savagnin; fermentation takes as long as 18 months in the naturally cool cellars; and the wine has to mature and oxidise gently in oak barrels for six years. It is a potentially wasteful process too, because, as in Jerez, any casks which fail to produce a layer of *voile* or flor yeast have to be discarded completely, or used for vinegar.

Below: *Vin Jaune maturing in the cellars at Château-Chalon in the Jura. The wine will remain in these barrels for six years, during which time a significant proportion will evaporate.*

Even the successful barrels suffer wastage, with nearly 20% of the contents evaporating over the six years, and the Juraciens make quite certain that their customers know about – and pay for – this loss; the traditional clavelin bottles used for Vin Jaune (usually) contain only 62cl instead of the 70 or 75cl customary elsewhere in France.

As for Vin de Paille, this is more reminiscent of the Recioto wines of Italy, tasting of raisins, but again with a bite of acidity to prevent it from cloying. Grapes for Vin de Paille – a mixture of Poulsard, Trousseau, Pinot Noir, Chardonnay and Savagnin – all used to be dried on the straw mats from which the wine has taken its name, but today it is as likely that the bunches are simply hung in a well-aired barn or loft for a couple of months. Fermentation is patience-testingly slow, taking between 12 and 24 months, and the wine then spends a further period of four years in barrel before bottling. This lengthy process unfortunately has to be paid for and a half bottle of Vin de Paille can cost as much as a very classy Sauternes. This is perhaps understandable when you consider that it takes over a kilo and a half of grapes to make one of those half bottles, and that its contents are amongst the longest-lived of any wine in the world. It is one of the most interesting and alcoholic – the strength can be as high as 17° – non-fortified wines in the world, and one of the most delicious.

L'Etoile produces both Vin de Paille and Vin Jaune, but this small appellation, to the south-west of Château-Chalon, also has the distinction of using the black Poulsard grape to make white wine; either, rarely, in blends with the Savagnin and the Chardonnay, or by itself. Here too, the key flavour of these cask-matured wines is ''nutty'', a characteristic which is more apparent the greater the proportion of Savagnin there is in the blend.

Right: Sloping vineyards just beneath the appellation of Château-Chalon, one of the smallest in France, and the source of the rarely seen, but very best, Vin Jaune of all.

Left: *Château d'Arlay, a source of good, traditional Jura wines, including rich Vin Jaune. This property has been one of the few to maintain the Jura tradition of winemaking.*

L'Etoile is also, according to its inhabitants, the place to look for the best sparkling wine in the whole Jura region.

The Savagnin is not used in these sparkling wines, which are produced by the Champagne or Rural Method in most of the appellations, because its flavour is too full-bodied for fizz. The sparkling wines which are produced, from the Chardonnay and Pinot Blanc, are fresh and attractive, with the floral style sometimes found in the region's still white wines.

Thanks to the enthusiasm of Henri Maire, the efforts of such traditionalists as Château d'Arlay, and the success of the local co-operatives, the apparently inexorable slide of the Jura into the pages of history has, one hopes, been halted. Even so, with less than five million bottles of wine made each year, the Jura is bound to continue to be one of France's more eccentric winemaking regions producing – for those who have acquired the taste for them – some of the country's most deliciously eccentric wines.

Jura Wines

Grapes	(White) Chardonnay (known here as Melon d'Arbois), Savagnin (also called Nature, and possibly related to the Traminer) and Pinot Blanc. (Rosé) Poulsard, Trousseau and Pinot Noir.
Soil	Jurassic limestone, with silicious clay topsoil
Appellations	Arbois (AOC 1936, red, rosé, sparkling and still dry white). Arbois Pupillin (AOC 1970, as above, but from 13 communes around Arbois and including Vin de Paille and Vin Jaune). Château-Chalon (AOC 1936, 45,000 bottles exclusively of Vin Jaune, made from Savagnin at yields of 30hl/ha.) Côtes du Jura (AOC 1937, red, rosé, vin gris and, mostly, dry white.) Côtes du Jura Mousseux (*Méthode Champenoise*, made mostly from Chardonnay and Pinot Blanc). L'Etoile (AOC 1937, a tiny [34ha] appellation producing characterful white. Good Vin Jaune and Vin de Paille and very good Mousseux). Vin de Paille (produced in various communes always from a blend of Poulsard, Trousseau, Pinot Noir, Chardonnay and Savagnin in tiny quantities). Vin Gris (see Arbois). Vin Jaune (made in several communes – see Château-Chalon)
Recommended producers	(Arbois) Henri Maire, Dom de la Grange-Grillard; Roger Lornet; Caveau des Bacchus, Lucien Aviet; Jacques Tissot; Dom Rolley; Jacques Forêt; Rolet Père et Fils; Arbois Coopérative, Dom Petit. (Arbois Pupillin) Désiré Petit; Dom Bouillere. (Château-Chalon) Maison Courbet et Fils; Marius Perron; Jean Maclé; Jean Bourdy. (Côtes du Jura) Château d'Arlay; Badoz Père & Fils; Jean Bourdy; Côtes du Jura Coopérative; Marius Perron; Courbet & Fils; Jean Maclé. (L'Etoile) Château de l'Etoile; Dom de Montbourgeau. (Vin Jaune) Château d'Arlay; Jean Bourdy; Dom Rolet.
Best vintages	1943, 1953, 1976, 1978, 1983, 1985. These recommendations are for white wines; rosés are seldom worth keeping for more than two years.

SAVOIE

Key to map
1 Vins de Savoie.
2 Crépy.
3 Roussette de Savoie.
4 Seyssel.

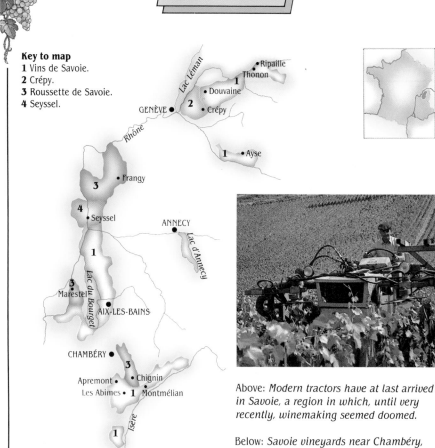

Above: *Modern tractors have at last arrived in Savoie, a region in which, until very recently, winemaking seemed doomed.*

Below: *Savoie vineyards near Chambéry, overlooked by brooding hills. In winter, this is the preserve of holiday skiers.*

*I*t has been said of Crépy, that it is "Greatest of France's lesser wines; least of its great ones." Well, Crépy and the nearby commune of Seyssel may reasonably claim membership of the league of France's best wines – both were after all awarded *Appellation Contrôlée* status around 40 years ago – but quite how the rest of Savoie's wines managed to achieve promotion from the chorus line of the VDQS to the starring roles of the AOC, is another matter entirely. These are delicious, light, refreshing country wines and just the stuff to gulp back after a hard day on the pistes of Val d'Isère, but they are hardly what many would consider truly worthy of Appellation quality.

The recent promotion to AOC of Vin de Savoie probably has more to do with tourism than wine law. Everything in this corner of the French Alps is rather chic, and rather expensive. So perhaps it is not surprising that the region's wine growers managed to persuade the authorities that they ought to be able to remove the "country wine" stigma from their wines. Besides, if you take a charitable view, AOC may have saved Savoie's vineyards from disappearing completely, a fate which earlier this century seemed all too possible.

The Romans knew Savoie well, apparently liking what Pliny described as the resinous quality of the region's wines. Whether this characteristic did indeed come from the influence of the nearby forests as he suggested, or whether it was the result of the local style of winemaking remains unclear. By the 11th century, when the vineyard of Monterminod was given to the Burgundian abbey of Cluny, they had gained a name for being good for the digestion and, during the following centuries, they established a reliable if unspectacular market for themselves throughout the region. In 1768, on the eve of the revolution, the local *député* established that Savoie had some 9,000ha of vines. Today, the figure stands at 1,200 and, despite the allocation to the region of VDQS status in 1945 and full AOC in 1973 (some communes having received their appellation a little earlier), there is little hope of the vineyards expanding to their former size.

The problem lies in the way in which the vines have been planted, dotted around in patches in the valleys and mountains of Savoie and Haute-Savoie, in such a disorganised fashion that there can be little chance of a cohesive wine industry being created. The climate does not help either; it can be very warm in summer, but damp, cold and frosty during the winter and spring, making winemaking an unpredictable affair. Often the grapes simply fail to ripen, producing thin, acidic and slightly fizzy wine. This is a region where warm vintages and skilled winemaking are vital.

Of the Savoie appellations, the best known are probably the Vin de Savoie itself, Crépy, Seyssel and Roussette. The style and quality of Vin de Savoie depends to a great extent on the grapes from which it is made. Amongst the whites, those made from the Jacquère are probably the most fruitily refreshing and the Roussettes the most honeyed and rich. Of particular interest is the local "*Spontanée en Bouteille*", where Crépy offers the usually dull Chasselas a chance to make some really attractive and slightly floral-flavoured wines which gain in freshness from the slightly *perlant* or *pétillant* bubble which is the result of the wine having been bottled "*sur lie*".

The vineyards of Seyssel were, for many years, covered with irises. Situated high on south-facing slopes and planted uniquely with Roussette, they produce white wines which genuinely do smell of violets, and have a slight flavour of quince or pear.

Right: *Roussanne grapes. This is a variety almost exclusive to Savoie, and used to produce Chignin-Bergeron in the commune of Chignin.*

Savoie Wines

Soil	Mostly schistous clay-chalk, top soil at an angle of at least 40%.
Grapes	(White) Roussette (also known as Altesse), Gringet, Mondeuse, Chasselas, Roussanne, Molette, Cacabboué, Jacquère, Chardonnay (also known as Petite-Sainte-Marie). (Rosé) Gamay, Pinot Noir, Mondeuse Rouge, Persan.
Main appellations	Crépy (AOC 1948, 800,000 bottles of dry white, slightly sparkling "crépitant" wine, made from Chasselas). Roussette de Savoie (AOC 1973, 250,000 bottles of floral, very dry, white, made from Chardonnay – up to 50 per cent – Altesse and Mondeuse Blanche). Roussette de Savoie + Cru (as above but made exclusively from Altesse and in specified communes). Roussette de Frangy (big, honeyed, pure Altesse). Seyssel (AOC 1942, 180,000 bottles of floral, dry wine made from the Altesse). Seyssel Mousseux (as above, but sparkling and made from Altesse, Molette Blanc and Chardonnay). Vin de Savoie (AOC 1973, red, rosé and dry white, made from the Mondeuse, Pinot Noir, Gamay (for rosé) and Jacquère, Altesse, Chasselas, Aligoté and Chardonnay). Vin de Savoie + Cru (as above, but of a higher natural strength, and from specified communes). Vin de Savoie Mousseux (as Vin de Savoie). Vin de Savoie Ayze Mousseux (the only "cru" name to appear on a mousseux label. Made from Gringet, Mondeuse Blanche and at least 30 per cent Altesse.)
Recommended producers	(Abymes) Gerard Ollivier; Marcel Viallet. (Apremont) Jean Masson; Gilbert Perrier; Le Vigneron Savoyard; J. C. Perret; Pierre Boniface; Dom des Rocailles. (Chignin/Chignin-Coteaux Les Château) André & Raymond Quenard; Les Fils Réné Quenard. (Crépy) S. A. Fichin. (Mondeuse d'Arbin) Louis Magnin. (Roussette de Savoie) Noel Dupasquier; Michel Million Rousseau; Dom Roussillon Père et Fils; GAEC Les Aricoques; Michel Jean-Paul Neyroud. (Roussette de Seyssel) Varichon et Clerc. (Vin de Savoie Cruet) Philippe et André Tiollier.
Best vintages	1978, 1983, 1985 (most Savoie is however best drunk young).

*T*he wines of Bugey are, if anything, over-shadowed by their only slightly better known Savoyard neighbours. Apart from the destruction of the vineyards by barbarians, the history of the region, like its grape varieties and climate are very similar to those of Savoie, but the wines, some of which are made quite close to the Mâconnais and Beaujolais, can bear a family resemblance to the wines of those Burgundian regions. Though only qualifying for the rank of VDQS – as opposed to Savoie's *Appellation Contrôlée* – these wines can be just as characterful and just as good as the better wines of that appellation.

The best wines are the sparkling and *pétillant* Vins du Bugey, of which little is made, most particularly Cerdon which, like the other Bugey fizz, is either made by the *Méthode Rurale* or by the *Méthode Champenoise*, but is invariably red or rosé. Still Vin du Bugey itself can vary enormously depending on the grape variety from which it has been made (labels often refer to a single variety) with some Beaujolais-like reds and Mâcon-like whites being made from the Gamay and Chardonnay respectively.

The soil, climate and grape varieties of Bugey wines are the same as in Savoie. All of Bugey's wines are VDQS; the table below lists the characteristics of the varieties available.

Right: *A typically old-fashioned wine shop in Vongnes in Savoie. Sparkling, pink and white are all on show; all sell well to holidaymakers.*

Bugey Wines

Vin du Bugey	Red, rosé and white. 60 per cent of the total production (1m bottles) is white; up to 20 per cent white grapes (Jacquère, Aligoté, Chardonnay, Altesse, Mondeuse Blanche, Pinot Gris) can be used in the making of rosé. Some single grape varietals are made. Minimum strength: 9°. Maximum yield: 45hl/ha.
Vin du Bugey Cru	The best Vin du Bugey, from the following villages, is allowed this VDQS: Montagnieu (only white); Cerdon (invariably red or rosé); Virieu-le-Grand; Manicle; Machuraz. Minimum strength: 9.5°. Maximum yield: 40hl/ha.
Roussette de Bugey	A light, floral-tasting blend of Chardonnay and Altesse. Minimum strength: 10°. Minimum yield: 32hl/ha.
Roussette de Bugey + Cru	Similar to Roussette de Bugey, but produced in the villages of Arbignieu, Chanay, d'Anglefort, Montagnieu and Lantignieu. Minimum strength: 10.5°.
Vin du Bugey Mousseux / Pétillant	Good, fresh, sparkling and semi-sparkling wines made by the local form of *Méthode Champenoise*. The best come from Montagnieu and Cerdon. Minimum strength: 9°.
Recommended producers	(Bugey Brut) GAEC Dupont Frères. (Cellier du Bel-Air) Dom Ferrier. (Cerdon) Dom Renardat-Fache. (Vin du Bugey) Dom Monin.

RHÔNE

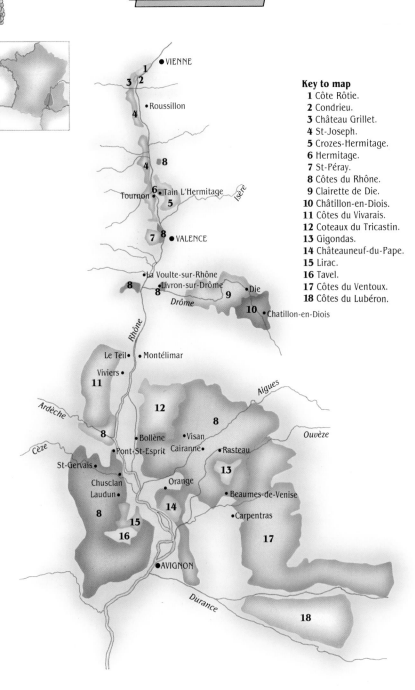

• VIENNE

1 Côte Rôtie.

3 2

• Roussillon

4

Key to map
1 Côte Rôtie.
2 Condrieu.
3 Château Grillet.
4 St-Joseph.
5 Crozes-Hermitage.
6 Hermitage.
7 St-Péray.
8 Côtes du Rhône.
9 Clairette de Die.
10 Châtillon-en-Diois.
11 Côtes du Vivarais.
12 Coteaux du Tricastin.
13 Gigondas.
14 Châteauneuf-du-Pape.
15 Lirac.
16 Tavel.
17 Côtes du Ventoux.
18 Côtes du Lubéron.

4 ● 8

Tournon • 6 • Tain L'Hermitage   *Isère*
5

7 8 ● VALENCE

• La Voulte-sur-Rhône
8 • Livron-sur-Drôme
8   9 • Die
Drôme   10 ● Chatillon-en-Diois

Rhône

Le Teil • • Montélimar

Viviers •
11

Ardèche

8

Aigues

12

8

Ouvèze

8   • Bollène • Visan
Cèze • Pont-St-Esprit Cairanne • • Rasteau
St-Gervais •   13
Chusclan   • Orange
Laudun •   • Beaumes-de-Venise
8   14   • Carpentras
15
16   17

● AVIGNON

Durance

18

Grape Varieties

White	**(northern)** Viognier, Roussanne, Roussette, Marsanne, Aligoté, Chardonnay, Muscat à Petit Grains.
White	**(southern)** Bourboulenc, Ugni Blanc, Clairette, Roussanne, Picpoul, Viognier, Pascal Blanc, Grenache Blanc, Marsanne, Muscat.
Red	**(northern)** Syrah, Grenache, Mourvèdre, Cinsault, Counoise, Muscardin, Vaccarèse, Terret Noir, Camarèse, Carignan.
Red	**(southern)** Grenache Noir, Mourvèdre, Cinsault, Pinot Noir, Picpoul Noir, Aubun, Counoise, Carignan, Gamay.

Of all France's wine regions, the Rhône must be one of the most typecast; very few people imagine that the stretch of vine-growing land which separates the Beaujolais and Mâconnais from the southern Mediterranean coast and its beaches, actually makes anything other than the spicy-leathery red wines of Hermitage and Châteauneuf-du-Pape and the lighter, more peppery examples of Côtes du Rhône. To most people, this is red wine territory.

The more experienced wine drinker might recall the fact that two of France's best-known rosés are produced down here in Tavel and Lirac, but even then the chances of him waxing lyrical about *white* Châteauneuf or Hermitage, let alone the exclusively dry white Condrieu and Château Grillet, the sparkling Clairette de Die, and the honeyed Muscat de Beaumes de Venise, are very slim indeed.

Statistically of course, the "Rhône-is-red" believers are well supported by the facts: of the 205 million bottles of Côtes du Rhône produced each year, only 3 million or so are white. In Châteauneuf the figure is 3 per cent in Crozes-Hermitage 10 per cent. Only in Hermitage itself does the figure rise to a respectable third, but then, there is very little Hermitage made.

The white and pink wines of the Rhône have no real equivalent anywhere else. And lest anyone suppose that their existence is a result of the white wine boom of the second half of the 20th century, it is worth pointing out that the Châteauneuf-du-Pape drunk by both of the popes who gave the village its name would almost certainly have been white.

Much of the unique quality of these wines stems from the traditional grape varieties which are used, and rarely grown elsewhere in France: Viognier, Clairette, Roussanne, Marsanne, Bourboulenc, Ugni Blanc, Grenache, Syrah, Mourvèdre, Cinsault.

Above: *The village of Beaumes de Venise and its vineyards which produce spicy rosé as well as the luscious sweet Muscat for which Beaumes de Venise is best known around the world.*

The earliest history we have of the Rhône is of its occupation by the nomadic Asian Ligurians in 1600 BC. A thousand years later, vineyards had been planted and were being tended by the Phoenicians who had established themselves at a city they called Massilia and which we now know as Marseilles. In the 14th century, it was the Catholic church – in the form of the papacy which briefly had to transfer its headquarters from Rome to Avignon – which was to provide the name of what is probably the Rhône's best-known wine. The few ruined walls which stand imposingly outside the overgrown village now known as Châteauneuf-du-Pape, and whose stone mullioned windows still overlook the surrounding vines, are all that now remains of Pope John XXII's summer palace, the building from which the village derived its name.

In the 18th century, the opening of the Canal du Midi established a commercial route that permitted Rhône wines to be shipped north to Paris and even as far as Britain, but this commercial boom was to be curtailed by the arrival, in 1863, of the phylloxera beetle which devastated the entire area, following the inadvertent importation from the United States of some infected vines by Château de Clary in Lirac.

In 1923, Châteauneuf distinguished itself by more or less creating the *Appellation Contrôlée* legislation which would, 13 years later extend its influence to most of the rest of winegrowing France, and today the range of individual Rhône appellations and styles stands as a worthy monument to the efforts of those early legislators.

Just as the Loire is divided into separate sub-regions, so too the Rhône is quite clearly separated into two sections, the northern Rhône which greets the south-ward-bound motorist as soon as he hits Vienne, twenty minutes closer to the sun than Lyon, and the southern Rhône which peters out in Avignon 200km further south. As if to emphasise their independence, the two sections are separated by around 50 vineless kilometres between the towns of Valence and Donzère.

The Northern Rhône has more in common with the port-producing vineyards of the Douro and the great Riesling slopes of the Rhine and Mosel than it does with either Burgundy or Bordeaux. The best view of these slopes is from the river itself; the steepness of the slopes seems almost unreal – if the wine were not good and unusual, no one would ever willingly work these fields when easier, flatter land could be found.

The climate here is continental, like an exaggerated version of that of Southern Burgundy, and the baking summers (Côte Rôtie certainly lives up to its name) can be

Above: Château Grillet, the only single-proprietor appellation in France, and the source of great, expensive wine.

matched by frozen winters, as was proven in 1985 when large sections of the vineyard were devastated by frost. The effects of the cold weather can be made far worse by the one climatic drawback to life in southern France, the Mistral which blows up the river and makes some of the seasonal vineyard tasks extremely difficult to perform. On the other hand the latitude (45°) is reckoned to be ideal for growing vines and, when well made, wines of the Rhône can achieve an enviable balance of freshness and natural ripeness.

Of all the Rhône's white wines the most sought after by wine buffs must be Château Grillet. This is, like Château-Chalon in the Jura, one of the most perfect justifications for *appellation contrôlée* legislation: a set of vineyards covering just 2.5ha, a little larger than a British country landowner's garden, with its very own appellation and an annual production of just 8,000 bottles of wine each year. The wine is, by any standards, a curiosity. Taking a flavour of almonds, flowers and spice from the Viognier, it gains a woody edge from the 18 months it spends in barrel before transfer into the dark yellow, 70cl "Rhine" bottles which further serve to emphasise Château Grillet's separateness from the other wines produced nearby.

The entire appellation belongs to a single estate so, unlike the vast majority of France's other appellations, every bottle from a particular vintage should resemble the next. Unfortunately, however, regular comparisons can prove expensive, rarity value and an increasing demand having led to high prices. Whether Château Grillet is worth the premium one has to pay in comparison with the neighbouring appellation of Condrieu is open to question. Like Château Grillet, Condrieu is grown on sandy-granite soil with a fine topsoil locally known as "*arzelle*" which is formed from decomposed mica. This, coupled with the Viognier, a variety which is grown almost nowhere else, makes for a spicy wine which is as successful as an aperitif as it is when matched with a fairly full flavoured plate of fish.

It is, however, an under-exploited appellation. Only 20ha are currently planted, with expansion to 25 or 30 planned, despite the legal potential of 200ha. So the annual production is only around 50,000 bottles (375hl). The problem is partly the proximity of Lyon – apartments are more profitable than vineyards – and the ease with which the other kinds of fruit grown here can be sold. Fundamentally, though, the main problem lies in the Viognier which, in some years, sulkily refuses to produce more than 20hl/ha, or, in other words, a third to a half of the amount produced in an average year in an equivalent appellation in Burgundy.

The flavour is demanding too. According to the books, the keynotes are pears, ripe fruit and spice; I perversely find a pleasant cheesiness to it. Whatever the specific taste, its individuality and the fatty 13 or 14° of alcohol it often boasts (a result of the low yields) make this a wine one has to grow to like. It almost tastes as though it ought to be sweet, and a naturally sweet version was made until the beginning of the 1960s. Just one word of caution: if you want to enjoy those flavours at their best, make sure that you drink Condrieu young.

Left: *The vines at Condrieu slope down almost to the banks of the Rhône, only a short drive south of Lyon. Working the vineyards here is difficult, and still a task for men rather than machines. Condrieu's wines are more affordable than the nearby Château Grillet.*

*I*f Château Grillet and Condrieu are two of the greatest of the white wines of the Rhône, they are matched by Hermitage, almost unarguably the Rhône's finest red. Whether or not Saint Patrick planted the first vines here is uncertain, but the wine does owe its name to a 13th century knight-turned-hermit, called Gaspard de Sterimberg, who settled here on his return from the crusades and (it is said) generously introduced his many illustrious visitors to the wine of his new home. Most of this would have been red, but a third of the wine made here is white, thanks to the fact that 40 or so of the 125ha of Hermitage vines are planted on soil with a greater proportion of clay which is better suited to the Marsanne and Roussanne grapes than to the Syrah, the variety exclusively used to make red wine in this part of the Rhône.

Winemaking styles vary greatly and the final flavour of white Hermitage will depend as much on the temperature of the fermentation, whether or not it has taken place in barrel and whether or not the wine has been bottled after six months or longer in barrel, as on the precise proportions of the grape varieties. When well-made, and from a good vintage, these wines can be kept for up to ten or even 20 years, during which time the

Above: *White Côtes du Rhône maturing in barrel – most matures in tank though.*

floral, spicy flavours associated with young white Hermitage soften into a peachy nuttiness. Between youth and age, there is often a duller phase however. A true Hermitage rarity worth seeking out is the Vin de Paille made from dried grapes which was once frequently made here but which had virtually died out until Gerard Chave recently decided to revive the tradition. (Fuller details of the making of Vin de Paille appear in the section on the Jura).

Often confused with Hermitage, Crozes-Hermitage is very much the poor relation. The largest appellation in the northern Rhône, grown in 11 communes a short way into the hills behind the slopes of Hermitage itself, Crozes is a very variable feast, depending on the soil – granitic, clay or sandy – in which it is produced. Only a tenth of the vines

Below: *The Hermitage vines slope steeply down to the edge of the Rhône, overlooking the town of Tain l'Hermitage.*

Northern Côtes du Rhône Wines

Grapes	(White) Clairette, Roussanne, Marsanne, Grenache Blanc, Bourboulenc, Viognier (Red) Grenache, Syrah, Mourvèdre, Cinsault, Counoise, Muscardin, Vaccarèse, Terret Noir, Camarèse, Carignan
Soil	Sub-soil is granite or gneiss; vines are planted on the steep slopes of the rocky hillsides.
Appellations	Côtes du Rhône (AOC, this covers red, rosé and white wines made throughout the Rhône, 2,072,000hl of red and rosé, and 48,200hl of white). Château Grillet (AOC 1936, 91hl of white). Condrieu (AOC 1936, 900hl of white). Crozes-Hermitage (AOC 1936, mainly red, 10 per cent – 4,000hl is white). Hermitage (AOC 1936, 1,200hl of white). St-Joseph (AOC 1956, 1,500hl of white). St-Péray (AOC 1936, 2,800hl of white, 80 per cent is Méthode Champenoise).
Recommended producers	(Condrieu) Georges Vernay; Delas Frères; André Dezormeaux; Paul Multier, Château du Rozay. (Crozes-Hermitage) Paul Jaboulet Aîné, Domaine Thalabert; Jean Louis Pradelle, Domaine des Clairmonts; Chapoutier et Cie, Les Meysonniers. (Hermitage) Jean Louis Chave; Henri Sorrel; Jean Louis Grippat; Cave Coopérative de Vins Fins. (St-Joseph) Pierre Coursodon; Raymond Trollot; Cave de Saint Desirat.

(80ha) are planted with white grapes, mostly Marsanne and Roussanne, the rest being Syrah.

Where the soil is sandy, as at Mercurol, and where the personality of the Marsanne is allowed to show through, the wines can be nuttily attractive, particularly when bottled early. Only the very best are worth ageing, and shortage of acidity can be a problem; for this reason, malolactic fermentation is discouraged by most producers.

A little further south, one comes to St-Joseph, an appellation which comprises a peculiarly long stretch of vineyards which run along 65km of the eastern bank of the Rhône, south from Condrieu, in a mixture of gently sloping to flattish land in the north, and steep terrace in the south, on soils of granite, sand and clay. Around a sixth of the total production of St-Joseph is white, coming from vineyards throughout the appellation though it is generally acknowledged that the best are from sites closest to Tournon and Hermitage.

As with red St-Joseph, quality can vary enormously. At their best, these wines are at once spicy and peachy; lesser examples, however, can be completely unbalanced, either lacking acidity to the extent that they are flat and flavourless or, by contrast, being unpleasantly acidic and fruitless. The profitability here has traditionally been poor, the wine is still relatively little known, prices are consequently modest, so there is limited motivation for winegrowers to produce really good wine but, by the same token, there are tasty bargains to be found.

St-Péray is usually thought of as producing exclusively sparkling white wine. In fact, however, a fifth of the production from these 60ha of vineyards is produced as still wine of a kind which was apparently well liked by King Henri IV, though the list of wines he is said to have disliked is far shorter than that of his favourites. The composer, Richard Wagner, was another fan.

The bubbles were first introduced into this Marsanne/Roussanne blend in 1829 by Louis-Alexandre Fauré, a cellar master who had moved to the Rhône from Champagne. Despite having a decidedly coarser style than the wine Monsieur Fauré was used to making, the new fizz proved successful with the Parisians who readily took to its gold-colour and its full spicy-floral flavour. Picked early, the Marsanne and Roussanne have the essential acidity required for sparkling wine; picked late they can also, very occasionally, benefit from an attack of *pourriture noble* to make an individual sweet wine. Sadly, the expansion of Valence, just across the river, threatens the future of St-Péray's vineyards in a more irreversible way than ever the phylloxera beetle did.

Clairette de Die, the Rhône's other sparkling wine, is confusingly named. Still, dry Clairette is, as you might expect, made exclusively from the Clairette grape. It is, however, produced in very small quantities, while the sparkling Clairette de Die Méthode Dioise or "Tradition", has, by law to contain at least 50 per cent Muscat and usually contains 75-80 per cent and even, in a few cases, 100 per cent of this grape.

Another curiosity here is the way in which the sparkling wine is made: the "*méthode dioise*". Supposedly derived from the tribal custom of the post-Roman inhabitants who were said to sink barrels of white wine in cold streams to make them "*pétillant*", the method of making Clairette de Die still involves chilling the must. The freshly pressed and lightly filtered juice is cooled to -3°C for 48 hours, before being partly fermented at a very low temperature for up to 4 months, at which point the still-sweet wine is put into bottle where the continuing fermentation will create carbon dioxide. At least four months later, the solids which have developed in the bottle are removed under pressure, and the wine is filtered under CO_2 pressurization so as to maintain the natural gas. It is then re-bottled and sold a year later.

A truly delicious pudding wine, Clairette de Die Tradition or Méthode Dioise must not

---

Below: *The tiny village of Amourdedieu where Marsanne grapes are grown to produce St-Péray, one of France's least known sparkling wines. Picked early, the Marsanne produces high-acid wine, which is ideally suited for making into sparkling wine. Picked later, it can be hit by noble rot and make good sweet wine.*

using Aligoté (90 per cent) and Chardonnay (10 per cent). This light, undemanding wine, most of which is drunk locally, is better thought of than the red, though the rosé, made from Gamay (75 per cent), Pinot Noir and Syrah, of which 900-1,350hl is produced annually, can be attractively light and fruity when caught young.

The Côtes du Vivarais VDQS is a wine region awaiting the promotion to AOC status already accorded to its neighbours, Coteaux de Tricastin and Côtes du Ventoux. In the meantime, it produces a trickle of good, flowery white and rather more rosé, the best of which comes from the *"crus"* of Orgnac, St-Remèze and St-Montant.

Perversely, however, this region's vinous future may depend more on its Vin de Pays des Coteaux de l'Ardèche than on promotion to the ranks of the *Appellation Contrôlée*. This is because Burgundian *négociants*, most notably Louis Latour, have discovered that Chardonnay made carefully here can be sold to customers who balk at the price of white burgundy.

Now the biggest communal appellation in the Rhône, Châteauneuf-du-Pape produces some 3,000hl of wine each year, of which only 100hl is white, made principally from the Grenache Blanc and the Clairette. Like the red, Châteauneuf Blanc can benefit from the effect of the large pebbles which cover most of the vineyards, which both keep the soil moist and warm at night. Elsewhere, however, white grapes are planted in the more sandy and clayey soil to the east and northeast of the town, and in the gravelly soil to the south. Often disappointingly heavy in character, when young the best white Châteauneuf can, nevertheless, be both rich and floral in character and a good compromise choice for occasions when it is difficult to choose between red and white.

be confused with Clairette de Die Méthode Champenoise, a dry, mostly Clairette-based, and rarely inspiring sparkling wine.

In the Central Rhône, in the *départements* of the Drôme and the Ardèche, there is the 70ha appellation of Châtillon-en-Diois which produces red, rosé and white wine. Only 100-150hl of white wine are made each year,

Central Rhône Wines

Grapes	As for northern Rhône with the addition of Aligoté, Chardonnay, Muscat à Petit Grains, Picpoul Blanc, Ugni Blanc (white) and Gamay and Picpoul Noir (red).
Soil	Chalk and clay with "pudding stone" pebbles in some vineyards.
Appellations	Côtes du Rhône (AOC, as for Northern Rhône). Châtillon-en-Diois (AOC 1975, mainly red and rosé, only 30 per cent of production, 850hl, is for white). Clairette de Die (AOC 1971, 57,900hl of still and sparkling white). Clairette de Die Tradition/Méthode Dioise (AOC as above, sparkling white that must be made from at least 50 per cent Muscat). Coteaux du Tricastin (AOC 1973, 86,000hl of mainly red, some white, 880hl, and rosé).
VDQS wine	Côtes du Vivarais (VDQS 1962, 35,000hl of red, rosé and a tiny amount, 1,200hl, of white).
Recommended producers	Mme Bour, Domaine de Grangeneuve; Cave Coopérative "La Suzienne", Suze la Rousse; Michel Gallety, Domaine "La Montagne"; SCV de Saint Remèze-Gras, Bourg-Saint-Andeol; Domaine Gallety, Viviers; M. Francis Dupré, Domaine du Vigier.

*U*narguably the best-known rosé in France, and with a heritage which stretches back into the middle ages, Tavel Rosé is, according to its proponents, one of the few pink wines in the world which improves with age. Perhaps it is a question of personal taste, but to my mind, the attractively spicy-peppery style of good young Tavel only develops into a flatter, flabbier, less spicy and less peppery style after an extra few years in bottle.

Lirac always seems to stand in Tavel's shadow as "the other Rhône rosé", which is a pity, considering firstly that Roquemaure in the heart of this appellation was an important wine market for the southern Rhône as early as the middle of the 18th century (although today pink and white account for only around 10 per cent of the wine made in this appellation), and secondly that good Lirac rosé easily outclasses some of the "commercial" Tavel on the market.

In one sense, however, Lirac rosé does deserve its secondary status: it was only because of the determination, on their repatriation from Algeria, of the Pons-Mure family to promote the pink wine they made at their Domaine de Castel-Oualou that the style ever began to catch on at all.

Above: *Grenache grapes being loaded into a trailer near Tavel in the Rhône. Tavel is the one rosé reputed to improve with age. The wine derives a distinctive spicy style from the constituent grapes.*

Only a quarter of the appellation's potential 3,500ha is planted with vines and white Lirac represents only 3-4 per cent of the total production and is rarely found outside France. It is made from the Clairette, Bourboulenc, Picpoul, Calitor, Maccabeu and Ugni Blanc and when drunk young, this can be one of the most attractively aromatic light wines of the region.

Only half of the 10,000ha of potential vineyard of Côtes du Ventoux are planted, and of the 200,000hl produced, rosé and white respectively represent a tiny and an even tinier proportion. Both are worth looking for in the region as they can be lighter and more directly fruity than many other Rhônes of either style. Much the same could be said of Coteaux du Tricastin, an expanding young (1973) appellation, 95 per cent of whose wine is red. The white, almost all of which is drunk locally, can be soft and quite floral in style while the rosé is one of the lightest and most delicate of the region.

Gigondas is one of those wines which serves to prove the flexibility of the *Appellation Contrôlée* system. Until 1971, this was just another Côtes du Rhône Village, albeit one which had a reputation for making some of the region's better wine; now, however, it has an appellation all to itself and can claim prices far higher than those paid for wines from less exalted neighbouring villages. White wine produced here is sold as Côtes du Rhône, and rosé forms only a small part of the annual production. Often quite full-bodied for pink wine – a red wine drinker's rosé – Gigondas rosé can be one of the Rhône's most attractively fruity and peppery wines, provided it is drunk young.

Above: *A Bourboulenc vine growing in the sun-baked soil near Tavel. The warm climate here produces very ripe grapes.*

Of the other Côtes du Rhône-Villages, Rasteau and Beaumes de Venise demand special mention for their *vins doux naturels,* made from grapes harvested late in September with a potential alcohol of at least 15°. The juice is fermented cool to maintain the maximum grapiness, and fermentation is stopped with the addition of a little pure alcohol so as to produce a very sweet wine with the alcoholic strength of vermouth. Beaumes de Venise was producing this kind of sweet Muscat in the middle ages, but the style almost died out following the onslaught of phylloxera in the late 19th and early 20th Centuries. Only the efforts of the co-operative, whose square screw-top bottles have taken the world by storm, prevented Muscat de Beaumes de Venise from joining the ranks of the vinous dodos. A pleasant grapey dessert wine, when served properly young and cold, Muscat de Beaumes de Venise is, if the most successful, not actually one of the most interesting of France's *vins doux naturels.* Rasteau, though launched to compete with Muscat de Beaumes de Venise, differs in being made from Grenache Noir, Gris or Blanc, Cairanne and Sablet, in both red and white, sometimes with oak ageing. Very rare, this is still an interesting variation on the sweet theme and one worth tasting if you ever have the chance.

Under the appellations Côtes du Rhône and Côtes du Rhône-Villages – which latter encompasses wines from the best 17 communes – white and rosé are still a minority interest. Even so, examples of Côtes du Rhône which are not over-alcoholic and/or short of acidity (both frequent faults) can be pleasant, provided they are drunk young. White and rosé Côtes du Rhône-Villages can be more than a cut above plain Côtes du Rhône but no easier to find. Ones to look for are Côtes du Rhône-Cairanne for its white; Côtes du Rhône-Chusclan for a truly outstanding rosé which outclasses many a Tavel and Lirac; Côtes du Rhône-Laudun for big, Châteauneuf-style whites and good rosé; and Côtes du Rhône-St-Gervais for its rosé.

Southern Côtes du Rhône Wines

Grapes	(White) Bourboulenc, Ugni Blanc, Clairette, Roussanne, Picpoul, Viognier, Pascal Blanc, Grenache Blanc, Marsanne, Muscat, Maccabeu. (Red) Grenache Noir, Mourvèdre, Cinsault, Pinot Noir, Picpoul Noir, Aubun, Counoise, Carignan, Calitor.
Soil	The valley is much wider here and the soil is made up of alluvial deposits overlaid with pebbles or stone. Some areas are sandy; other limestone.
Appellations	Châteauneuf-du-Pape (AOC 1936, mainly red, only 4,700hl of white). Gigondas (AOC 1971, mainly red, and a small proportion of rosé). Lirac (AOC 1947, 19,500hl of red and rosé, 830hl of white). Tavel (AOC 1936, 37,500hl of earthy, fairly heavy rosé). Côtes du Ventoux (AOC 1973, 254,200hl of red including a little rosé, and 2,800hl of white). Côtes du Rhône-Villages (AOC 1937, 217,000hl of red and rosé, and 4,100hl of white from 17 communes).
Recommended producers	(Châteauneuf-du-Pape) Domaine de Nalys; Domaine de Mont-Redon; Domaine de la Serrière; Domaine du Père Caboche; Domaine Trintignan; La Terre Ferme; Domaine de la Solitude; Domaine de Cabrières. (Beaumes de Venise) Domaine du Cayron, Gigondas; Pierre Amadieu, Gigondas; La Cave des Vignerons; Domaine Les Goubert. (Lirac) Marie Pons-Mure, Domaine Castel-Oualou; Antoine Verda et Fils; Château Saint-Roch. (Côtes du Ventoux) Cave Gely et Fils, Domaine de Champ-Long; Jean-Pierre Perrin, La Vieille Ferme. (Côtes du Rhône-Villages) Coopératives de Rochegude and Cairanne; Domaine Bouchard (Valréas); Cave Coopérative des Coteaux (Visan); Les Vigneronnes de Chusclan and Laudun; Domaine Ste-Anne (St-Gervais).

Winemaking in Provence has a very long history, dating back to the time of the Greeks in about 600 BC and subsequent Roman occupiers, and, thanks to the arrival of the English in the 13th and 14th centuries, there is a long history of wine trading too. More recently, the development of the Côte d'Azur as a tourist resort has led to a boom in sales of dry rosé, the style with which Provence is now inextricably linked. This is a pity really, because, although some of those pink wines can be unbeatable summer drinks, the region has many more interesting wines to offer.

Half of the wine bearing Côtes de Provence labels is made by the region's 57 co-operatives, and over two thirds of the 10 million bottles produced each year are pink. They vary from the most basic rosé, produced largely from the Carignan, to truly delicious wine made from the peppery Grenache, spicy Syrah and blackcurranty Cabernet Sauvignon. And even if precisely the same grapes were used, the variations of climate would preclude a truly consistent style. Thankfully, the Carignan content is being reduced. White wine represents less than 10 per cent of the crop and its quality depends on growers picking early enough to retain some freshness in the potentially dull Clairette and Ugni Blanc.

To discover exactly what Provence rosé, and indeed rich, Sémillon-based white, can be like, lash out on a couple of bottles from Domaine Ott. Despite the list of 21 "Grands Crus" claimed by the growers of Provence, the Ott wines are the nearest to real greatness the appellation affords. However, they are heavily overpriced.

For a more affordable bottle, it is worth going to Cassis. This is such a pretty little pleasure port that there seems little need for anyone to go to the trouble of making wine; tourism ought to pay most of the bills. But vinegrowing has a long tradition here, and the locals like to say that the region has a staircase to heaven built by God so as to facilitate deliveries of His favourite wine. Picked early, the Ugni Blanc (forming a maximum of 50 per cent of the blend), Sauvignon and local varieties can produce attractively full-flavoured, fresh, floral wine. The rosé by contrast, which some producers persist in ageing in wood, can be heavy and dull.

Nearby, Palette once had a reputation for its *vin cuit*, a sweet wine traditionally drunk in Marseilles as a Christmas treat. Sadly, that style is only to be found in history books; today, the commune's two producers concentrate on dry red, white and rosé. Or to be more precise, *one* of the producers does,

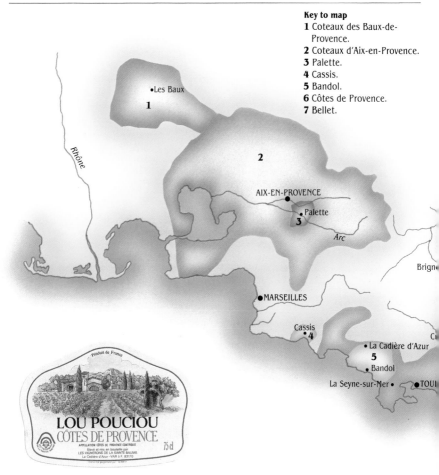

Key to map
1 Coteaux des Baux-de-Provence.
2 Coteaux d'Aix-en-Provence.
3 Palette.
4 Cassis.
5 Bandol.
6 Côtes de Provence.
7 Bellet.

•Les Baux
1

Rhône

2

AIX-EN-PROVENCE
•Palette
3
Arc

Brign

•MARSEILLES

Cassis
•4
• La Cadière d'Azur
5
• Bandol
La Seyne-sur-Mer •   •TOU

Produit de France

LOU POUCIOU
CÔTES DE PROVENCE
APPELLATION CÔTES DE PROVENCE CONTRÔLÉE
75 cl
Élevé et mis en bouteille par
LES VIGNERONS DE LA SAINTE BAUME
La Cadière d'Azur - VAR à F. 83170

because Château Simone makes all of the rosé and white Palette. The white – principally made from Clairette (80 per cent), Ugni Blanc, Sémillon and Muscat, aged for a year in barrel – is good, but it is the rosé, made from Grenache, Cinsault and Mourvèdre, which has given the property its reputation. Despite a sojourn of up to two years in cask, this is a beautifully refreshing wine, smelling of boiled sweets and all kinds of ripe fruit.

In the 11th century, the wines of Bandol were known as Vins de la Cadière after the nearby commune, but, following the example of Bordeaux and Oporto, the producers soon saw the advantage of naming a wine after the port from which it was shipped.

Above: *Neatly tended vineyards in the Côtes de Provence. This is a region where careful vineyard-tending and winemaking are paying dividends.*

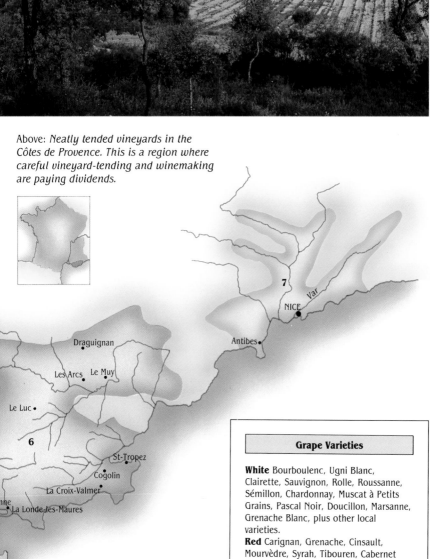

Grape Varieties

White Bourboulenc, Ugni Blanc, Clairette, Sauvignon, Rolle, Roussanne, Sémillon, Chardonnay, Muscat à Petits Grains, Pascal Noir, Doucillon, Marsanne, Grenache Blanc, plus other local varieties.
Red Carignan, Grenache, Cinsault, Mourvèdre, Syrah, Tibouren, Cabernet Sauvignon, Folle Noire, Braquet, Barbaroux.

The principal must have worked, because in the 19th century over 60,000 barrels left Bandol's quays, every one bearing a "B" brand to identify its provenance. Bandol enjoys the best climate of the whole Côte d'Azur, with 3,000 hours of sunshine a year. The winegrowers here like to say that they have never had a bad vintage, only the occasional smaller one. There are some 280 growers, of whom around 250 are members of the co-operative; rosé forms 35 per cent of their crop. Unlike some southern appellations, the amount of Bandol produced is increasing: from 260,000 bottles before the war to nearly 4 million today, with even further expansion in prospect.

The late-maturing Mourvèdre (50 per cent of the blend), which was reintroduced to the region with the arrival of *Appellation Contrôlée* legislation, likes the climate here where the weather is kind enough to allow harvesting in October. With a little help from the Grenache, Syrah, Carignan and the local Tibouren and Calitor, and despite eight months' obligatory barrel ageing, it produces unusually tangy, spicy wine. The white, which is mostly made from the Clairette (60 per cent), Sauvignon, Ugni Blanc and Bourboulenc, is pleasant, provided that it is drunk very young. Since 1985, neither "B"-branded barrels nor any kind of bulk shipment has left Bandol; to guarantee authenticity, the regulations decree that all the commune's wine has to be bottled on the spot.

In contrast to Bandol, Bellet is a tiny appellation (50ha out of a possible 700) which has been at risk of growing even smaller. Situated close to Nice, where most of its wine is sold at outrageously high prices, this commune took such little care of the quality of its wines that, in 1947, it actually had its

Above: *The vineyards of the Côtes de Provence, source of spicy rosé, possibly made even spicier by the presence of herbs growing close to the vines.*

appellation rescinded. It was only thanks to the efforts of a producer called Jean Bagnis that Bellet was allowed to rejoin the ranks of AOC. Whether these rosé and white wines represent value-for-money is very questionable, but the steeply sloping vineyards and hill-protected, sea-cooled microclimate do seem to allow the two dozen producers to produce crisper wines than many in this region. Besides, the white provides a rare chance to taste wine made from the unusual Rolle, Roussanne, Mayorquin and Pignerol grapes, while the rosé owes its character to the Braquet and the Folle Noire.

Two wines unjustly denied AOC when that status was accorded in 1977 to the far less

Provence Wines

Grapes	(See listing on pages 136/7).
Soil	Mainly schistous with mineral deposits along the coast, the rest of the area is chalky or clay-chalk.
Appellation	Bandol (AOC 1941, 33,000hl of red and rosé, and 1,500hl of white). Bellet (AOC 1941, 700hl of red and rosé, and 375hl of white). Cassis (AOC 1936, 1,900hl of red and rosé, 4,500hl of dry white). Coteaux d'Aix-en-Provence (AOC 1985, 105,000hl of red, white and rosé). Coteaux des Baux-de-Provence (AOC 1985, red, white and rosé). Côtes de Provence (AOC 1977, 643,000hl red and dry, fruity rosé, 44,000hl of white). Palette (AOC 1948, 560hl of red, white and rosé).
VDQS wines	Coteaux de Pierrevert (VDQS 1959, 10,000hl of mainly rosé, some white and red). Coteaux Varois (VDQS 1985, 48,400hl of mainly red, minimal amount of white and rosé).
Recommended producers	(Bandol) Château Ste-Anne; Moulin des Costes. (Bellet) Château de Bellet; Château de Crémat. (Cassis) La Ferme Blanche; Château de Beaupré. (Coteaux d'Aix-en-Provence) Domaine les Bastides. (Coteaux des Baux) Domaine des Terres Blanches. (Côtes de Provence) Domaine de Bertaud. (Palette) Château Simone. (Coteaux de Pierrevert) Domaine de la Blaque.

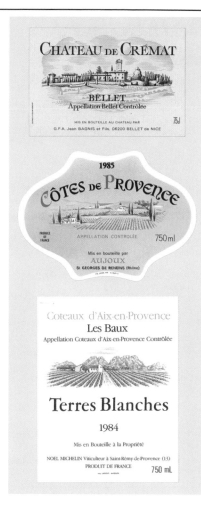

worthy Côtes de Provence, Coteaux d'Aix-en-Provence and Coteaux des Baux-de-Provence, have since received their due recognition. The former wine, takes its name from "Aquae Sextiae", the (hot spa) waters of Sextius, the Roman consul who was here in 122 BC. The rosé can be made from Cabernet Sauvignon (up to 60 per cent), Cinsault, Mourvèdre, Grenache, Syrah, Carignan, Counoise, and up to 20 per cent white grapes. The white wine (10 per cent of the crop) owes its character to the fact that 60 per cent of every bottle has to consist of the local Bourboulenc and/or Clairette, with the remainder being made up by Ugni Blanc, Sémillon, Sauvignon and Grenache Blanc. The wines produced around the mediaeval ruined village of Baux-de-Provence are similar in style, but the use of Grenache is greater here.

The Côtes du Luberon, a former VDQS which has recently turned AOC, is on the fringe of the Rhône both in its geographic location to the south of the Vaucluse, and in the style of its wines which owe their character to a harsh microclimate. Although the co-operative produces reliable wine, the one estate which has undoubtedly done more to improve the image of the region as a whole is Jean-Louis Chancel's Château Val Joanis which makes a lovely spicy, dry rosé and an improving Chardonnay-influenced white.

Less inspiring, but possibly with similar potential, the nearby Coteaux de Pierrevert uses all of the local varieties, and a few more surprising ones, to make rosé and white, almost all of which is sold by the co-operative. Burgundian merchants apparently come here to buy wine made from the Pinot Noir, Gamay, Chardonnay and Aligoté. What use they make of their purchases is anyone's guess.

Below: *Modern pressing equipment in operation at the Domaine de Jarras, one of the properties which belongs to the massive Listel wine company.*

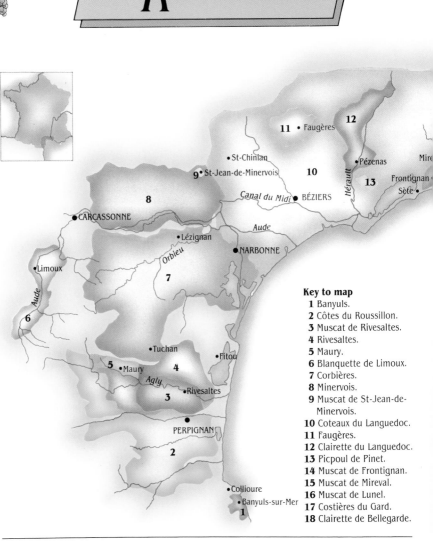

Key to map
1 Banyuls.
2 Côtes du Roussillon.
3 Muscat de Rivesaltes.
4 Rivesaltes.
5 Maury.
6 Blanquette de Limoux.
7 Corbières.
8 Minervois.
9 Muscat de St-Jean-de-Minervois.
10 Coteaux du Languedoc.
11 Faugères.
12 Clairette du Languedoc.
13 Picpoul de Pinet.
14 Muscat de Frontignan.
15 Muscat de Mireval.
16 Muscat de Lunel.
17 Costières du Gard.
18 Clairette de Bellegarde.

*I*f there is one theme which seems to link the diversity of wines produced in the Languedoc-Roussillon, it is the question of the grape varieties which should or should not be grown. Traditionally a large proportion of the red, and thus the rosé, was made from the dull but productive Carignan, while the Mauzac and Ugni Blanc conspired to make some similarly uninspired whites. But that is all changing, and with the changes there are being developed wines which have more truly regional character than ever was the case before.

Before considering these, it is perhaps worth looking at the one style which has remained largely unaltered. The success of Muscat de Beaumes de Venise from the Rhône has unquestionably helped to promote the four Muscat wines of Languedoc-Roussillon. These vary in style, both because of the climate and soil in which they are grown, and in the variety of Muscat they use. The Muscat de Frontignan, which has given its name to the finer Muscat à Petits Grains is, as one would expect, made 100 per cent from that variety. Ninety per cent of the total production comes from the co-operative,

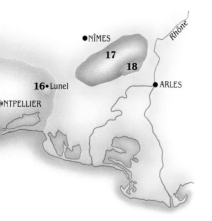

Below: *Vines budding in the Spring, near Calvisson in the Languedoc.*

but all the wine is tested every year by an independent jury, ensuring regular quality. Muscat de Miréval, promoted as a favourite wine of Rabelais' fictional hero Pantagruel, is also 100 per cent Petits Grains, but it is made in a slightly different way from Muscat de Frontignan. The modern co-operative which produces virtually all of the wine picks late for maximum sugar content, and then leaves the wine to mature at the outside temperature for two years before bottling. The resulting wine is bigger and richer in style.

St-Jean-de-Minervois produces a mere 200,000 bottles from extensive vineyards because of their poor soil, while Muscat de Lunel produces about a million bottles, 95 per cent of which come from the co-operative and are sold in distinctively shaped bottles. All of the wine benefits from three years' ageing and, to some people, is the best in France. Competing for that honour however is Rivesaltes, a *vin doux naturel* which perversely uses a wide range of grapes, including Grenache Blanc and/or Gris and Maccabeu to make Rivesaltes Doré, or Blanc. Both kinds of Muscat are used here to make some gloriously grapey wine but, on balance,

I find the most exciting Rivesaltes to be the pure Maccabeu.

More famous than the Muscats, Blanquette de Limoux is at once one of France's most traditional wines and one of the most successful alternatives to Champagne. But traditions change and while, until recently, this *Méthode Champenoise* used to include Clairette, that variety was banned in 1978; now the mixture is Mauzac with up to 30 per cent Chenin Blanc and Chardonnay. The co-operative which was founded in 1946 shares the production of 6 million bottles of Blanquette with a dozen other domaines. Different cuvées contain differing proportions of the three grape varieties used. Some samples of this wine can seem prematurely tired, but at their best they can have an appley freshness which allows them to do well in blind competition against Blanc de Blancs Champagne. Less worth buying, however, is Limoux Nature, a dry, still white wine which, like Coteaux Champenois in Champagne, explains the existence of the fizz. The Vin de Blanquette, a sparkling pure Mauzac, is dull.

Anyone interested to know what the Clairette which used to go into Blanquette de

Above: *Vineyards are overlooked by cliffs at the worryingly named La Clape, the biggest appellation in the Languedoc.*

Limoux tasted like should seek out Clairette du Languedoc. This pure Clairette, nearly all made by the region's co-operatives, is a long established white oasis in a desert of red. Most of the wine used to be used for vermouth; now there are some good, dry to semi-sweet wines and *vins doux naturels*, but better winemaking can improve them further, as has been proved by domaines such as Château de la Condamine-Bertrand. Duller Clairette can be found in the form of Clairette de Bellegarde, but some examples bottled *sur lie* keep their freshness more successfully.

Picpoul, another grape of little prestige, known in the Loire as the Gros Plant, and more generally used here to make vermouth, gives its name and flavour to Picpoul de Pinet. This delicate, grassy wine is a great deal more successful than most of the Loire examples, provided that it is drunk young.

The name Minervois – or rather of Minerve, its capital – is derived from "Men Erba", the woody rock, and the description suits it well; this is one of the most savagely bleak wine-growing corners of France. Despite being thought of as an exclusively red appellation, the mean soil and windy vineyards here produce good rosé, from the Carignan and Monastel, and white from the Marsanne and Maccabeu. The quality of the rosé will improve as the proportion of Carignan is reduced. Much the same could be said of St-Chinian, a big alcoholic rosé which, in the 19th century, was given to patients in Paris hospitals, presumably to "build them up". Grenache, Mourvèdre and Syrah are gradually supplanting the Carignan.

Pure Carignan rosé is still (unfortunately) being made in Corbières, a recent promotion to the ranks of the *Appellation Contrôlée*, but of the 80 million bottles of Corbières made, only 3 million are pink, so the style is clearly a sideline here. As for Corbières Blanc, this Grenache Blanc – Malvasia – Maccabeu – Clairette blend represents a mere 1 per cent of the total production. Conditions vary as much as the blends, and choosing good Corbières will be easier if and when a Corbières-Villages appellation is created. Corbières Supérieur is simply a little more alcoholic than Corbières.

The wine of the biggest appellation in the Languedoc, La Clape, is produced on what

was in the middle ages an island linked to the mainland. Vinegrowing is no accident here; the meagre soil permits no other form of agriculture. Whites are made from Malvasia and Terret Blanc and can be grapily attractive. The rosé is less interesting.

For really good rosé, and some first class, pure Sémillon whites, one has to go to Costières du Gard, an appellation which also makes a traditional Clairette de Die-style fizz from Clairette and Muscat, and the Rasiguères co-operative in Côtes du Roussillon, where a Carignan-Grenache-Maccabeu-Cinsault blend, shows what the Carignan can achieve when grown in the right conditions, and when really well handled. In the same appellation, the Taichat co-operative does similarly well with a Maccabeu-Malvasia white. Faugères, by contrast, makes a very little rosé or white; little in quantity, little in quality.

As elsewhere, the vineyards of the Coteaux du Languedoc offer a ragbag of grape varieties, of which the Merlot is currently in the ascendency, coupled with a gaggle of indigenous varieties, including the Lladoner Pelut Noir. New laws are tidying the situation up and rosés should be spicier and more flavoursome than some of the dullish examples of the past.

Cabrières was known for its "bronze" rosé in the 14th century. Today 45 per cent of the blend is supposed to be made of Oeillade, though this condition is not always respected. Pic-St-Loup used to be made of pure Carignan, but that variety now represents less than 50 per cent of the blend. The white here is not bad either. Both wines are similar to those of Quatourze, though the latter tend to be a little fuller in style. St-Drézery, smallest commune in the region, producing 260,000 bottles, has long been famous for its rosé, a wine which ferments for only 24 hours. St-Saturnin has a good, dynamic co-operative and makes decent rosé; as can Coteaux de la Mejanelle.

St-Christol, well liked by the Tsar Nicholas II of Russia, makes reasonable rosé, but not as good as Coteaux de Verargues, a commune near Lunel. Finally, there is Malepère's Merlot-dominated rosé and Côtes de Cabardès et de l'Orbiel near Carcassonne, where the proportion of Carignan has been reduced to a third of the blend.

Languedoc-Roussillon Wines

Grapes	(See separate listing on pages 140/1).
Soil	A lot of schist, with clay and gravel deposits.
Appellations	(Roussillon) Côtes de Roussillon (AOC 1977, 305,000hl of red and rosé, 10,400hl of white). Rivesaltes (AOC 1972, 295,000hl of white and rosé vin doux naturel). (Languedoc) Clairette de Languedoc (AOC 1965, 9,300hl of sweet white). Faugères (AOC 1982, 54,500hl of mainly red, a little white and rosé). Muscat de Frontignan (AOC 1936, 22,100hl of sweet, white vdn). Muscat de Lunel (AOC 1943, 7,900hl of earthy, sweet white vdn). Muscat de Miréval (AOC 1959, 6,500hl of sweet, golden vdn). Muscat de St-Jean-de-Minervois (AOC 1972, 2,700hl of sweet white vdn). (Aude and Gard) Blanquette de Limoux (AOC 1981, 45,400hl of soft, fruity white made Méthode Champenoise). Vin de Blanquette Méthode Rurale (AOC 1981, 1,500hl of sparkling white). Limoux (AOC 1981, 50hl of still white). Corbières (AOC 1985, 635,600hl of red and rosé, 26,000hl of white). Minervois (AOC 1985, 252,600hl of red and rosé, 6,300hl of white). Vin Noble du Minervois (AOC 1985, a small amount of sweet white dessert wine). Clairette de Bellegarde (AOC 1949, 3,000hl of dry white).
VDQS wines	Coteaux du Languedoc (1980); Coteaux du Languedoc-Villages which incorporates the following: La Clape (1951), Quatourze (1951), St Georges d'Orques (1951), Cabrières (1980), Coteaux de la Mejanelle (1980), Montpeyroux (1980), St-Saturnin (1980), Pic-St-Loup (1980), Coteaux de Verargues (1980); Picpoul de Pinet (1954); Cabardès (1973); Côtes de la Malepère; Costières du Gard (1951).
Recommended producers	(Côtes de Roussillon) Vignerons Catalan. (Rivesaltes vdn) Domaine Sarda-Malet. (Clairette de Languedoc) Château de la Condamine-Bertrand. (Faugères) Domaine Gilbert Alquier. (Muscat de Frontignan) Coopérative de Frontignan; Château de la Peyrade. (Muscat de Lunel) Cave Coopérative et Domaine de Belle Côte. (Muscat de St-Jean-de-Minervois) Cave Camman. (Blanquette de Limoux) Coopérative de Sieur d'Arques. (Corbières) Château de Caraguilhes. (Minervois) Château de Paraza. (Cabardès) Domaine de Rayssac. (Clairette de Bellegarde) Domaine de St-Louis-la-Perdrix. (Costières du Gard) Domaine de Mas Carlot.

THE SOUTH-WEST

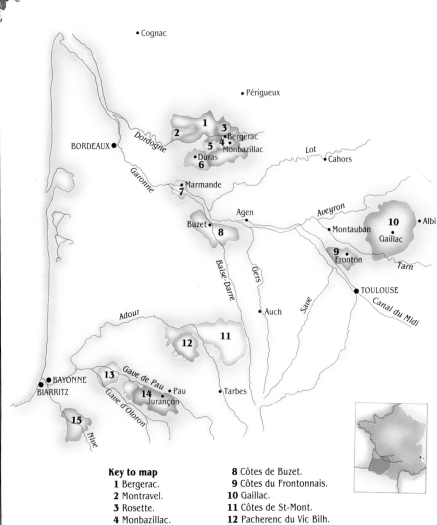

• Cognac

• Périgueux

BORDEAUX •

Dordogne

Garonne

1

2

3
• Bergerac

5 4
• Monbazillac

• Duras
6

• Marmande
7

Lot

• Cahors

Agen

Buzet •
8

Aveyron

• Montauban

10
• Gaillac

• Albi

9
• Fronton

Tarn

Baïse-Darré

Gers

Save

• Auch

TOULOUSE

Canal du Midi

Adour

12

11

• BAYONNE
BIARRITZ

13

Gave de Pau

14
Jurançon

• Pau

• Tarbes

Gave d'Oloron

15

Nive

Key to map
1 Bergerac.
2 Montravel.
3 Rosette.
4 Monbazillac.
5 Côtes de Saussignac.
6 Côtes de Duras.
7 Côtes du Marmandais.
8 Côtes de Buzet.
9 Côtes du Frontonnais.
10 Gaillac.
11 Côtes de St-Mont.
12 Pacherenc du Vic Bilh.
13 Béarn.
14 Jurançon.
15 Irouléguy

S outh-west France is an explorer's paradise. Small towns and hidden villages are still making wines in the same way (and with the same gloriously obscure grape varieties) as they were five or more centuries ago. And, at the same time, alongside these traditional concerns, you will find some of the most go-ahead co-operatives in France. In short, this is the place for anyone who likes to see what happens when past and future meet.

Being thought of as "poor man's Bordeaux" has never really pleased the winegrowers of Bergerac, but this lovely, calm, hilly country has feuded with the Bordelais since even before the English king Edward III prohibited the passage of wine, fruit, men, women and children – in other words, *anything* – across the river to Bordeaux. But the people of Bergerac survived. After all, they had their fruit (one French strawberry in six is grown here), tobacco (where else would you find a tobacco museum?) and *foie gras*. Des-

pite the Bordeaux requirement that Bergerac use smaller barrels for their wine (tax was paid *per cask* in the 17th century), two thirds of the region's wine was still successfully sold to Holland.

Following the last war, however, Bergerac's sweet white wines fell out of favour, and the dry wine which was made to replace it remains of inferior quality. Sadly, over a third of the wine is made by less than dynamic co-operatives, and over half is then sold to, and by, Bordeaux *négociants* who have done little to improve quality.

It says a great deal that my request for the best Bergerac from the wine list of that town's finest restaurant elicited a wine made by an Englishman, Nick Ryman, with expertise picked up by his son in Australia. Ryman's Château La Jaubertie shows what can be done here, with the Sémillon, the Sauvignon and even, as an experiment, with the Muscadelle, both as varietal wines and as a blend. These are wines that they fear as competition in the Graves, but there are few other Bergeracs over which the Bordelais lose sleep. Dry white Bergerac now represents 10 million bottles against some 250,000 of rarely inspiring rosé, nearly all of which is made by the co-operatives. Côtes de Bergerac rosé is rather better, since it has to

Below: *Compressing grapes for white Bergerac to be made by a co-operative. This traditional procedure can lead to the grapes oxidizing in the vineyard.*

be made from Merlot and Cabernet, but Côtes de Bergerac Moelleux, a usually honeyed but flabby style whose production has halved in recent years, accounts for just 5 million bottles.

Other sweet and semi-sweet wines made within the confines of Bergerac, but carrying their own appellations, are the tiny (26,000 bottles) Rosette; Saussignac (once called Bergerac-Côtes de Saussignac), a slightly less sweet version of Monbazillac; Montravel; Côtes de Montravel and Haut Montravel.

These *semi-sec* styles are rarely worth much attention, and for really sweet wine made at Bergerac one has to look to Monbazillac. The name alludes to a "mountain of gold", and this could, and should, be one of France's truly great sweet wines.

In the 18th and 19th centuries, Monbazillac became the almost exclusive preserve of the Dutch, hence labels which read "Marque Hollandaise", but, following the attack of phylloxera at the turn of the century, the quality of the wine deteriorated. Sweet wine was out of fashion and the growers cut corners in order to compete with the cheapest wines on the market. Too much wine was produced per acre, permitted yields are still twice those allowed for Sauternes – and too little care was taken over planting the right grape varieties and picking carefully.

Above: *The beautiful Château de Monbazillac, once almost exclusively the preserve of the Dutch, and still the source of some of the best sweet wine in France. It is essential to choose wines from the best vintages.*

Today, there are a few good estates; the co-operative which sells a third of the wine and owns the beautiful Château de Monbazillac can also make fine wine in good vintages, but this remains an under-exploited asset.

Like Bergerac, Côtes de Duras is often thought of as "alternative Bordeaux" and its 10 million bottles of dry white certainly have little difficulty in competing with most basic Bordeaux Blanc. This is a region which derives much of its income from fruit growing and tourism, and which seemed for a while to have given up trying to make quality wine. It was only in the 1960s that hybrid vines were torn up and the run-down appellation put to rights. The best whites are very influenced by the Sauvignon; the best rosé (of which there is little made) by both Cabernets.

A far more traditional appellation, Gaillac (the name means either "fertile place" or "Gallois") also went through a period of decline, despite its very distinguished history. Plague, war and finally phylloxera all

took their toll and this century it looked as though the old market town had relinquished its place in the wine industry. Fortunately, a new spirit of quality consciousness was born in the 1970s with the development of the co-operatives which now sell over two thirds of Gaillac production. Almost every style of wine is made, using a bizarre set of indigenous grapes including the wonderfully named, freshly tangy, "Len de l'El" (Loin de l'Oeil or "far from the eye"), but the best tend to be the dry *perlé,* whose slight bubbles serve to counteract the potential flatness of the Mauzac, the semi sweet *Méthode Rurale* fizz (made in the same way as Clairette de Die), and two sweet, low alcohol wines, a 6° and the Pétillant de Raisin which has only 3°.

Of the other appellations in the South-West, the Côtes de Buzet co-operatives which handles 95 per cent of the crop, produces only 40,000 bottles of white, made from the Sémillon, Sauvignon and Muscadelle, and less than 260,000 bottles of rosé, made from the Merlot, both Cabernets and Malbec. Côtes de Marmandais, a region known for fruit, has two co-operatives which sell over 95 per cent of the wine. One of the two, the Cave de Cocumont, is experimenting with new grape varieties which may help to improve quality. At present, however, very little rosé and white wine is made.

At Lavilledieu, the situation is even clearer: no rosé and virtually no white are made, but this is a tiny appellation (five hectares) which is busily planning to expand. If, and when, rosé is made, it will be from the Negrette, Gamay, Syrah and Tannat. The white is made from the Mauzac and is likened to Gaillac. For a taste of what Lavilledieu's Negrette rosé might be like, look for a bottle of Côtes du Frontonnais. Pink wine accounts for only 5 per cent of a 25 million bottle-production, but the spicy Negrette makes up 50-70 per cent of the blend.

South-West Wines

Grapes	(See separate listing on pages 144/5. As the area is so large, the wines are extremely varied, and the grape varieties used come from all over France, principally from the Rhône, Loire, and Bordeaux.)
Appellations	Béarn (AOC 1975, 10,000hl of red and rosé, 375hl of white). Bergerac (AOC 1936, 236,600hl of red and rosé). Bergerac Sec (AOC 1936, 89,000hl of dry, fruity white). Côtes de Bergerac Moelleux (AOC 1936, 38,000hl of sweet white). Côtes de Bergerac/ Côtes de Saussignac (AOC 1936, 2,250hl of dry-sweet white). Côtes de Buzet (AOC 1973, 75,000hl of red and rosé, 1,100hl of white). Côtes de Duras (AOC 1937, 43,000hl of red and rosé and 33,200hl of white). Côtes de Montravel-Haut Montravel (AOC 1937, a small appellation producing 6,000hl of sweet liqueur white wine). Montravel (AOC 1937, 30,400hl of dry – sweet white). Côtes du Frontonnais (AOC 1975, 79,000hl of mainly red, only 5 per cent of this is rosé). Gaillac (AOC 1979, 54,000hl of red and rosé, and 39,500hl of white). Gaillac Mousseux (AOC 1979, sparkling wine made by the méthode "Gaillacoise"). Gaillac Perlé (AOC 1979, light dry *pétillant* white). Gaillac Premières Côtes (AOC 1979, a small appellation producing dry/semi-sweet white). Le Pétillant du Raisin (52,500hl of red, white and rosé, slightly sparkling). Irouléguy (AOC 1970, 3,900hl of lively full-flavoured rosé). Jurançon (AOC 1975, sweet perfumed white). Jurançon Sec (AOC 1975, dry white, in all Jurançon produces 31,000hl of white wine per year). Monbazillac (AOC 1936, 57,000hl of sweet white). Pacherenc du Vic-Bihl (AOC 1975, 3,250hl of dry-sweet white). Rosette (AOC 1946, 1,350hl of medium dry to semi-sweet white).
Recommended producers	(Béarn) Coopérative at Salies-Bellocq; Clos Mirabel-Jurançon. (Bergerac) Château Panisseau; Château la Jaubertie. (Bergerac Sec) Pierre Alard et Fils; Domaine de la Vaure. (Côtes de Buzet) Coopérative Vinicole de Buzet-sur-Baïse. (Côtes de Duras) Château les Savignattes; Domaine Amblard; Domaine de Ferrant; Domaine des Cours; Domaine de Laulan. (Montravel) Château de Bloy; Domaine de Fontfrede. (Gaillac) Château Larroze; Domaine Jean Cros; Cave Coopérative Labastide de Lévis; Château Lastours. (Jurançon Sec) Mondinat et Fils; Château Jolys; Cru Lamouroux. (Monbazillac) Château Monbazillac; Château Paulvere; Château le Fage. (Pacherenc du Vic-Bihl) Domaine Bouscasse; Clos de L'Eglise.

There has always been a golden rule for wine bargain hunters: go for the unpronounceable names: no one else will, and prices will reflect the lack of commercial success! Pacherenc du Vic-Bihl ought to be just such a wine, possibly the ugliest-named wine in France, sounding more like a cider from Brittany than a wine. The derivation is apparently from "pichet-en-renc" (*piquets en rangs*) and refers to the fact that the vines here were trained in rows. Vic-Bihl, by the way, is the village. In real terms though, this is white wine from the Madiran region, made from the local Arrufiat (or Ruffiac), Gros Manseng and Petit Manseng grapes, on 25ha of land which might otherwise be producing Madiran. About half the wine comes from the co-operative which, like this appellation's other producers, offers both *sec* and *moelleux*. Of the two, the *sec* is the one to go for, particularly when, as in some domaines, it is bottled *sur lie*. If anything, this quirky wine could become quirkier in the future as the percentage of the Arrufiat is increased.

Subject to the same rules as Pacherenc, but more commercially successful at the moment, is Côtes de St-Mont. Thanks to the

highly modern Producteurs de Plaimont co-operative which produces two thirds of the wine, and also thanks to the co-operative's level of quality control, the white (25 per cent of the production) is reliably good and lemony-crisp. The rosé, of which there is very little made, is similarly reliable.

Henri IV's fondness for wine has been mentioned more than once in this book. However many endorsements he may have given during his lifetime, there is no question about the very first wine he ever tasted; it was his grandfather, Albert, King of Navarre, who gave him a mouthful of Jurançon, and rubbed his lips with garlic for good measure. Not surprisingly, the sweet white wine instantly became "le vin du roi" and babies throughout France found themselves being introduced to alcohol at rather an early age. Then everything went wrong. During this century, Jurançon went into what seemed to be a terminal decline during which quality fell to such an extent that sugar was even used in the sweet winemaking. The decline was halted only by the arrival of Henri Meyer who not only started the co-operative, but also invited the great Professor Peynaud to travel across from Bordeaux in order to tell the growers how to put things right.

The answer lay in giving people what they wanted, rather than what their parents had wanted; Meyer (and Peynaud) invented dry Jurançon, using the Gros Manseng rather than the Petit Manseng whose small berries give sweet Jurançon its concentrated flavour. Today, Jurançon is in far better health, thanks largely to the success of Jurançon Sec (50 per cent of the total production and 75 per cent of the wine from the co-operative). The *moelleux* has not faded away entirely, and fine, sweet Jurançon is developing a new following. Well-made sweet Jurançon can maintain its spicy flavour for as long as, or longer than, any sweet wine, thanks to a level of acidity twice as high as that of Sauternes. On the other hand, concentration of flavour is often less than that of Bordeaux since, like Monbazillac, Jurançon is allowed a far higher yield per acre. One final word of warning: normally, dry Jurançon will be labelled Jurançon Sec while the sweet will simply call itself Jurançon. Where a dry wine has a strength of over 12.5° (often the case for the best sites) its wine legally has to be labelled in the same way as sweet Jurançon. It is all rather confusing.

There are three other rareish wines of varying interest to consider from this part of France. The Irouléguy co-operative makes wine from grapes grown almost on the Spanish border. There is no white and the Cabernet-dominated rosé is mostly sold to hill-walking tourists, the local Basque population, and Basque expatriates in the USA.

Béarn, the birthplace of Sauce Béarnaise, however, should have some Rosé de Béarn to sell. This style, launched in 1948 in Paris by Henri Meyer, saviour of Jurançon, sold at thrice the price of the region's other wines. Quality fell when Meyer left the co-operative in the 70s, but it has since improved following his return. The old-style rosé is made of traditional local grapes; a newer, better blend contains more Cabernet and has a deeper colour.

An appellation which used to be 100 per cent white, but which now produces a quarter of a million bottles of (Tannat-dominated, and rather dull) rosé, Tursan is the place to come if you want to taste the spicy but short-lived white wines made principally from the local Baroque. Hurry though; vines are being uprooted to make way for other forms of agriculture.

Left: *The well-regimented vineyards of Tursan, one of the least-known appellations in France. Other kinds of farming are taking over here.*

CORSICA

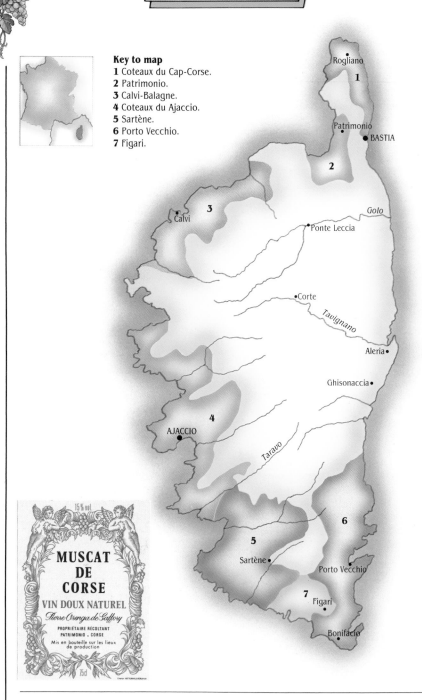

Key to map
1 Coteaux du Cap-Corse.
2 Patrimonio.
3 Calvi-Balagne.
4 Coteaux du Ajaccio.
5 Sartène.
6 Porto Vecchio.
7 Figari.

MUSCAT DE CORSE
VIN DOUX NATUREL
Pierre Orenga de Gaffory
PROPRIÉTAIRE RÉCOLTANT
PATRIMONIO . CORSE
Mis en bouteille sur les lieux de production

Quite apart from the range of its wines, France contains within its boundaries a unique spectrum of national characteristics, from the precise Nordic coolness of Champagne, to the fiery Latin blood of the south. In Alsace, the centuries of German occupation have created a semi-Germanic people who still speak in a Germanic dialect; in Corsica, the influence is Italian. The names of the over three dozen indigenous grape varieties all sound as though they should be spoken in the accent of the Piedmont, while the relaxed allocation of Appellation Contrôlée status (does this smallish island really warrant *eight* separate appellations?) has everything in common with the largesse with which the authorities in Rome have dished out their DOCs.

That Latin influence is not surprising, given the length of time Corsica spent as an Italian province, but more recent input came with the arrival of 17,000 French ex-colonials following the granting of independence to Algeria. The experience of making wine in North Africa, most of which was used to beef up French wine from cooler climes, proved unhelpful during the first years of their presence, as did the importation of the Carignan grape, a variety previously not used here.

Over the last decade or so, however, quality has improved greatly, thanks to the efforts of the co-operatives and of a number

150

Corsican Wines

Grapes	(White) Vermentino, Ugni Blanc and other local varieties. (Red) Nielluccio, Sciacarello, Grenache, and other local varieties.
Appellations	Vin de Corse-Patrimonio (AOC 1963, 3,750hl of white and 12,000hl of red and rosé). Vin de Corse-Ajaccio (AOC 1976, 7,500hl of red, white and rosé). Vin de Corse-Sartène (AOC 1976, 26,250hl of red, white and rosé). Vin de Corse-Calvi (AOC 1976, 45,000hl of red, white and rosé). Vin de Corse-Figari Pianottoli (AOC 1976, 15,000hl of red, white and rosé). Vin de Corse-Porto-Vecchio (AOC 1976, 15,000hl of red, white and rosé). Vin de Corse-Coteaux du Cap-Corse (AOC 1976, 450hl of red, white and rosé). Vin de Corse (AOC 1976, 135,000hl of red, white and rosé).
Recommended producers	M. de Bernardi (Patrimonio); Domaine Peraldi; Domaine de Torraccia; Clos Nicrosi.

Above: *The vineyards of the Domaine de Torraccia are found in a magnificent natural setting 10km to the north of Porto Vecchio. White wines from here are made from the local Malvoisie grape.*

of individual estates. Whites and rosés, fermented cooler and bottled earlier, have and maintain a freshness previously unfound in Corsica. Even so, many of these wines are still better suited for drinking young, and *sur place*.

Anyone wanting to taste the kind of wine the Greek settlers who imported the first vines here may have enjoyed should try Vin de Corse-Patrimonio which is probably as authentic as any. More interesting though is the grapey-spicy *vin doux naturel* made here from Muscat and Malvoisie.

Vermentino is used to make white Vin de Corse-Ajaccio, a pleasant, crisp enough wine which should, however, not be allowed to age, while Coteaux d'Ajaccio can produce attractively spicy rosé, using at least 30 per cent of the local Sciacarello.

Like Vin de Corse-Sartène, Vin de Corse-Calvi is an appellation covering wines which have enough fruit and flavour to be enjoyed by visitors but which seem to flatten out remarkably quickly once those visitors have carried them home and left them in a rack for a few months.

The rosés and whites of the Vin de Corse-Figari, on the other hand, though grown in the driest, most unpromising part of the island and, not surprisingly a little hefty in style, have a flavour which can last. Even so, my advice is "drink young".

Arguably, the best winemaking in Corsica is to be found at the Domaine de Torraccia in the Vin de Corse-Porto-Vecchio, where temperature-controlled vats effectively combat the natural tendency towards flabbiness, while similarly good, if softer, whites are made by the Clos Nicrosi in Vin de Corse-Coteaux du Cap-Corse.

The general Vin de Corse appellation is a blanket designation, covering 50 communes on the coast as well as inland. Styles, as elsewhere, can vary from the light, peppery and Provençal, to heavy, flabby and forgettable.

VINS DE PAYS

Until 1968, there were only three kinds of French wine: Appellation Contrôlée, VDQS and Vin de Table. This last category was very much a catch-all, covering as it did the litre bottles of caustic, anonymous stuff sold cheaply in supermarkets and the wine made from the newly planted vines at Château Latour. Somewhere between the two lay a wealth of characterful wine which, by rights, ought at least to be a VDQS.

In 1968, the situation was finally remedied, with the invention of three types of *vin de pays*. Suddenly there was a place in the hierarchy for country wines, and a better chance for some of those country wines to climb the ladder to VDQS and even, in time, fully-blown Appellation Contrôlée status. The system works well and certainly far better than any equivalent designation in any other country, specifying controlled levels of alcohol, acidity and sulphur dioxide, authorized grapes and, perhaps most important of all, officially organised tasting panels before which every would-be *vin de pays* must pass.

The success of the *vins de pays* designation is proven by the number of wines which have managed to achieve promotion to

Above: *Receiving grapes at the Listel winery at Villeroy. The Listel company, which produces excellent vins de pays, grows all its vines on sandbars in the Rhône delta and on the coast near the port of Sète.*

VDQS. But it would be wrong to take too rosy a view. On the one hand, although there is a list of permitted grape varieties for each *vin de pays*, some of these lists run to 20, 30 and even 60 varieties. Given that selection, how can any wine be expected to display a truly regional characteristic?

The numbers can work against consistency of quality too. The Vin de Pays du Jardin de la France is potentially a reliable source of Sauvignon (though Chenin, Chardonnay and company are allowed too) but its wine can come from any one of 11 *départements* and now represents some 30 million bottles per

Below: *Spraying the vines to protect them against disease and attack by insects is a regular chore. Failure to treat properly can lead to vines being hit by rot, for example. Spraying shortly before picking is forbidden.*

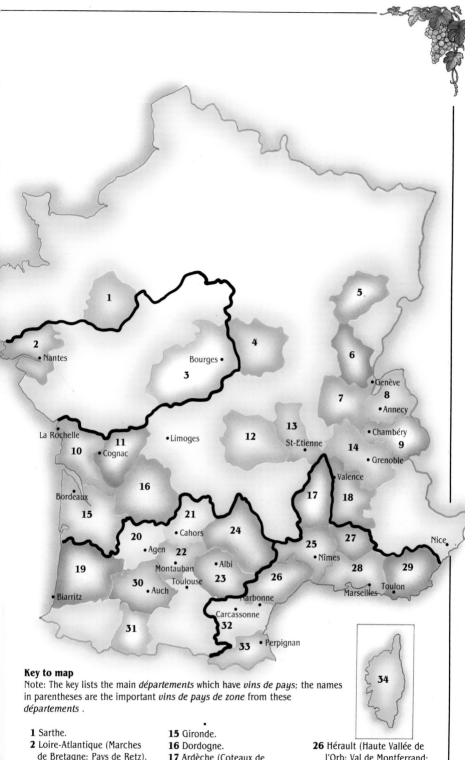

Key to map

Note: The key lists the main *départements* which have *vins de pays*; the names in parentheses are the important *vins de pays de zone* from these *départements*.

1 Sarthe.
2 Loire-Atlantique (Marches de Bretagne; Pays de Retz).
3 Cher/Indre (Coteaux du Cher et de l'Arnon).
4 Nièvre.
5 Haute-Saône (Franche Comté).
6 Jura (Franche Comté).
7 Ain.
8 Haute-Savoie.
9 Savoie (Allobrogie; Balmes Dauphinoises; Coteaux du Gresivaudan).
10 Charente-Maritime.
11 Charente.
12 Puy-de-Dôme.
13 Loire (Urfé).
14 Isère.

15 Gironde.
16 Dordogne.
17 Ardèche (Coteaux de l'Ardèche; Ardèche).
18 Drôme (Comté de Grignan; Coteaux des Baronnies; Collines Rhodaniennes).
19 Landes.
20 Lot-et-Garonne (Agenais).
21 Lot (Coteaux des Glanes).
22 Tarn-et-Garonne (Coteaux du Quercy; St-Sardos; Coteaux et Terrasses de Montauban).
23 Tarn (Côtes de Tarn).
24 Aveyron (Gorges et Côtes de Millau).
25 Gard (Sables du Golfe du Lion).

26 Hérault (Haute Vallée de l'Orb; Val de Montferrand; Collines de la Moure).
27 Vaucluse (Principauté d'Orange).
28 Bouches-du-Rhône.
29 Var (Mont Caume; Argens; Les Maures).
30 Gers (Côtes de Gascogne; Condomois; Montestruc).
31 Hautes-Pyrénées (Bigorre).
32 Aude (Hauterive en Pays d'Aude; Haute Vallée de l'Aude; Val d'Orbieu; Vallée du Paradis).
33 Pyrénées-Orientales (Catalan).
34 Corsica (Ile de Beauté).

year. Is it any wonder that bottles can vary so much from one producer to the next?

There is another problem. Nearly two thirds of all the *vins de pays* are produced by Caves Coopératives, some of which control entire *vin de pays* designations. While, in a number of areas, these co-operatives have been wholly instrumental in elevating a wine from *vin de table* level to something a great deal better, the monopolistic situation which inevitably arises can be as constricting as the system which went before.

Given these variables, there seems little point here in analysing the *vins de pays* one by one – there are over 70 of them, some enormous, others barely used – rather than in picking the ones which seem to stand the best chance of hitting the big time and of joining the ranks of the VDQS and AC.

Champagne, Bordeaux, Burgundy and Alsace have no *vins de pays* of their own. In the South-West, though, my money would be on Vins de Pays de la Dordogne which produces some good Sémillon-based whites and on the rosés of the Côtes du Tarn (in the Tarn *département*) but above all, I would be betting on the Ugni Blanc and Colombard wines of the Côtes de Gascogne (from Gers) which have already proved such a major success in Britain. If I had to choose one inexpensive white wine in France with which to bang the

Above: Vineyards in the south-west of France, source of some of the most interesting vins de pays.

producer of poor Muscadet over the head, this would be it. The South-West's blanket Vin de Pays de Comté Tolosan is too much of a mixed bag of regions and grape varieties to recommend or criticise easily.

Corsica seems likely to make further progress with Pinot Noir rosé and Chardonnay and Sauvignon whites under the Ile de Beauté label, while the Rhône can expect much from the Chardonnay used to make Vin de Pays des Coteaux de l'Ardèche. Among the other likely Rhône success stories, I would pick out the Coteaux des Baronnies and the Collines Rhodaniennes (both from the Drôme *département*), which are using Chardonnay and Aligoté to add zing to the rather flatter local varieties.

The Loire has, apart from the variable blanket Vin de Pays du Jardin de la France, good rosés and Sauvignon whites from Indre-et-Loire and pleasant gooseberryish Sauvignon from the *département* of the Cher. Maine-et-Loire and Coteaux du Cher et de l'Arnon are two other names to watch.

Inevitably however, it is in the Midi and Provence that the largest selection of *vins de*

pays is to be found. Of these, it is worth looking out for the rosés of Catalan, near Perpignan (Pyrénées Orientales), and of Coteaux de Peyriac (Aube/Hérault) and Val d'Orbieu (Aude) in Languedoc. The whites of the Haute Vallée de l'Aude, made from the Terret Gris, Chardonnay, Chenin and Sémillon are good and characterful.

Other good rosés from the south are Mont Caume (Var), Coteaux du Pont-du-Gard, Vaunage (both Gard), Caux (Hérault) Côtes

de Céressou and Côtes de Thongue (both Hérault), while the Terret Gris produces good white wine at Littoral Orb-Hérault (Hérault).

Standing apart from all these, however, are the pink, "gris" and white wines of the Sables du Golfe du Lion (Gard). Planted in the sand dunes, and thus immune to attack from the phylloxera beetle, the vines here deserve immediate promotion to VDQS or AC status. Probably the only reason for this not having already happened is the varied and experimental nature of some of the wines made here, and the fact that the appellation if, and when, it is accorded stands to benefit one company, Listel, which has more or less created the designation.

Below: *Harvesting by machine at Listel, where the sandy soil has protected the vines from the ravages of phylloxera.*

INDEX

156